NEW COLLEGE DURHAM
D0177889

Managing Value for Money in the Public Sector

# Managing Value for Money in the Public Sector

Jonathan G. Bates BSc ACA

Head of Finance
Education Department
London Borough of Bromley

CHAPMAN & HALL
London · Glasgow · New York · Tokyo · Melbourne · Madras

**Published by Chapman & Hall, 2–6 Boundary Row, London SE1 8HN**

Chapman & Hall, 2–6 Boundary Row, London SE1 8HN, UK

Blackie Academic & Professional, Wester Cleddens Road, Bishopbriggs, Glasgow G64 2NZ, UK

Chapman & Hall Inc, 29 West 35th Street, New York NY10001, USA

Chapman & Hall Japan, Thomson Publishing Japan, Hirakawacho Nemoto Building, 6F, 1-7-11 Hirakawa-cho, Chiyoda-ku, Tokyo 102, Japan

Chapman & Hall Australia, Thomas Nelson Australia, 102 Dodds Street, South Melbourne, Victoria 3205, Australia

Chapman & Hall India, R. Seshadri, 32 Second Main Road, CIT East, Madras 600 035, India

First edition 1993



Typeset in $9\frac{1}{2}/11\frac{1}{2}$ Meridien by Excel Typesetters Company, Hong Kong
Printed in England by Clays Ltd, St Ives plc

ISBN 0 412 46360 1



A catalogue record for this book is available from the British Library

Library of Congress Cataloging-in-Publication Data

Bates, J.G.(Jonathan G.)
Managing value for money in the public sector / Jonathan G. Bates. – 1st ed.
p. cm.
Includes bibliographical references (p. 243) and index.
ISBN 0-412-46360-1 (acid-free paper)
1. Administrative agencies—Great Britain—Management. 2. Government productivity—Great Britain. 3. Total quality management—Great Britain. 4. Management audit. I. Title.
JN318.B38 1993
354.4107'5—dc20 92-38464
CIP

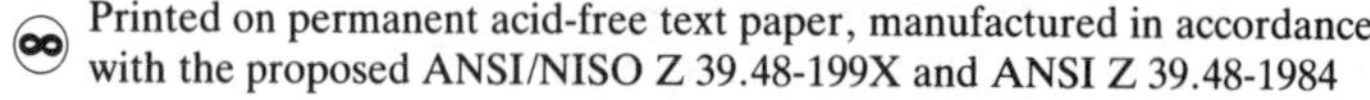
Printed on permanent acid-free text paper, manufactured in accordance with the proposed ANSI/NISO Z 39.48-199X and ANSI Z 39.48-1984

# Contents

# Foreword

In an eye-catching recent advertisement to recruit a Director of Education we pictured a group of young school children running vigorously down a flight of steps towards you, the viewer. The bye-line said – '. . . with things moving this fast, you need a strong sense of direction.' The message was clear and strong: in these times of ever-accelerating change in the public sector you need nifty footwork and a youthful sense of balance if you are to reach your goals.

In this book, Jonathan Bates offers a way ahead for management in today's and tomorrow's public sector. His key concern is the achievement of quality at best value prices throughout the public sector environment. To that end he describes the management tools which an organization can deploy to ensure that its purposes are clearly focussed and articulated, and the methods which may be used to ensure that each individual employee has a sense of that purpose and a deep involvement in her or his work. The model Jonathan Bates describes is complete in the sense that it considers the dimensions of how to decide where the organization is going, how to set clear targets for achievement, and how to plot the extent to which the organization arrived at its chosen destination. He is careful also to examine the various environments in which the organization should examine its competence; that is, the perspectives of quality, measurement, competition and accountability.

This is a book fit for the moment. Like all good management it is timely. As the public sector negotiates the sea-change of an urgent re-orientation towards customer and quality issues, its managers could usefully take time to read Jonathan Bates's book. After all, it might just be the steps needed to prevent one falling down and being trampled underfoot in the charge for better public services.

Nigel Palk
Chief Executive
London Borough of Bromley

# Foreword

# Preface

At what age do you expect to retire? Probably, it will be before your sixtieth birthday. Your parents will be in their eighties and your grandchildren may be at school. In this situation – difficult though it is to imagine, your family will be drawing heavily on state services through education, health care and pensions.

If three out of four generations are using state services you will very much hope that the quality of provision is high. How then will the public sector of the future cope with this demand?

This book is about managing change in a public sector which is facing these demands now.

## Demographic change

The public sector is facing the most difficult period of its history. The challenge is not political. It is not about one political party being against public provision and another being supportive. Rather demographic and economic changes such as those described above are forcing reorganization of the main public sector industries and making reform imperative.

The major changes at present at work in our society include:

1. Reduction in birth rates.
2. Increase in the number of retired people.
3. Increasing need for an educated workforce.
4. Rapidly increasing productivity in much of the economy.
5. Low productivity increases in the service industries.
6. Public demand for higher quality services.

The effect of these deep-rooted changes is to inexorably increase the cost of public services. Lower birth rates translate into higher salaries, an older population means increased costs as do most of the other changes. Hardly one of the trends we are seeing benefits the public sector in terms of costs. Without a major change in the way we manage our operations, real expenditure on public services will rise by as much as 30% over the next ten years without any increase in the quality of service provided.

Of course in that time the economy should have expanded significantly. This will help ease the situation. But we will still be paying more for less in a world where we will be used to paying less for more as technology reduces the real cost of living.

# What are the solutions?

The scope for policy changes are small because political parties cannot stop major changes in society midstream. Since it is impossible to legislate to prevent the onset of old age or the demand for an increasingly educated workforce, what are our options?

The change we need must come from within the public services via radical managerial reform. More public services of higher quality must be produced from the same amount of money. This is a tall order. How can such a demand be defended? Put simply there are some things which the public sector tends to do well and there are others where the standards are lower. The former tend to be the actual provision of a service – perhaps emergency medical care, and the latter, *management* of those services. By improving achievement in those areas that are weak very substantial savings are available. As we describe in Chapter 9 savings of up to 40% are potentially available.

Britain has a history dotted with examples of weak management. A prime case is the decline of the Lancashire cotton industry where as an example, the mother of a colleague of mine was working in 1960 on a loom designed in the 1870s. In the public sector all over the world we are seeing the same types of management failing. For instance many local authorities have accounting systems that provide information that a manufacturing business would have considered archaic in the 1920s.

But before we get too self-deprecating, the management weaknesses seen in the British public sector are far from specific to this country. They are common to all public sector systems the world over, and Britain rather than lagging behind its competitors is almost certainly ahead of them.

# Value for money

Management weakness in the public services has been recognized for a long time. Everyone has a story about waste and inefficiency in a public sector body. In order to combat waste the concept of value for money and value for money audit evolved. The idea was to seek out unnecessary costs and to ensure that expenditure of the same type was not wasted again.

This type of value for money work has saved millions of pounds. But it has not produced benefits on the scale needed to prevent the crisis that is now looming over public services. Value for money (VFM) report after report has said that for innumerable government services:

1. Objectives are not adequately set.
2. Management information is inadequate.
3. Control and decision making is poor.

But because each service is looked at individually the overall point that management systems are weak is missed.

This book looks at how public sector management systems can be improved so that managers can preempt auditors in revealing poor practice. It proposes that the professionals who actually provide services should manage reform. VFM auditors and management consultants are always amateurs dabbling in a professional's area of expertise. This book encourages professionals whether they be administrators, social workers, school teachers, army officers or doctors to assess their organization's achievement and to manage reform from the inside seeking out better ways of using the resources available.

# Structure of the book

Public sector management is rooted in tradition and myth. There are very strong philosophies governing the ways that things are organized. In an era of enforced change many of these traditions need selectively to be called into question. The public servant is trained to be unsusceptible to fraud but is also inculcated with a deep suspicion about business methods. The former view needs reinforcing whereas the latter trait needs to be washed away as soon as possible. The public sector will never be like a commercial organization but it must be business-like if it is to make the most of the resources available.

So that the reader can see how the present-day culture within the public sector was formed, the first part of the book provides a brief history of public enterprise. This is followed by an analysis of the situation now facing the public sector and a chapter on the factors that govern public servants' actions. These first three chapters aim to provide an analysis of government services and the problems that they now face.

Chapters 4–7 then describe how new techniques can be used to promote value for money in any public body. Examples are taken from a wide selection of organizations. This middle section of the book provides the theory of managing for improved VFM, albeit in a very practical form.

Chapters 8 and 9 are substantial sections that show how to put theory into practice. Full-length case studies covering the main areas of public provision, including health and education, are given in both chapters. Chapter 8 deals with managing for better use of resources, that is increased productivity; Chapter 9 covers managing for increased quality.

Throughout the book examples are given from a wide range of services to illustrate the management techniques discussed in the text. It is important that readers appreciate that these examples and the case studies are designed to show how various management methods can be used. They are *not* meant to provide details about specific performance in a specific service. Thus the case studies on education are not intended to show costs that teachers should aim for and neither are they intended to support any educational theories or philosophies. The examples and case studies are for all readers regardless of their own professional backgrounds and their only purpose is to illustrate modern management techniques in practice.

Lastly, Chapter 10 attempts to place the practical measures discussed in the body of the text in the context of a wider managerial reform programme and the factors discussed at the beginning of the book.

# Part One

## Putting Management Reform in Context

# 1

# The rise of the public sector

This introductory chapter charts the rise of the public sector in the Western world over the last 150 years. Much of the present-day functioning of central and local government is innately linked to its past. Present-day organizations are moulded from their predecessors, but perhaps more importantly the attitudes of public servants, politicians and the electorate are all grounded in an historic conception of the role of the public sector. As we shall see much of this view of the past is grounded in fact. Other conceptions of the role of public bodies are present-day distortions of history. But whether historically correct or not the general view held of public enterprise is essentially conservative. In the later chapters of this book this aspect is considered in much greater detail as we look at how the public sector can become once again a more lively and confident generator of wealth and well-being.

Between 1890 and 1955 public expenditure per person in the UK rose seven times in real terms. A comparable statistic is the rise of the electronics industry from the 1960s to date. Just as for computers, the market for public goods has been meteoric: it has been a major success story.

The extraordinary rise of the public sector in the developed world was commented upon at the turn of the century by a German, Adolf Wagner (*Finanzwissenshaft*, Leipzig, 1890). He saw that as the economy as a whole expanded, the proportion taken by the public sector grew faster. In 1976, for instance in the UK, public sector spending represented 48% of gross domestic product (GDP). In 1890 it was just 9%. Wagner gave three reasons for the phenomena he could see occurring.

First, there was an 'inevitable' need for centralization of administration in a complex modern state. There needs to be strong control over economic policy and controls over factory and product safety require to be worked out and administered. State security needs to be guarded internally by the police and courts; externally by the armed services. Jobs related to these concerns proliferate as governments attempt to balance the requirements of an expanding number of new and powerful interest groups.

Second, technical advances give rise to great opportunities. Many of these require enormous amounts of capital for proper exploitation. Examples include telephone systems, electricity supply and major sewerage systems in cities. To obtain a unified sewerage system for a major city most governments decided state provision was necessary. Lastly, Wagner noted that where economic benefits are difficult to measure, or where monopolies were natural, government provision was considered best. Examples include social services and education, as well as many of the new technological utilities already mentioned.

It is the purpose of this chapter to look more carefully at the evolution of the modern public sector using Wagner's three categories as a convenient basis for analysis. But there is also another aspect of the public sector which Wagner takes for granted. Government administration, major industry and the welfare services all employ clerical and manual staff in a way very similar to that in private industry; that is, they require a technocratic expertise very different from the purely political skills of statesmen. Thus as the public sector became more successful its nature inevitably changed from that of political retainers supporting a strong man (a king, queen or minister) to the role of a servant serving the public at large. The extent to which public servants are in fact political retainers is a complex and highly relevant issue. Before we consider public sector development in detail we must first look at the issue of independence and technical excellence.

## The link between independence and technical excellence

For centuries, governments have hired public servants. In the most primitive cultures the division between servant and political supporter existed but was rather arbitrary. The bodyguard of the tribal chief carries out the service role of a security man. However, if he does not support the political leanings of his master he is unlikely to volunteer or be selected for the job. This mix of roles continues to a greater or lesser extent even today. In Britain, few right-wingers hold high administrative office in local authorities with left-wing administrations. However, the idea of a formal separation of the roles of servant and retainer began to take root at the end of the 1700s. The American politician James Madison echoing the views of the English philosopher, John Locke put forward the idea in his 'Federalist Papers' that the legislature (i.e. parliament) should be separate from the executive, one being accountable to the other. This was embodied within the American constitution. While this did not necessitate an apolitical executive, it did mark an important division between decision taking and administering the practical consequences of decisions already made.

An entirely different rationale was used by Napoleon when setting up the French civil service after the revolution. He required technical excellence to administer his policies. He recruited his civil service under the slogan 'careers open to talent' a phrase still very relevant to the modern French civil service. We see then two strands of thought affecting the development of the professional public servant, the Anglo-american concept of independence and the concept of technical excellence, perhaps best exemplified by the French. The quest for technical excellence in the public sector had arisen many times before in other countries. A good example is the English longbowmen in medieval times who were required to practice regularly on village greens so as to be ready for war. Other examples include the Ottoman tile and carpet factories which were set up to provide the highest quality products in Iznik and Cairo.

In Britain independence and technical excellence were brought to the civil service after the Northcote–Trevelyn Report of 1853. The report was produced by a politician, Sir Stafford Northcote who was to become a Chancellor of the Exchequer under Disraeli, and a civil servant, Sir Charles Trevelyn, Assistant Secretary to the Treasury. It marked the culmination of a series of campaigns concerned with removing patronage from public appointments. Northcote and Trevelyn made four major recommendations which were to mould the British civil service until the present day. First, there should be a classification of work in 'intellectual' and 'mechanical' duties. Graduates were to perform the intellectual work. Second, entry to the civil service should be through competitive examination of young people. Third, separate departments of state should all be staffed from a single civil service through which staff could progress. Lastly, promotion should be on merit.

In fact their recommendations were only slowly adopted. However, the concepts of independence (examination and merit promotion) and technical excellence (the 'intellectual' duties requiring graduates) had been set. In the United States development of an effective public sector was more chequered. It was not until the 1900s that the Progressive Movement started to push for the reform of an inefficient and corrupt public administration. Change was to a large extent on a city-by-city basis and was, as a result, piecemeal. The progressives promulgated the concept of 'neutral-competence', the same combination of independence and technical excellence suggested in the Northcote–Trevelyn Report. Since that time the vast majority of civil service reforms throughout the world have been based on this maxim.

We can see then that although ideas of independence and excellence were not new, major reform of the public service did not take place until the end of the 19th century; that is at the beginning of the period of major growth in the public sector. To see why this occurred we need to look at the function of the public sector over the period.

# The business of the public services

Wagner divided the then emerging public sector into three categories. We can best refer to these three roles as:

1. State administration and control, e.g. the Inland Revenue and the Army;
2. Nationalized industries, e.g. electricity supply;
3. Welfare expenditure, e.g. education.

There is also another important item on which governments spend money – the cost of borrowing, that is, servicing the national debt.

In Britain public expenditure became a significant element of the economy during the Napoleonic wars. In order to finance Britain's role the Prime Minister, Pitt the

Younger was forced to introduce income tax. It was not until the 1890s that expenditure exceeded the level of 1814.

Expenditure even in 1890 was small compared to the economy as a whole – a mere 9% of GDP. By 1955 though, radical change had occurred and spending represented 37% of GDP. And in Britain public spending did not peak until 1976 when the figure was 48.5%.

To see how expenditure has developed we must look at each of the above categories in turn.

## State administration and control

In this category Wagner describes those services necessary for markets to function. He includes enforcement of law and order internally and externally. We can thus include the following:

1. Public administration.
2. Law and order.
3. Defence.

In Table 1.1, we can see how expenditure on these items varied over the last 100 years.

In fact Wagner was only partially correct when he predicted an inevitable rise in public administration. Spending in this category rose by only 35% from 1910 as a proportion of GDP. Peacetime defence expenditure did increase until the 1950s. Thereafter it declined as countries lost overseas possessions and consequently costly military commitments. It also reduced heavily as a result of substantial investment in electronic warfare and nuclear weapons. More recently, in contrast we are seeing increased expenditure on law and order, a result of the high crime rates that seem to be inevitable in modern free societies.

Public administration and control has the longest history and perhaps is the least likely to change in the future. A very wide political concensus supports traditional state provision of the armed services, regulation of industry and the judicial system.

**Table 1.1** Public expenditure relating to public administration, law and order and defence, 1890–1989

| | *% of GDP in Britain* | | | | |
|---|---|---|---|---|---|
| | *1890* | *1910* | *1935* | *1955* | *1989* |
| Public administration* | 2.4 | 3.5 | 4.7 | 5.4 | 4.6 |
| Law and order | 0.6 | 0.6 | 0.7 | 0.7 | 1.8 |
| Defence | 2.4 | 3.6 | 3.1 | 10.1 | 4.0 |
| TOTALS | 5.4 | 7.7 | 8.5 | 16.2 | 10.4 |

*Note*: * Figures for pure administration work are not available.
Figures given include a certain element of other work.

Although organization of police forces is a more contentious issue most support the general view that law and order is very much a public sector concern.

# Nationalized industries

States have always tended towards some form of production or commerce under their direct control. In Britain, Henry V (1413–22) built a fleet using hired labour and oak from the Royal forests. By the end of the next century, Henry VIII (1509–47) had set up dockyards at Portsmouth, Woolwich and Deptford. A completely different form of nationalized industry was initiated by the Kings of France. Louis XI (1461–83) formed the French postal service and in 1756, Louis XV (1715–74) set up the famous Sèvres porcelain factory. However, it was not until the 19th century that governments became involved in major commercial products.

The history of state production falls into two quite separate elements with very different origins. While nowadays we consider nationalized industries to be the preserve of central government, the first major forays into 'state capitalism' were undertaken by local government. As towns developed in the 19th century it naturally fell to city councils to improve and rationalize the utilities available to the inhabitants of the area. It is interesting to look at how these public utilities developed.

## Public utilities

The major utilities in an industrialized state are: water, gas, transport, and electricity.

Although the ancient Romans and Persians had piped water in their cities the first water company was set up in Britain in 1805. In the years that followed many small companies were formed with major cities each being supplied by a number of private suppliers. As early as 1837 Leeds corporation took partial control of the local water company and in 1847 Liverpool council purchased two local companies after the Liverpool Waterworks Act. It subsequently invested over £1 million in a reservoir scheme near Chorley. This was municipal capitalism on a substantial scale. It was followed by Bradford in 1854, Birmingham in 1876 and London in 1902.

Gas supply has a similar history to water. In 1812 the London Gas and Coke Company was formed and by 1843 Manchester had its own municipal gas company. In 1870 there were 50 municipal gas undertakings.

The scale of this public investment was enormous. In Birmingham, a city famous for the scale and range of its commercial dealings, the city debt was increased from £50 000 to £2 million when the local gas undertakings were purchased. In mid-Victorian times this was a formidable sum.

In 1870 the Tramways Act allowed local authorities and private individuals to build tramways. Initially, councils were not permitted to manage them. Again local authorities in Britain took to an entrepreneurial task with great energy and by 1913 there were 3 426 000 000 passenger journeys and three-quarters of all tramways were owned and managed by local authorities.

The last area of municipal involvement in public utilities was regarding electricity companies. The legal power for local authorities to produce and sell electricity came relatively early in 1882 with the Electric Lighting Act. By 1902 there were six municipal electricity companies which included production for the cities of Manchester, Liverpool and Birmingham.

The great period of municipal control of public utilities came to an end with the Great War although substantial change did not occur until the 1940s. The essential fragmentation associated with city based provision was inconsistent with national needs as so obviously illustrated by a world war. Another more forceful reason was the rise of socialist national governments in Europe. For many left-wing thinkers nationalization was an ideal form for community based production. But most importantly the end of municipal enterprise coincided with a feeling that essentially the pioneering work had been done. You do not have to be a socialist to be driven to provide essential services for all. Providing the first running water to an estate of tenements is a great achievement. But the excitement wears thin when social and technical pioneering is replaced by controlling costs, providing maintenance and developing corporatism. By 1918 the public utilities had reached this stage, and from then on new solutions were required.

## Central government

Production and commerce under the control of central government varies both within individual states and between them. Some industries became nationalized through purchase from the private sector. The most interesting such case relates to Italy where historically the major banks owned the majority of shares in industry. By nationalizing the banks the Italian government effectively nationalized Italian industry. But in general we can identify three major forms of central government production.

1. Government initiated industry, e.g. Ship-building, chemical weapons, Sèvres porcelain.
2. *Ad hoc* government purchases from private industry, e.g. Rolls Royce.
3. Nationalization by Act of Parliament, e.g. French Railways.

As we have already discussed states have traditionally organized some major industries. This was normally the case when substantial capital investment was needed. Rulers were also fond of state production of luxuries. However, today modern governments have tended to disinvest in arms production except in the highly risky and emotive fields of nuclear and chemical weapons. Luxury goods are no longer an area of state interest.

As economies became more complex in the last century major business failures started to become politically important. If a bank threatens to collapse votes can be won by saving it. In France the Banque Nationale de Credit was saved by the government when bankruptcy threatened in 1929. And in the early 1970s the British government prevented the loss of Britain's aeroengine manufacturing capacity by nationalizing Rolls Royce. Throughout the 20th century Western countries have taken into national ownership all sorts of industries to prevent bankruptcy: shipping companies, railway companies, mining and mineral concerns have all been subject to *ad hoc* nationalization.

Most important, however, was the compulsory nationalization of key industries by act of parliament. In 1936 the legislation was passed in France to form SNCF, the modern French nationalized railways, from five private companies and some state owned concerns. After the war nationalization became more prevalent. Most states of Europe nationalized electricity and gas production and supply, coal mining, central banking, steel production and railways. Other candidates in many countries were commercial banking, insurance, automobile production, aircraft industries, oil and chemicals. By the mid-1960s a very substantial proportion of production in Europe was in state hands.

The impetus for industrial nationalization was politically rather than commercially motivated. It was motivated by a great desire across the whole of war-worn Europe (but not the USA) to give the populous indirect ownership of capital. More rational reasons for nationalization such as control of key state resources or direct control of the economy did not seriously enter into politicians' calculations.

In retrospect compulsory nationalization of industry was a relatively short-term and unsuccessful movement. In Great Britain nationalized industries are few, in France substantial disinvestment has taken place, and in the Eastern Block massive privatization is likely.

While municipal control of public utilities was in the main a great success, central government controlled industry shared none of the same flair and enthusiasm. There are a great number of reasons for this but there is one major cause. Municipal enterprise was the result of essentially rational consideration of how to provide services to the people. Nationalization in contrast was just a political dream. It was not designed to provide operational benefits and in the main it did not.

## In summary

Government owned industry showed enormous expansion during the nineteenth century. Wagner's observation that vast sums of capital were needed to properly exploit technical advances was essentially correct. Municipal enterprise provided the emerging public utilities with stability and finance. The same has been true regarding central government control over massive technological investment in the nuclear armament industries. The other area of state interest in commerce – that is state ownership of core industries is in contrast a political rather than rational response to real need.

In most major countries local government enterprises were among the first to be subject to central government takeover. Since this transfer was only a partial success, government control of industry is rapidly becoming a thing of the past. Historically we cannot ignore the successes and failures of municipal and state ownership. But as an area for current study there is at present little scope!

# Welfare expenditure

If state administration costs have only increased moderately and if the nationalized industries are in heavy decline, a very different picture is presented by welfare expenditure. In Britain, home of the 'welfare state', nearly 22% of GDP is devoted to welfare expenditure. It now represent 55% of all government spending.

Welfare expenditure includes:

1. State education.
2. Health care.
3. Unemployment benefit and social security payments.
4. State provided housing.

In Britain, we can analyse expenditure in these categories as shown in Table 1.2.

In all Western countries very substantial expenditure is devoted to education, health and social security. It is worth looking at how governments managed the revolution necessary to devote such large sums to these areas.

It is probably a surprise to discover that welfare expenditure has been a major area of public expenditure for centuries. In Britain local government became formally responsible with the Poor's Rate Act 1601. It appears that local government had become involved in poor relief after the dissolution of the monasteries in Henry VIII's reign. Up until that time the church had looked after the poor at its own expense. By 1834 poor relief totalled £6 029 371, about 10% of expenditure excluding repayments on the national debt. It was, however, only about 1.5% of GDP. If social security (the 'workhouse') was a major area of public expenditure, education and health care were not. Education was provided by charitable trusts and sunday schools. Health care was a purely private affair based on ability to pay supplemented to an extent by charitable trusts.

It was not until the 19th century that society began to take an interest in alleviation of hardship. This interest was based on a positive concern for betterment of mankind. Consequently it involved education – a preventative measure (to prevent future hardship), and concern for conditions of life including the relief of poverty – curative measures. All through the 19th century large numbers of Royal Commissions delved into the problems of the poor, the lot of women and the education and care of children. It was during that century of terrible urban poverty that many of the ideas we now take for granted were formulated. Up until the end of the 'Enlightenment' the poor were considered a necessary evil that would always be with us. In contrast the Victorians formulated the idea and practice of philanthropy. In doing so they fundamentally changed mankind's view of the world. The early economists such as Ricardo and Smith considered the poor necessarily part

**Table 1.2** Analysis of expenditure categories

| | *% increase over period* | *% of GDP* | | | |
|---|---|---|---|---|---|
| | | *1920* | *1935* | *1955* | *1989* |
| Education | 300 | 1.6 | 2.6 | 3.9 | 4.8 |
| Health | 713 | 0.8 | 1.7 | 3.4 | 5.7 |
| Social security | 300 | 3.5 | 5.9 | 6.4 | 10.5 |
| Housing | −22 | 0.9 | 1.1 | 2.4 | 0.7 |
| Food subsidies | — | — | — | 0.2 | — |
| TOTALS | | 6.8 | 11.3 | 16.3 | 21.7 |

of a market system. It was in revulsion against this that liberal thinkers looked for alternatives. Marx's economic writings provided a more heavy-handed answer. At the same time as Marx was advocating forceful revolution a much more tentative revolution was taking place, for as early as 1833 the government was providing education in a small way.

Slowly, these beginnings were added to. To start with many improvements were based on government regulations policed by various inspectors. A succession of factory acts limited working hours for children, women and miners. The Child Labour Act 1833 controlled children's working hours and made education for child workers mandatory. An inspectorate with very substantial powers was set up to police the regulations. Other changes were related to environmental health. The building of sewers and buildings in the great cities provided a public good which particularly benefited the less well off.

However, it was not until the 1890s that legislation started to provide substantial financial assistance. A change in attitude had occurred and *laissez-faire* liberalism gave way to a socialist liberalism. Regulatory legislation such as the Child Labour Act gave way to service based legislation. The Board of Education Act 1899 was a trigger for a long series of acts which all had the effect of improving the funding of state education. The Liberal government of 1905 brought in some of the most radical changes affecting public spending. In 1908 it provided pensions for all those over 70 and whose annual income was below £31.10s. The maximum rate of pension was five shillings a week. In 1909 labour exchanges were set up by the Board of Trade to assist those attempting to find work. And in 1911 a joint government and worker national insurance system was set up to provide against ill health. A man on wages in excess of 1s.6d a working day contributed 7d a week. The government contributed 2d. In return the worker obtained 'medical treatment and attendence', treatment in a sanatorium for tuberculosis, 26 weeks of sickness benefit and if unable to work due to illness a disabled benefit from the 27th week onwards. Thirty shillings maternity benefit was also payable. Sickness benefit was at a top rate of 10s a week for men; lower rates were paid to women.

The series of reforms that have led to a public expenditure equivalent to just under half of the output of the state (48.5% of GNP in 1975/6) began in the 1830s. This was the decade of the Reform Act, the abolition of slavery, the Child Labour Act and the Poor Law Amendment Act. Clearly a change of outlook had taken place. People no longer lived in the 'best of all possible worlds'; active government based reform would provide solutions to grave social ills.

The next critical period is at the turn of the century. Primary school education had become mandatory for all children, state pensions were introduced and national medical insurance was conceived. Whereas previously reform very much involved controlling and assisting in the actions of third parties, at the turn of the century the role of government increased to provide real services at a mass level. The three areas of social spending that now accounts for so much of the expenditure of the governments of developed nations were introduced. That is education for all, medical services for all and social security payment for the elderly and sick. To start with expenditure in these areas was strictly limited and quality of service was low. The next great change in government spending did not take place until the 1940s.

The 1942 Education Act and the 1945 National Health Act represent the completion of the reforms begun over 100 years previously. Every man, woman and child was to be given free at the point of service a first rate health service and education. Throughout the civilized world governments strive to provide education and health care as well as financial assistance to the least well off. It is an enormous challenge.

# Summary

There are few important areas of human activity in which governments have not at one time or other become directly involved. At the same time that involvement, at least in total, steadily increased up until 1980.

Modern government began to take shape in Britain in the 1830s after the Reform Act 1832. During the Victorian era right up until 1980 governments invested heavily in state-run industries and welfare expenditure. This investment was on a very large scale so that by 1975 public spending was nearly half of British GDP. In Table 1.3 we give the figures for 1989.

The crucial point to understand is that the activities of Western governments (as well as the old Eastern block regimes) are firmly based in the supply of goods and services. The formulation of public policy and regulation of the economy hold a very low precedence in the league of public undertakings. As Table 1.3 shows about 87%

**Table 1.3** British public spending as a percentage of GDP (excluding privatization proceeds)

| | % | % | % | *% of total* |
|---|---|---|---|---|
| Defence | | 4.0 | | 10.3 |
| Law and order | | 1.8 | | 4.7 |
| Public administration | | | | |
| Agriculture | 0.5 | | | 1.2 |
| Trade and energy | 1.7 | | | 4.4 |
| Environment (not covered below) | 1.3 | | | 3.2 |
| Other | 1.1 | | | 2.9 |
| | | 4.6 | | |
| TOTAL State administration and control | | | 10.4 | 26.7 |
| Housing | | 0.7 | | 1.7 |
| Education | | 4.8 | | 12.2 |
| Health | | 5.7 | | 14.5 |
| Social security | | 10.5 | | 26.8 |
| TOTAL for welfare services | | | 21.7 | 55.2 |
| Transport and highways | | 1.2 | | 3.2 |
| Overseas development | | 0.5 | | 1.2 |
| Arts | | 0.2 | | 0.6 |
| TOTAL other services | | | 1.9 | 5.0 |
| TOTAL service expenditure | | | 34.0 | 86.9 |
| Interest on national debt and other | | | 5.0 | 13.1 |
| TOTAL British Government expenditure as a percentage of GDP | | | 39.0 | 100.0 |

of total spending is of a service or product based nature (simplistically taken as all activities excluding debt interest). This excludes the remaining nationalized industries.

With the advent of major technological wars, it was only natural that the public sector should have evolved the way it did. What is far more difficult to understand is the consistently repeated sentiment that governments and their public servants essentially govern. Much of their role is clearly akin to that of traditional business people who manage productive organizations on a day-to-day basis. Of course doctors, teachers and policemen spend their time producing concrete material results. In rather stark contrast, for most of this century, senior public servants and politicians have had very little interest in this field. It was not until the 'Next Steps' report was published in 1987 that this crushingly obvious failing was officially recognized in Britain.

In the following chapters we look at why this is and we attempt to suggest methods which could help to make the public sector continue its historic success. As the next chapter makes clear there is still an increasing demand for the services the public sector offers. The challenge is to make the provision of those services as efficient and as effective as is humanly possible.

# 2

# Why value for money is important

## Introduction

In the last ten years the phrase 'value for money' has become almost indelibly associated with public sector management and audit issues. Why is this?

Some consider that VFM is linked to a prolonged period of 'penny pinching Conservative rule' in Britain. Others believe that all public sector organizations need to be constantly encouraged to perform and that repetition of VFM 'clichés' is a way of trying to achieve this. A third view might be that the Audit Commission and National Audit Office used the phrase VFM as a marketing slogan for their newly formed organizations.

All these explanations for the importance of value for money probably contain an element of truth. But the most solid indication that value for money is important is given in the OECD report, *Social Expenditure, 1960–90* (OECD, Paris, 1985). This report concluded that the Western democracies could not afford increases in 'welfare expenditure' levels without a 'conflict with the aim of sustained economic growth'. In the face of warnings of this type governments of all persuasions will strive hard to increase the achievement of public services while maintaining expenditure levels. This can only be done by increasing value for money.

But you do not have to believe the OECD to be convinced of the importance of value for money in the public services. There are plenty of good reasons for economy, efficiency and effectiveness. This chapter examines them and places the public sector in the context of some of the changes that are taking place in the industrialized world.

## What is value for money?

A thorough description of value for money is given by P. C. Jones and J. G. Bates in their book *Public Sector Auditing* (Chapman and Hall, 1990). It says the following:

> Value for money is achieved when a public body carries out its duties to high standards at low cost. This can be summarized colloquially by saying that a good job is being done.
>
> Slightly more technically, value for money is achieved when administration and service provision is 'economic, efficient and effective'. These three concepts are interrelated. Economy and efficiency are similar: both relate to saving resources. Economy ensures that input costs are minimized. Efficiency ensures that maximum output is achieved at the minimum level of input cost sufficient to be effective. Efficiency, therefore, subsumes economy. A body cannot be efficient and uneconomic, but it can be both economic (i.e. cheap) and inefficient. Effectiveness is a far more positive idea. Effectiveness means that a service provided properly caters for a real need. (pp. 222–23)

Value for money is the requirement to maximize the use of scarce resources. Just as a successful commercial product will provide good value for money – if it did not no one would buy it – so public goods should also be successful in meeting the real needs they are designed for at an attractive cost.

## The reasons

If we want to discover more about why VFM is important it is perhaps best first to consider the question in conventional public sector terms.

Using the concept of philanthropy, which was responsible for the formation of the welfare services, we would consider that poor value for money equated to stealing from the needy. Waste is always immoral but wasting the little that the poor have for their use is all but unforgivable. Unfortunately this sound moral view has never been adequate and the public sector has always had its share of inefficiency and ineffectiveness.

The other public sector view that was discussed in Chapter 1 was the requirement for technical competence. This provides an equally unequivocal answer. Waste and

**Table 2.1** Output growth per employee in Britain

| | *5 years to 1990* % | *Average per year* % |
|---|---|---|
| Manufacturing industries | 24.0 | 4.8 |
| Service industries | 1.5* | 0.3* |
| Whole economy | 9.0 | 1.8 |

*Note*: * Estimated by author.
*Source*: *Employment Gazette*, **99** (8) August 1991, S16.

lack of fitness for purpose should form no part of the professional's work since the professional aims to provide the best possible from the available resources. Again this view has not been adequate for the needs of public enterprise. Why this should be is discussed in Chapter 3.

But there are now much more challenging reasons for value for money which are neither morally or professionally based. They are democratically and economically forced upon us. They can best be illustrated as follows.

## The productivity divide

Over the five years from 1985 to 1990 the British economy and that of most other Western countries expanded strongly. One measure of this expansion is the productivity achieved per person employed. This is detailed in Table 2.1.

The striking fact from these statistics is that the vast majority of productivity growth has been achieved by manufacturing industry. Remember manufacturing only accounts for about 30% of the British economy estimated on the basis of employees. But of what relevance to VFM in the public sector are these figures?

The public sector is composed mainly of service industries. Although the real level of productivity increase in the public sector cannot be effectively measured we can assume that it mirrors the rest of the service sector economy and increases at about 0.3% a year.

If we assume productivity increases at these rates in both the economy as a whole and the public sector for the next ten years then an extraordinary situation occurs. Taxpayers will be paying over £30 billion more than they do now for an almost unchanged quality of service. This is a staggering statistic which will have very wide implications for the economy as a whole and for the public sector in particular. We can call it the 'productivity divide', and it will become an increasingly big issue in the next few years.

Table 2.2 illustrates its effect. Put bluntly, in a period of increasing expectations the public are going to be asked to pay another £32 billion for the same semi-adequate

**Table 2.2** The mechanics of the productivity divide

| | *Yearly productivity increases at* | |
|---|---|---|
| | *0.3%* *Public sector* | *1.8%* *Whole economy* |
| Year 0 | 100.0 | 100.0 |
| Year 1 | 100.3 | 101.8 |
| Year 2 | 100.6 | 103.6 |
| Year 5 | 101.5 | 109.3 |
| Year 10 | 103.0 | 119.5 |

Relative decline of the public sector compared to the economy as a whole:
119.5/103.0 = 16.0%
Value of that decline measured at 1991 values:
approx. £200 billion × 16.0% = £32 billion

public services we have now. Let us put this in proportion. To keep public expenditure at present real levels, we would have to completely eliminate *all* public spending on the National Health Service or all types of education. It is not a pleasant prospect.

## Productivity changes in manufacturing and services

Without some thought it is difficult to see why these great changes are happening. An example might be of use in illustrating the changes that have occurred and are still occurring.

A neighbour of mine started work at the age of 14 as a wagoner. This was also the trade of his father. Up until the last war he used to transport agricultural produce using a cart and two heavy horses. The total tonnage transported in a year by this method can be calculated and compared to that of a modern lorry (see Table 2.3).

In comparison to a modern 38-ton lorry the horse and cart was 500 times less productive. This comparison is crude but it is instructive because it shows the magnitude of productivity increases that have been achieved in many areas of industry.

But how much of this productivity increase has been shared by the public services? Class sizes in schools have reduced in the same period, so productivity here has certainly not increased. And in the health service there have been no dramatic productivity improvements. There is no 500-fold increase in achievement. This is not to belittle the *quality* improvements that have occurred in all the public services. Rather we are stating the fact that a surgeon cannot do 500 times as many operations a day now as his predecessor did 50 years ago.

Of course there are areas of the public sector that have seen very rapid rises in productivity. Surprisingly, the armed services probably provide the best example. The prime cause has been the reliance on nuclear deterrent to cut the numbers of conventional forces needed for a given defence capacity. Very high levels of research and development have also helped by producing sophisticated electronic aircraft and missiles which have reduced the reliance on ground troops that, in the First World War, for instance, took so large a part in the action.

**Table 2.3** Comparison of a cart to a modern lorry

*Cart*
Total hauled a year:
2 tons carried 6 days × 51 weeks × 10 miles a day
= 2 tons for 3060 miles or 1 ton for 6120 miles.

*Lorry*
Total hauled a year:
38 tons carried 5 days × 46 weeks × 350 miles a day
= 38 tons for 80 500 miles or 1 ton for 3 059 000 miles.
Increase in productivity
3 059 000/6120 = 499.8 times or a 50 000% increase

Another area with much increased productivity is road construction. But most of the administrative services have been only little helped by computerization and until the last ten years most social benefits have been processed with a heavy manual input.

## Pressures on public enterprise

We can see that there are going to be great pressures on the public sector to increase productivity. Many will almost certainly have felt the beginnings of this squeeze already in the form of government legislation, managerial reorganization and VFM auditing. This book attempts to define the causes of the changes that are to come and suggest practical methods of obtaining the productivity increases that are clearly needed.

In this chapter we look at the specific pressures that the public sector will face as the world about it changes.

## The 'Triple Squeeze'

The 'productivity divide' is not the only pressure that there is for better value for money in the public sector. There are three main changes in the way we live that are forcing change on public enterprises. We will look at these changes one by one. Together they form the 'Triple Squeeze' that is beginning to frighten governments but has yet to trouble public servants.

The first squeeze is the 'productivity divide'. We have already looked at the problems this is going to cause.

The second squeeze is the so-called 'demographic timebomb'. Birthrates in Europe have consistently fallen since the early 1960s. There are therefore fewer children and consequently there will be fewer young people ready and able to take up work. The situation is made more dramatic by the fact that people are living for much longer. The result is that fewer and fewer people are having to support more and more dependants.

To illustrate the effect of the reduction in birth rates the Audit Commission report *Towards Better Management of Schools* published in 1986 showed that the number of secondary school pupils would drop by 1.1 million or 27% between 1979 and 1991. This is a pretty impressive statistic. More impressive still is some recent data from Italy showing that Italian women are now on average producing just 1.29 children each. In Britain the rate is about 1.7 but this is well short of the 2.1 needed to keep a stable population. At the other end of the age range people are living much longer. At one local authority I visited recently two individuals who were born in the 1880s were applying for exemption from the poll tax. Soon one in five people will be of pensionable age and in the next century Germany is expecting there to be only two people working to support every retired person.

For the public services this is a two-fold problem. First, labour is becoming more and more expensive. Second, the requirement for welfare services and state pensions continually increases. The only way out of this tightening net is highly productive use of employees. In other words, value for money must be maximized.

The third pressure can be termed the 'brain lust'. There is an unceasing demand for better educated and trained people to work in the new increasingly computerized workplace. In a poem, Thomas Hardy describes a country girl's work based on cutting swedes in the rain.

> How it rained
> When we worked at Flintcomb-Ash,
> And could not stand upon the hill
> Trimming swedes for the slicing mill.
> The wet washed through us – plash, plash, plash:
> How it rained!

You do not need much education for this type of employment. But many of the descendants of the people he describes now work in the local district council in the accounts department or on a word processor. For this a good secondary education is needed. The next generation though will need some form of tertiary education. If machines can be made to do most of the routine work then the people will have to solve the complex problems the machines cannot handle. They will also have to program the machines. You need more that a GCSE in maths for this type of work; you must have a diploma or a degree and very probably a professional qualification on top.

Modern society may not enjoy educating its children and young people but the world it has created has a insatiable lust for highly educated personnel.

The public sector is particularly hard hit by the 'brain lust' because of the rapid increase in service industries. For instance health, public administration and the police are all industries that require copious quantities of 'white blouse' workers. This is rather unpleasant jargon for young women school leavers with A levels but who have chosen not to go into tertiary education. These are the people that the high street banks want behind their fashionable new open counters. They must be courteous, computer literate and must be able to think for themselves. But there is a shortage of them for the reasons we have already discussed but also because the service industries are employing more and more people. Only about 10 000 girls leave school every year with just A levels. When it comes to competing with the banks, building societies and insurance industry many elements of the public sector find themselves poorly placed. The health service has been the first to feel the effects of the battle for these high quality staff because of the endless demand in the National Health Service (NHS) for good nurses.

## The practical effects of the 'Triple Squeeze'

We have discussed the major influences that are affecting the public sector in general terms. But what are the practical steps we should take to counter these inexorable changes that are inching up on us all? Below we list the changes that must happen in the public sector if it is to remain viable.

### *Practical effects of the 'Triple Squeeze'*

1. Major reductions in the full-time work force;
2. Use of contract staff to cover peeks in workload;
3. Use of external consultants to provide specialist expertise when needed;
4. Introduction of effective management information systems to provide for increased requirements in control and decision making;
5. Increased delegation of responsibilities and duties to staff;
6. Formation of organizations with only four or five levels of management hierarchy;
7. A complete commitment by senior staff to the quality of service delivered;
8. The introduction of
   (a) accountability, and
   (b) competition;
   into the supply of public services.

To some readers these changes will seem revolutionary. In a sense they are. But it will be a very benign revolution. Individuals will have more freedom of action and hence more self-respect. Work will become more interesting and the quality of service provided will improve.

Those that are used to a public sector which guarantees a job for life, that is highly unionized and where promotion is incremental and of right through a thousand different levels of management will be alarmed. This alarm is unfortunate but there is consolation. If these changes do not take place the quality of service the public sector could offer would decline inexorably. In the author's view hopeless decline would alarm the traditionalists even more than the changes outlined above.

Clearly, the list raises a range of major issues that cannot be considered briefly. In this chapter we discuss some of the staffing issues raised (points 1–3 above). We then consider the central role of management information (4). Much of the contents of the book revolves around the issue of accounting for the achievements of public sector organizations. Ideas regarding management information affect the whole philosophy of public provision and readers should not therefore expect a dry numerical view.

Points 5–8 in the above list cover management changes which should accompany a much more rigorous view of public sector productivity and quality of service. Chapter 9 looks at these issues and illustrates them with case studies. Lastly, Chapter 10 places all the foregoing issues in the context of public accountability and a competitive environment in which to provide services to a relatively wealthy public with ever-increasing expectations.

## Staffing changes

If a commodity is expensive a wise user aims to minimize consumption. Unfortunately, this is the situation most of the public sector faces regarding the rather special resource of staff. The 'productivity divide', the 'demographic timebomb' and the 'brain lust' have all ensured that employees are becoming a luxury.

There are a number of ways to reduce staff costs and they were listed in points 1–3 above. (Reducing salaries is usually not an option!)

Clearly, the first requirement is to reduce the workforce to a working minimum. But if this is done two problems arise. First, when there are variations in workload there may be insufficient cover. Second, specialist staff may be under-worked. As an example, a computer maintenance person may have breakdowns to deal with only three days a week.

The solutions to these problems are a further reduction in the permanent workforce combined with the use of contract staff or subcontractors when needed.

It is interesting to understand why contract staff have so recently become an important element of modern industry. In the past the majority of employees worked in factories. When demand for the product fluctuated it was not necessary to lay off people. They were retained and their production was put into stock. But with service industries it is not possible to make for stock. A few spare appendicitis operations kept in a cupboard in case demand picks up represents a rather interesting surrealist idea. It is not, unfortunately, a viable way of running a health service.

It is worth looking at a small example illustrating the benefits of using contract staff and subcontractors combined with a small highly professional permanent staff.

## The value of contracted staff

Consider a small government department that issues licences. Normally, it processes 100 licences a week, but often there are 120 to do. So as to provide an adequate service staffing levels are set to be able to cater for 120 licences a week. We can illustrate this numerically.

| | *Week 1* | *Week 2* | *Week 3* | *Week 4* | *Total* |
|---|---|---|---|---|---|
| Number of licences | 100 | 120 | 100 | 100 | 420 |
| Employee costs (£) | 1000 | 1000 | 1000 | 1000 | 4000 |
| Cost per licence (£) | 10 | 8.33 | 10 | 10 | 9.52 |

Now the department could reorganize its affairs to reduce its core staff and to cover the fairly frequent peak periods that occur using part-time contract personnel. These contract staff could be retired former employees who are keen for some work every now and then and perhaps young mothers who while their children are young do not wish to work full-time.

The department's costs would now look like this:

| | *Week 1* | *Week 2* | *Week 3* | *Week 4* | *Total* |
|---|---|---|---|---|---|
| Number of licences | 100 | 120 | 100 | 100 | 420 |
| Employee costs (£) | 833 | 1000 | 833 | 833 | 3499 |
| Cost per licence (£) | 8.33 | 10 | 8.33 | 8.33 | 8.33 |

For the four-week period costs have been reduced by £501 or about 12.5%. This may appear a modest achievement but when service sector productivity increases are limited to only 0.3% a year this represents 40 years of 'improvement' achieved in one go.

Some will say that a number of real jobs have been destroyed by the use of a low pay and low rights part-time labour force. This view is out of date for many reasons. First, there will always be full-time work for good office workers. The 'demographic timebomb' will ensure this. Second, since people are living much longer they will want less demanding work on a part-time basis during much of their retirement. This is the 'demographic timebomb' again. Lastly, the rates of pay available to effective part-time staff will seldom be low. When skilled people are in short supply wage rates are good. These changes are the result of shortages of high quality staff; it is the public sector which is under pressure not the employees.

In the examples and case studies throughout the book the issue of how to manage staff is discussed more fully. The example here is designed to illustrate in a simple way how change can be made effectively and painlessly.

## Management information

The full costs of processing licence applications is only known if the cost per licence is calculated as it was in the example. So often in the public services this type of calculation is avoided with the result that the benefits of change are never properly comprehended. In Chapter 4 the reasons for the lack of management information in the public sector are discussed and in the following chapters we review the issues and then the practice of obtaining management information in the public sector.

The influential philosopher Karl Popper said, 'If you cannot measure it, it does not exist.' Some theologians might not agree but the evidence is that the majority of the population in developed countries do.

People want hard tangible measurable benefits – shorter NHS waiting lists, lower rates of tax, more child allowance, longer holidays. They are little interested in assurances that education is actually rather good in Britain or that British roads are continually improving and are the envy of the developed world. Electorates have learned that measured achievement is infinitely preferable to subjective assessments of bureaucratic performance made by politicians or public servants.

But the capacity of most public organizations to measure their own achievements is pathetic. Much of the hope for the future success of public enterprise hinges on their capacity to improve the recording and measurement of their achievements and not just their costs. Only by measurement can organizations assess where there are opportunities and where resources are being wasted. People must measure in order to be able to control and take decisions. In the public sector it can be safely asserted that control and decision making are suboptimal. The results are ignorance and waste.

# Changes to date in public sector management

During the 1980s there were a large number of reform measures aimed at the public sector. These included privatization of the nationalized industries, compulsory competitive tendering for many local authority services and the formation of 'Next Steps' agencies in the civil service.

It is worth reviewing these changes because they represent the first attempts of government to come to grips with the reality of the 'Triple Squeeze' on public services. Many of these reforms were deeply unpopular when they were introduced. In particular, many people resented the ideology that fired most of the changes. Those in power gave the very strong impression that if an organization was publicly owned it was bad almost to the extent of being corrupt. Naturally many people, particularly those who worked in the public services, resented this view. However, in retrospect many of the changes of the 1980s are now accepted and are generally seen to benefit the public interest.

## The ideology that initiated reform

If there is a single phrase that can sum up the political mood of the reformers it is 'that there is no such thing as a free lunch'. For those that have a romantic notion of the human spirit this view is uncompromisingly materialistic. But in their heart of hearts the public believe that the public sector is based on the materialistic use of taxpayers' money. Although perhaps distasteful, a thoroughly materialistic review of public enterprise was and still is needed. It is a matter of rendering unto Caesar what is Caesar's and this always has required hard cash.

The essence of the reform in the 1980s was that subsidy should be removed and managers should be given full responsibility for the financial repercussions of their actions. To the politician this was right-wing thought at the expense of caring socialism. But to the economist it represented an attempt to measure and control the value placed upon services.

The issue of managerial responsibility was a prime element of the political dogma of the time. It was found that large branches of expenditure were effectively under nobody's control. Even as recently as in 1990 the annual report of the Ministry of Defence stated that fuel costs had been cut by 39% at a regimental headquarters in one year. Reductions of expenditure of this magnitude only occur because no one ever felt it was his or her responsibility to monitor the fuel budget before. Once some one did, the waste was immediately obvious and now can be prevented.

Let us review the major reforms or changes that have occurred in the last ten years. They are listed in Table 2.4.

Even 13 years after the first reforms were implemented it is still very difficult to view the changes with an open mind. However, a review of the present policies of the three main British political parties is instructive.

All agree that reform is still needed. None would return to the position in 1979. Compulsory competitive tendering is agreed as a useful tool. Most of the privatizations, although not the methods used, are now accepted. The 'Next Steps' reform to make central government departments into semi-independent agencies has received

**Table 2.4** Recent government reforms

| | |
|---|---|
| 1979–82 | Rayner Scrutiny Reports into Whitehall. |
| 1980 | Local Government Planning and Land Act – introduction of Compulsory Competitive Tendering for local authorities. |
| 1982 | Formation of Audit Commission for Local Authorities. |
| 1983 | Formation of National Audit Office. |
| 1984 | Privatization of British Telecom. |
| 1988 | 'Next Steps' reform of Central Government. |
| 1988 | Education Reform Act (Local Management in Schools). |
| 1990 | National Health Service and Community Care Act – the Health Service internal market. |
| 1991 | The Citizen's Charter. |

wide support as has the concept of the Audit Commission and National Audit Office. Local management in schools is generally accepted. Even the health service reforms are now not strongly disputed. The Citizen's Charter has the support of all parties, although the details are disputed. It is now possible to call all these changes to British bureaucracy 'reforms' as opposed to policy changes. Tory landowners did not like the 1832 Reform Act, but it was definitely reform. I think the same can be said of these reforms. Many may have found them unpalatable but in total they do form a real attempt to remove some of the problems that most people recognize are wrong with the way we run our public services.

## Value for money and the reforms

Before we can see how the reforms have attempted to tackle the problem of increasing value for money in the public services in response to public concern and the 'Triple Squeeze', we need to understand how value for money is achieved.

Value for money falls nicely into three elements. These are: *goal congruence; professional flair;* and *management information.*

## Goal congruence

Goal congruence is the most important aspect of value for money. It is also the most difficult to obtain. In essence goal congruence in the public sector means that public servants of all grades need to work with the public interest as paramount. Chapter 3 looks at this vital prerequisite of economy, efficiency, and effectiveness in detail and concludes that traditionally public servants, often unwittingly, have failed to place the public need before their own interests. A simple example illustrating this is the infuriating habit that many public offices have of opening at 10.30 am and closing at 4 pm. The opening practices of public offices can be contrasted to those of the suppliers of many other essential goods and services who tend to provide a much more flexible and consumer orientated service. The majority of people use petrol and it is obtainable 24 hours a day. Everybody needs food and supermarkets and corner shops usually stay open until at least 8 pm. The public sector often fails to meet consumer needs so directly.

Any system that is designed to promote VFM in the public sector must tackle the extremely difficult issue of goal congruence so that public bodies clearly serve the public interest.

## Management information

Lord Rayner, who carried out the 'scrutiny reports' into the operation of Whitehall (see Table 2.4) found a now famous rodent, the £30 Ministry of Agriculture laboratory rat. The market price of a laboratory rat was £2 but the Ministry bred its own for just 15 times the cost. How could this situation ever occur and then be allowed to continue? The truth is that no one ever knew how much the rats were costing to produce. There was no management information on the cost of breeding rats. If you run an organization where value for money is important then it is essential to have the information necessary to help make decisions and to control operations. If you know your own rats cost more than £2 then you stop breeding them and buy in. In this way it is impossible to arrive at a situation of paying 15 times the going rate.

If goal congruence is the most important prerequisite for improved public sector value for money then good management information runs a close second. The problem is that in practice it is sometimes difficult to introduce effective management information systems without having goal congruence first.

## Professional flair

There are lots of ways of conscientiously doing a job. However, some methods will be more efficient than others. Flair for a job is a major part of obtaining value for money. As an example a good valuer may suggest selling two pieces of land using the proceeds to buy a third so as to provide better services and reduced transport costs. A less enlightened individual might decide the status quo was an easier option.

Professional flair was the first area of public sector value for money that was investigated by reformers and numerous specific suggestions about how to do jobs better were made. However flair is inevitably less important than goal congruence because the public interest is clearly a public body's prime concern. It is also subsidiary to management information because unless you can measure the success of an idea it is not possible to be sure that it represents an improvement.

This book does not deal with the 'professional flair' aspects of value for money. Instead it concentrates on goal congruence and management information as the two main methods of promoting value for money. The problems the public sector faces are in the main management problems. Professional flair is thwarted again and again by a lack of management objectives, poor or non-existent management information and defective control and decision making procedures. In these circumstances we need to start tackling the management malaise as well as specific professional problems associated with individual services.

In the reform of the public sector there are some very substantial changes necessary. This book does not wish to suggest that public sector managers should sit back and wait for politicians or Whitehall to tackle the big issues before they start to change the way their own departments or organizations are managed. Work is needed at all levels. Now is the time to begin to develop management skills and techniques so that you are in the forefront of change.

Much has been written on specific VFM problems and readers are encouraged to obtain copies of works relevant to their fields. The Audit Commission have produced some excellent reports on areas of concern such as primary schools, use of motor vehicles, and leisure facilities. The National Audit Office have published many studies on individual government departments. Whatever area of public service you are in you will find both local and central government focused VFM audit reports useful when used in conjunction with the techniques described in the book. (A list of VFM publications is given in the Bibliography.)

## The reforms

The reforms of the early 1980s were primarily concerned with the problem of professional flair or the lack of it. The Rayner reviews were detailed scrutinies of over 150 civil service operations in an attempt to find poor professional practice and root it out. This view of the civil service was not radical and in essence followed the doctrine of technical competence. Where practices were deficient they should be changed to provide a more professional service. A typical Rayner report was written by Clive Ponting who worked for Lord Rayner briefly before later becoming better known for not breaching s2 Official Secrets Act 1911. This report is quoted in Peter Hennessy's book *Whitehall.*

> I had found glaring examples of waste and inefficiency everywhere – warehouses full of food that was stored for years, three separate distribution organisations, and nobody in charge of the system.

Rayner's work was taken over in 1983 by the newly formed National Audit Office and in 1982 for local government by the Audit Commission. These two bodies have worked since their formation to root out examples of poor value for money and to instill best practice methods into all the various trades that make up central and local government. Much of their work has been successful but as explained above it cannot quite get to the core of the value for money problem because that involves reform of the management system as well as specific improvements to services.

The next attempt to strike at the value for money problem involved management accounting and Michael Heseltine's Management Information System for Ministers (MINIS). The Financial Management Initiative that followed was designed to carry MINIS throughout the Civil Service. The initiative was much less successful than was expected. It was not that the reforms were wrong it was that nobody was implementing them. The solution to this problem was the 'Next Steps' initiative which is discussed later.

## Privatization

In the face of this relative lack of success the privatization campaign that started with British Telecom was likely to be more successful.

As public sector reform the privatization of the nationalized industries was effective for two reasons. First, it uncoupled the management of major industries from the political process. Second, where a genuinely monopoly-free market existed for the goods and services the industry provided, much of the problem of goal congruence was solved. In some of the privatizations a free or nearly free market had long existed. Examples include British Steel, Rolls Royce and British Petroleum. In others there was no market and attempts were made to create one. Power generation appears to be a relatively successful market whereas for water there is a severe shortage of competition.

As reform of the public sector, privatization has given a clear rule. If a public service can be provided effectively outside the public sector using regulation as a means of control then this is usually preferable to government ownership. Paradoxically perhaps, goal congruence and the public interest are often better served when organizations are free from direct government control.

## Compulsory competitive tendering

Compulsory competitive tendering is the mandatory requirement for public bodies to seek bids on the open market for contract type work even if the body has its own workforce capable of doing the job. As early as 1980 legislation was passed that required local authorities to tender proportions of their council house maintenance and highways maintenance work. So that the inhouse workforce can compete in the tender they are required to set themselves up as a quasi company called a 'Direct Service Organization' which must make a 5% return on the capital employed in the business.

Subsequently more and more aspects of the services provided by local authorities have become subject to compulsory competitive tendering. Now it covers all manual work from school meals to refuse collection. The Citizen's Charter and subsequent government publications make clear that tendering may soon be introduced into many clerical and professional services provided by local authorities.

The strength of compulsory tendering is that by using the free market, goal congruence becomes more likely. A company tendering in a free market for street sweeping will have as its goal efficient street sweeping as a method of earning good profits in the long run. In contrast an inhouse workforce working without the discipline of a market tends to have staff welfare as its first concern. Clearly, staff must be looked after and given a decent wage. Unfortunately, the inhouse system did this to excess. As an example it was well known that refuse collectors in many authorities could finish work at lunch time. I personally knew one such individual who ran a successful jewellery business in the afternoons after his round was finished.

The problems with tendering relate to the market that is formed. Many people feel that there are significant cartels among the providers of local authority services. The story goes that once the tender is published all the local builders, for instance, sit round a table and divide the available work up between themselves to avoid bidding against each other. My view is that these fears are excessive. Supporting this contention is the fact that the prices submitted for tenders over the last few years have been very keen. There is, however, a long history of corruption regarding government contracts of all kinds. Profiteers in the First World War are a particularly well-known example. The solution to this is not the old equally corrupt inhouse system but proper care and vigilance in drawing up tenders.

If greater goal congruence has been one VFM benefit another has been better management information. Under the inhouse system work was done until the money ran out. No one knew how much was achieved with the money spent. It was assumed that it was all used wisely and that was good enough.

But once it became necessary to draw up tenders for work a great change took place. Often for the first time someone had to consider how much work needed to be done to reach an acceptable standard. As an example people had to find out how much grass there was to cut whereas before they had just cut the grass they had found. Tendering forces standards to be explicitly set. Should the grass on housing estates be one inch long or is two inches quite acceptable? It matters because the cost of short grass is much higher than that of long.

The compulsory tendering process now means that costs have been calculated and standards set for many local authority services for the first time. With the benefit of much increased goal congruence and hopefully some flair on the part of the winning companies and direct service organizations compulsory competitive tendering meets many of the requirements for improved value for money. There are limits as to the suitability of tendering but to those services to which it is applicable it is a useful VFM tool.

## The 'Next Steps' initiative

In 1987 Sir Robin Ibbs who was in charge of the central government Financial Management Initiative asked the Efficiency Unit to produce a report to the prime minister on the success of the reforms on the management of Whitehall. The second sentence of the report read 'there is a long way to go'.

One of the main findings was that 'most civil servants are very conscious that senior management is dominated by people whose skills are in policy formation and who have little experience of managing or working where services are actually delivered'. This was about as clear a message as could be given that the civil service lacked that all important ingredient of goal congruence. The implication was that the real aim of senior civil servants was often self-development through directing political events rather than the provision of services in the public interest. The suggested solution to this problem was a scheme to break the civil service up into units 'which focus on the job to be done'.

The idea was to divide the provision of services from the formulation of policy by devolving public services to quasi-independent units or agencies. The benefit was an increase in goal congruence to be followed hopefully by improved management information and professional flair. As yet it is difficult to assess the success of the new agencies because there are few of them and they have been in existence for so short a time. My guess is that they will mark a big improvement from the old system but fall short of the radical changes that are required as a result of the 'Triple Squeeze'. The main problem will still be a real lack of goal congruence.

## Local management in schools and the hospital reforms

These reforms are much more radical than the others we have already discussed. They attempt to bring a new ingredient into the provision of public services – competition, as a spur to much improved goal congruence without the use of competitive tendering.

In Chapter 10 we discuss the importance of competition. Throughout the book we see how work practices are naturally changing to promote very small semi-autonomous groups who are dedicated to providing a top-class service. Work is becoming more interesting and employees are being trusted to work without direct supervision. The totalitarian management of the old-fashioned employer is being slowly replaced by a more democratic workplace. Employees are being recognized as individuals by virtue of their real achievements. It is a change I find heartening.

In the context of these changes competition within public services is entirely apt. A headteacher of a locally managed school is a significant individual not just another county council employee. The same applies to hospital trusts. Employees see themselves as part of a finite organization all working for the same ends in the public interest. Two of the greatest producers of culture in Europe have been the city states of renaissance Italy and enlightenment Germany. Within a small organization people can realistically aspire to be recognized. The renaissance artists and the composers of Germany were the great achievements of this type of system. On a more prosaic scale a competing public service broken up into manageable units stands a chance of producing similar benefits.

## Citizen's Charter

The Citizen's Charter is a mixture of a large number of different measures covering the public services in the widest sense. Much of the charter gives commitments to more of the reforms we have considered above. But the main aspect which is new is the idea of a series of charters covering a number of key services – education, council tenants, social services, and so on.

Each charter sets down a series of broad standards, for instance clear publication of all assessment and exam results in a school, with an implied contract that failure to provide a service represents a breach of trust. Some Labour local authorities have developed the idea of a semi-formal customer contract between the council and the public. This takes the charter idea to its logical conclusion.

How the Citizen's Charter will develop is not yet clear. However there is clear cross-party political support for a system that provides accountability and sets targets.

The basis for this type of reform is an attempt to promote goal congruence and management accounting. Whether it will produce all the results hoped for is as yet conjecture but there is no doubt that as a basis for change in the core services of the public sector it will force reform.

## The situation now

Thirteen years of reform have had an effect on British public service organizations. The reforms have been the equivalent of gently waking a slumbering giant. Now he or possibly she has got dressed and has regretfully come to the conclusion that he must now go out and do something. Breakfast has been eaten but we are still waiting for the giant to leave the protection of a cosy domestic interior. If only he would go out and work the giant could achieve prodigious feats. As spectators we all think he probably will but there is still a rather unpleasant nagging doubt. The problem is we need his services so desperately badly.

So what has actually changed in the public services? There is certainly much more that has not changed than has. Most of the public sector fails to attract the best graduates. Whitehall highfliers are a numerically small exception. Management information is almost non-existent in local authorities, health authorities and much of the rest of the public sector. Enthusiasm for change and excellence is improving but is often at pitiful levels. Most public enterprises remain accountable to no one.

All this is beginning to change but the skills needed to manage this change are very scarce. For instance there are over 136 000 qualified accountants in the private sector. On a pro rata basis one might expect 25 000 in the public sector; in fact there are probably only 5000. The education service has never taught teachers to manage large organizations. The education diploma courses that train teachers contain no management or administrative theory. Doctors run hospital departments with no training in the use of resources and the same applies to most of the other skills employed in the public service. Whereas in industry the young recruit if he or she receives no management training can learn as second best from those around him or her, in the public sector this has never been possible in the same way. As a colleague of mine once remarked in the public sector people just get on with their work in splendid isolation.

## The opportunity

This chapter has attempted to analyse the challenge that the public sector faces over the next ten years. At various times the public services have provided great opportunities for the energetic and able. The reforms resulting from the Reform Act of 1832 are one such period as are the great Victorian investments in water, gas and public transport. In our own century the establishment of the welfare state after the Second World War was another period of opportunity and challenge. We are now entering another era of change. The opportunities available to those managing public sector services are as substantial as in those previous periods of reform. Organizations that are subject to reform provide great opportunities to the energetic and able. When skills are in short supply, competition within an organization is weak. And this means that success and recognition is that much more attainable. Now that the public sector is breaking up into smaller units it provides the opportunity for an exciting career in a working environment that can provide recognition for the effort you have put in.

## Summary

The public services are moving inexorably towards change. This change is being forced by economic and social factors that are largely outside the scope of governments to alter. The costs of public services are set to rise dramatically over the next ten years outstripping the benefits of economic growth.

The existing quality of service provision will be very difficult to finance. The additional quality of service that electors now expect will be impossible to achieve without radical increases in the value for money that services achieve. This book analyses the changes needed to unleash greater economy, efficiency and effectiveness. It then demonstrates how these qualities can be achieved.

The reforms that have occurred during the 1980s have set the stage for the change that is needed. Beneath the political bickering there is a consensus that radical change is vital. For the dedicated public servant the opportunities now available for managing change and benefiting one's fellow citizens are unparalleled since the formation of the welfare state 50 years ago.

## Reader questionnaire

We have looked at the changes that are influencing the public sector. Successful public sector organizations will be those that anticipate these changes early and actively plan effective strategies for the future.

To what extent is your organization or department planning for change?

The questionnaire that follows is designed to allow you to analyse your personal and organizational responses to the challenges that lie ahead. First, we consider *your* views on change. How radical or conservative are you?

Next, the questionnaire reviews the extent to which you and your organization is planning for the future:

1. Who will your clients be in the future;
2. What will their needs be;
3. Will your workload increase or decrease?

Last, we consider some of the operational changes that you should already be considering so that you can meet the demands that lie ahead. This part of the questionnaire is designed to lead on to the following chapters of the book where the organizational changes needed are discussed in much greater detail.

## Are you ready for change?

1. Do you see change as an opportunity to improve the service you provide or as a threat to your profession and those you serve?

ANSWERS

(a) Could your organization or department be better run?
(b) What are the major changes that should be made?
(c) Which of these changes would provide the best value to the public? Would they tackle the problems identified in the chapter?
(d) Would your welcome more responsibility to promote and be accountable for these changes?
(e) Would you welcome radical changes in the way your organization was run if you knew that these changes would be implemented and the public would benefit?
(f) Would you welcome other changes if it could be proved that they would benefit the public.
(g) In the light of the rapid changes in society discussed in the chapter (the 'Triple Squeeze') would you be prepared to initiate change before receiving firm proof that the public would in fact benefit?
(h) Do you consider waste in the social services immoral; is it the taxpayer that loses or the recipients of the service?
(i) Given that there is needless waste in most organizations, what type of changes should the public services make to improve the quality and quantity of the services they offer?

## Are you and your organization planning for change?

2. Are you already gathering information about how both,
   (i) your clients, and
   (ii) your costs,
   will change over the next ten years?

ANSWERS

(a) Are you in an expanding service or a declining one?
(b) Are the costs of salaries and supplies in your organization increasing in cost in real terms or only at the rate of inflation?
(c) Do you or your organization put time and resources aside to find answers to these types of questions?
(d) Is it your responsibility to consider these questions or is this type of work only done by central departments?
(e) In what way is your staff recruitment policy tailored to meet the medium and long-term (five to ten year) demands your department will face?

(f) Do you have a staff training policy aimed at providing your department with the skills it will need in the medium to long term?
(g) Has your investment in computers, buildings and other substantial capital equipment been planned to maximize efficiency in the medium to long term?
(h) Can you provide strong arguements to defend the recent staffing and capital investment policies of your department and organization?

## Is your organization changing to meet future challenges?

3. Is the management of your department flexible and adaptable?

ANSWERS

(a) Do you have effective and efficient methods of covering short-term increases in work load?
(b) Do you have management information systems so that you can closely monitor your department's outputs and costs?
(c) Do you have effective systems so that your department can cooperate with other departments within the organization?
(d) Do you make regular comparisons between the achievements of your department and others elsewhere which do the same work?
(e) What other methods do you use to ensure that your department operates effectively?

Some readers will be naturally concerned that change may be introduced for the sake of change itself and not to benefit the public interest. In this chapter we have analysed the challenges facing the public sector. In the next we look at some of the characteristics of public sector organizations that prevent the public interest being served. This is designed to further reassure those that doubt radical change is needed.

# 3

# Self-interest and shared objectives

Now we look in more detail at one of the most important aspects of effective public sector provision – the need for *all* members of a public body to work for the same goal. When this is achieved all members of the organization are said to be 'goal congruent'. First, we analyse the nature and benefits of motivation. This is followed by a discussion of how traditional public sector management philosophies have shaped the public sector's perception of goal congruence and motivation. Lastly, the prime importance of recognizing the role of 'self-interest' amongst senior and junior public sector staff is emphasized as the explanation for many of the examples given in the chapter.

On Polish building construction sites in the 1980s workers were reputed to have deliberately broken 30% of plate glass on delivery. The consignment would then be deemed defective to the extent that all of it would have to be returned. Result – no glass to use. All go home for the day.

This story illustrates a problem associated with all organizations. The people running the operation at different levels do not necessarily all share the same goals. The goal of the party man who commissioned a building in communist Poland would be amongst other things, to build the building. The goal of the glazier is to avoid work if he can. Take an example nearer to home illustrating the same point. Most of us, at least in our school days, have run for a bus, caught up with it, but then been quite unable to persuade the driver to open the doors to let us on. Or we have been at a request stop; we have waved frantically but the bus has sped past.

The goal of the school child is to get home safely and quickly. Society as a whole will generally hold the same view. The goal of the bus company is to make a reasonable return on investment, this may involve closing the bus route we use, if it is unprofitable. Lastly, the goal of the bus driver may often be to keep the bus moving avoiding stops whenever possible. After all he or she may have a spouse or children to get home to. Figure 3.1 shows diagrammatically the relationship between these sets of goals.

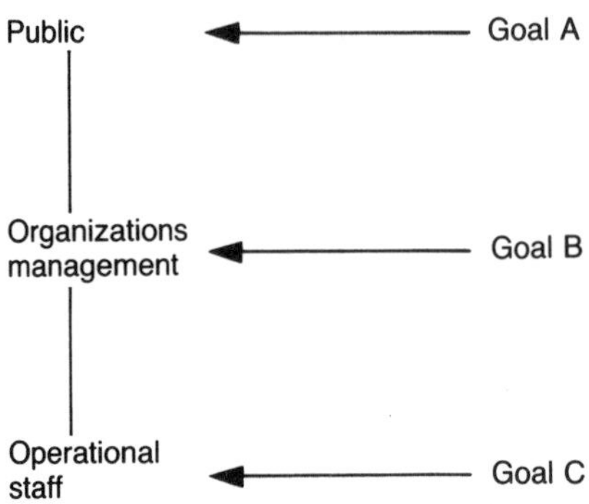


**Fig. 3.1** Goal relationships.

From Fig. 3.1, a number of possibilities now exist:

1. A = B = C
2. A = B ≠ C
3. A ≠ B = C
4. A ≠ B ≠ C

Possibility (1) represents the ideal situation. Everyone is working for a common goal. In (2) the operational staff and the management hold different goals. This is the position illustrated by the Polish glaziers. Possibility (3) might illustrate a company in the business of dumping toxic waste. Management and workforce might work together to dump the waste anywhere, regardless of public safety. Situation (4) represents the worst situation, perhaps the British car industry in the 1970s. The public wanted a good British car. The management designed cars few would buy. The workforce showed little interest in making the cars they were being asked to build.

# Benefits of goal congruence

Now we have defined goal congruence, let us look at its importance. Bertrand Russell in an essay entitled 'In Praise of Idleness' notes that the First World War 'showed conclusively that, by the scientific organisation of production . . . hours of work . . . could be cut down to four. Instead of that the old chaos was restored'. This passage illustrates two points:

1. The war effort was efficient and productive;
2. That once the stimulus of a common and pressing goal disappeared 'chaos was restored'.

Clearly, if Bertrand Russell is correct by all working for the same goal we might finish the working day at lunchtime. The benefits of goal congruence are potentially enormous. On a much smaller scale the English cricket side in the early 1980s under Mike Brierley enjoyed great success. Apart from Ian Botham the team was not noted for its talent, but with strong leadership and great determination it won test matches.

And at the level of the individual, those starting small businesses are driven by an infectious enthusiasm to succeed. When goals are clearly stated and are pursued vehemently by all those involved mankind can achieve extraordinary results. The Italian Renaissance was fuelled by the goal of discovering and understanding the classical world. Scholars, architects, painters and sculptors all worked with one aim. The result was a new view of the world based on logic rather than belief, some of the greatest art and architecture ever produced, and a massive and continuing tourist industry for Italy.

In commercial activities it is goal congruence that helps the Japanese to be so successful. Japanese society is pledged to Japanese commercial success: everyone shares the same goal.

By now it should be clear, whether we be concerned with a war effort, English cricket, Italian intellectual thought or just everyday economic activity, that strong allegiance to clear goals by all the players concerned reaps ample benefits.

## Goal congruence in the public sector

At times the public sector displays goal congruence of the highest order. In the early part of the Gulf crisis in 1990 two British diplomats voluntarily manned the British Embassy in Iraqi occupied Kuwait despite a seige. They were forced to dig their own well to obtain water. During the Second World War a British economy largely under state control was remarkably productive. Its success lead many from a wide spectrum of political thought to believe that an economy largely state run would be effective. From the mid-1940s to perhaps the early 1960s the Soviet state planning system showed great achievements. The common goal of repulsing the invader and then building the Soviet Union into a superpower strong enough to stand up to all comers produced extraordinary results, even if the human rights position was less appealing.

But we are all aware that in many areas of activity, state provision has not been the way to galvanize people into activity. As we saw in Chapter 1 municipal provision of utilities was a success. All could believe in the goal of clean water to every house. But a nationalized steel industry was far less successful. If the overall goal of the enterprise is dull – making steel efficiently in a world where many others do the same work, then traditionally in the public sector goal congruence has been lacking and success has been only partial.

Goal congruence has excelled in the public sector at times of crisis and when the greater public goal has been strongly understood by everybody. But for the everyday, the dull ordinariness of normal existence the public sector has exhibited a strong absence of goal congruence. In the early 1980s Italian state railways ran a train from Naples to Rome that was 24 hours late; the journey time is three hours! In the private sector some enterprises show a similar lack of goal congruence. But the message of the 1980s in Britain, France, Eastern Europe and in much of the rest of the world is that the private sector has been better at producing everyday products than the public sector. Somehow it motivates its staff at all levels to provide better goods and services needed by society.

The point being made is this: in many situations the public sector can be far more successful than the private sector *if* its staff are motivated and all share the same goal. What then can the public sector do to implement goal congruence from top to bottom? To obtain an answer to this we need to look at the management philosophy of public sector organizations.

## Public sector management influences

There have been three major influences on the management philosophy and practice of the public sector:

1. The philanthropic tradition.
2. The theory of 'neutral competence'.
3. The relationship between the public sector 'organizations' and the politicians.

The 'philanthropic tradition', has given the public sector its sense of 'public service', the feeling that it provides protection for those in need. The second, 'neutral competence' relates to the formation of a professional impartial public service. The history of this was discussed in Chapter 1 when we looked at the Northcote–Trevelyan reforms in Britain and the Progressive Movement in the USA. Lastly, the relationship between political master and public servant strongly affects the management of public services.

## The philanthropic tradition

In Chapter 1 we saw that 55% of public sector spending is welfare expenditure – social security, health care, and education. The very success of the modern public sector is based on provision of these services. Welfare became important after the Reform Acts as a more liberal parliament discovered the full horrors of social inequality. Philanthropy, the great Victorian contribution to European culture was born and generations of politicians have worked subsequently for the alleviation of poverty. The great public services were built up when the prominent concern of legislation was help for the needy. But since those formative times two major changes have taken place:

1. 'Philanthropic assistance' now costs at least 25% of the GDP of the UK;
2. The recipients of present-day 'philanthrophy' are in the majority of cases well off.

### *Economic changes*

It is a staggering thought that hospital care, education of children, social services and benefit payments cost 22% of GDP. Nevertheless, that is now the case. The National Health Service is often said to be the third largest organization in the world after the Soviet Army and Indian State Railways! How relevant then are the old altruistic ideas that formed these services in the first place?

Certainly care for the needy is an essential part of civilized life. But the way we interpret it in many of our public services is factious. The problem can be demonstrated like this.

If you give someone a present you tend not to measure the effect of that gift on the economy or society as a whole, since presents are normally given for emotional or political reasons. In many respects the public sector works on a similar basis. A school teacher works to help individual children, the policeman feels he is saving a defenceless society from evil and the social security clerk sees himself as a dispenser of charitable funds. The state charity that the public sector represents is in many ways equivalent to a godfather taking a benevolent interest in a child and sending presents every Christmas and birthday. The giver seeks to improve the lot of the receiver but the effect on society as a whole, particularly the economic effect is considered of no importance. For a godfather this view is quite reasonable; for the providers of public services it is highly damaging.

The problem with the philanthropic view of the public sector is that it does not take account of economic reality. Consequently, the goals of organizations following this view are essentially emotional rather than rational. The health service worker in modern Britain is often perplexed and angry if he is told a treatment is too expensive for National Health Service use. Of course it may be foolish not to use the treatment method in an ideal world. But in most countries public spending is limited to what can be afforded. In this context not all possible treatments will be appropriate if the maximum good is to be achieved. Individuals and organizations need to set goals based on economic reality. The philanthropic view of the public sector is hindering this increasingly.

It is worth giving a concrete example of how the emotional tradition is adversely affecting public services. In everyday life when an individual assists another it is unthinkable for the receiver of help to enquire of the wealth of his or her benefactor. And even in 1990s Britain, the wealth and achievements of a beneficient government tend to remain the subject of surmise alone. It is not only the public who are unaware of the economic or material output of much of the welfare state. Those who actively participate know almost as little as the public to whom they provide services. The nature of philanthropy is to give and not to count the cost and to only cursarily assess the benefit.

Later on in the book we look very carefully at how the public sector can improve its accounting for costs and achievements. But the point made here is that public sector organizations and staff often find it difficult to set sound economic goals for services that have traditionally been run on the basis of love for one's fellow men.

## *Change in clientele*

As the public sector has grown in size the clientele of its welfare functions has changed out of recognition. At the time of the Poor Law Amendment Act 1835, individuals had to be homeless and moneyless to receive assistance in a workhouse. Up until the 1944 Education Act the majority of the population could not consider secondary eduation for their children. And before the formation of the National Health, hospital treatment for the sick depended on the funding and policy of the local hospital. Up until very recently the public welfare organizations had to deal with real and pressing need.

But in the 50 years since the formation of the Welfare State there has been change. Good eduation and health care together with a strongly expanding economy have radically changed the social landscape. We now talk of the proverty trap and inner city problems. The poor are no longer the majority. For most poverty has been eliminated and remains only in economic and geographical pockets of suffering. So how does this affect the welfare state?

The welfare system was set up with the clear goal of assisting those in need. In the introduction to his famous report on 'Social Insurance and Allied Services' published in 1942, Sir William Beveridge is very clear about the status of those whom the new welfare state would help. 'Social insurance', he says, 'fully developed may provide income security: it is an attack upon Want. But Want is only one of the five giants on the road of reconstruction and in some ways the easiest to attack. The others are Disease, Ignorance, Squalor and Idleness'. Not for an instant does he include families with two cars, a video machine and healthy children with good exam results, in his view of those his report was to assist. Just as the public utilities had been a success in the 19th century because the cause was strong and simple so was the welfare state at the beginning of the second half of the 20th century. But where do we stand now with much of the initial task complete? What are the new goals that the major public bodies need to set for themselves and their staff?

This question will be answered by the later chapters of this book. But we can say here that a public service ethic based purely on help for the needy is no longer relevant. It is devisive; it is also inefficient. Let us take an example to illustrate the goal setting problems the welfare services have.

Diabetics periodically have to visit a hospital consultant. The National Health generally does not work on the basis of strict appointments. A patient may wait a considerable time before he sees the specialist. Because he is diabetic the doctor tells his patient to observe strict meal times so that blood sugar levels are kept constant. The irony of the situation is lost on the health service but because of the long wait the diabetic patient has already missed a meal. The old hospital system works on the basis that a doctor is better than no doctor for the suffering individual patient. Subtleties such as regular meal times are quite lost.

Take another example. An education system designed to educate the children of the uneducated is now facing the problem of educating sons and daughters of reasonably well-off families intent on going to polytechnic or university. The doctrine of philanthropy is hardly relevant here. As many teachers all too clearly realize, many of their pupils will finish their education and take a job earning much more than their old teachers. Even in the area of housing benefits paid to those who are eligible for assistance with housing costs, in a large minority of cases the individuals claiming are far from the traditional view of the impoverished. During the 1980s, housing benefit offices were forced to take a daily copy of the *Financial Times* so that they could check the share prices of those claiming benefits to ensure their investments were under the statutory maximum value.

## *Summary*

Up until the present day the prime motivation of public sector organizations and their staff has been a concern for the needs of the less fortunate. Now due very much to the success of policies based on that viewpoint a radical change is due. The twin effects of massive growth in services and a reduction in poverty has meant that now, much more sophisticated goals are needed. The old motivation is stifling the development of better services.

## Neutral competence

Up until the last ten years governments in most countries have attempted to modernize their bureaucracies and run them on a strongly hierarchical basis. Many of the problems of state administration were seen to be due to amateur and in some cases corrupt administration by public servants. The Northgate–Trevelyan Report in Britain and the Progressive Movement in the USA sought with considerable success, to improve public adminstration by introducing the concept of 'neutral competence'. Public servants were to be properly trained professionals working within a strict hierarchy so that decisions could only be made by authorized personnel.

In Chapter 1 we discussed neutral competence because technical excellence combined with an absence of direct political interest has been one of the most important and beneficial innovations in government administration. But although neutral competence was a breakthrough in the impartial furthering of good government it would be naive to imagine that it had solved once and for all the ills of a public service that was previously based on patronage.

The wholly rational view of the public service that neutral competence provides, in contrast to the problems associated with the philanthropic view, is also the cause of many of the difficulties associated with bureaucracies. The problem is this. Because neutral competence creates a divide between public servants and politicians there becomes an encouragement for public servants to foster their own interests at the expense of the task for which they are employed. So that we can fully understand the problems over goal congruence that 'neutral competence' encourages we must look at some examples of the behaviour of public bodies. These illustrate clearly some well-known 'disfunctional' behaviour patterns that we all know occur in public service. Some of the examples may be a little damaging to our professional pride. Although some people find it is easy to fall into the unpleasant habit of discrediting sound public sector achievement, this is not the object here. Rather by analysing some real problems associated with public provision one can hope to solve pressing needs.

### *Problems resulting from the principle of neutral competence*

The hierarchical professionalism that neutral competence entails is characterized by two traits. Regardless of the level of unsung success a public organization has had, many will hold the following view:

1. Public servants are poor at taking decisions and are slow at carrying out routine work. They often appear rude and unhelpful.
2. Public servants are empire builders pushing their interests into the lives of ordinary private people when it is neither necessary nor wanted.

A graphic example of the first trait is given by President Kennedy. During a confrontation with the Russians over Berlin in 1961 he requested advice from the State Department, the equivalent of the British Foreign Office. Despite the crisis an answer was not received for a month and when it did come it gave no useful advice listing only old foreign policy positions. Kennedy's response to the State Department after he had solved the Berlin problem was ruthless. He hired 30 private staff to give him up-to-date advice in their stead.

At the other extreme public servants are seen as officious and overzealous. Perhaps you telephone for tax advice and the next moment you are the subject of a major investigation surrounded by prying tax inspectors. In Britain the Cleveland child abuse affair is a well-known example of this phenomenon. Over a time local paediatric doctors and social workers developed a theory of diagnosing sexual abuse of children. Using this theory they found that many of the children who routinally used the health service or social services showed signs of sexual abuse. Consequently, large numbers of children were taken from their parents and placed in local authority care. Not altogether surprisingly many parents in and around Cleveland felt that their children were about to be taken from them and that they, the parents, would be branded as child molesters. The result was 'enormous concern . . . voiced not only by parents of the children involved but also nurses, police, members of parliament and through the press, the public both in Cleveland and nationally' (Report on the Inquiry into Child Abuse in Cleveland 1987 by Lord Justice Butler-Sloss CM 412, p. 1). The inquiry was critical of staff at the middle management level (doctors and social workers) and of senior management (directors of services) for not recognizing and controlling middle management's actions. The report states that 'the two paediatricians . . . are to be criticized for the . . . certainty and overconfidence with which they pursued the detection of sexual abuse in children referred to them'.

The efficiency of the public sector can be just as worrying to the public as its sloth. But how did the philanthropic public servant become characterized in these ways? And what is the link between worrying over-efficiency and a rather leisurely view of the job in hand?

How is it that public servants can show such contradictory and paradoxical characteristics and how is this related to neutral competence? It could be that some people are happy for a quiet life while others are interested in developing power. Using this theory the behaviour of a public body depends largely on luck. Clearly this is a factor. Not all children's doctors behave in the way described in the Bulter-Sloss report on the Cleveland affair. But we need to go beyond relying on luck to explain how public bodies perform.

In the early part of the chapter we said that there were three major elements to goal congruence; the goal of the public/politician (A), the goal of the organization (B) and the goal of the operational staff (C). Neutral competence directly effects both the A/B relationship, public and organization, and the B/C, the organization and its staff.

## *The goals of staff within an organization*

In both the examples we have looked at the goal of the public sector organization was not that of the public at large. So much is clear. But what were the goals of the staff in both the State Department and in Cleveland?

It is important to make clear now that the view of senior executive staff is synonymous with the organization's goal. They are the Bs referred to above. This group of people are theoretically quite separate from the majority of staff employed. These we will refer to as the 'operational staff', the Cs.

In the example of Kennedy's State Department it is clear that both the organization and its staff were generally in a state of slumber. Neither had goals congruent with the public interest as represented by the president. In the Cleveland case the social services authority and health authority were motivated very differently to their operational staff, the social workers and paediatricians.

The problem is, that neutral competence as a public sector management philosophy does not address the human need for motivation. To some extent it replaces the philanthropic motivation of the past with a general feeling that professional people are motivated by their professional calling.

Professional people are motivated by their vocations. Everyone knows that doctors and nurses, for instance, are usually dedicated to healing. But this somewhat simplistic view of the world is not adequate when a significant percentage of Western economies are at stake. Professional motivation is not a sufficient basis to run an economy. As an example bankers take professional examinations, but no bank considers this sufficient motivation for its employees. Cheap mortgages, regular staff assessments and other perks are used to direct the bankers best efforts in the direction the bank organization sees fit. Of course the public sector does not always leave its employees to motivate themselves through professional standards. As we will see the Federal Bureau of Intelligence in the United States certainly did not. But the trend in Britain has been to avoid managing to encourage goal congruence between employees and organizations. This is especially the case with education, health, social services – the areas with the highest proportions of professional staff.

Second, the philosophy of neutral competence tends to avoid issues of motivation and goal congruence because of an implicit but unvoiced fear that motivation except by professional standards is synonymous with politicalization of the service. The feeling is that services will cease to be neutral politically and will become corrupt. This view is essentially pessimistic. Motivation can be linked to political causes, but it can just as well be linked to pecuniary gain, honour or other attempts to increase an individual's well-being. In Britain, the armed services are very good at motivating their personnel by a combination of service and unit pride, lively competition between individuals and promotion prospects linked with opportunities for foreign travel. Yet few seriously consider the services politically partial as a result.

If 'neutral competence' has led to a general unwillingness to look seriously at the goal congruence of staff it has also contributed to problems over organizational goals. It is to this second half of the problem that we turn next.

## *The organization's goals*

Let us consider two examples that illustrate how public service organizational goals can be formed. The American Federal Bureau of Investigation (FBI) was headed by a certain J. Edgar Hoover from 1924 to 1972. This individual worked under the slogan of professional neutral competence in his, the security field. Because he was professional he was independent. On many occasions this 'independence' brought him into conflict with elected politicians. One of the most extraordinary episodes of such conflict related to Hoover's attitude to Martin Luther King (Victor S. Navasky, *Kennedy's Justice*, New York, Atheneum, 1997, p. 20). From 1963 to 1968, the year of his death, the FBI ran a campaign against Martin Luther King. They promoted their own 'safe' candidate for the leadership of the civil rights movement, and they attempted to blackmail King. All this happened while the American administration was supportive of King. The second example from Britain shows very similar characteristics, although in a much less contentious area.

Lesley Chapman's experience in the Property Services Agency (PSA) described in his book *Your Disobedient Servant* showed that public organizations can have very different goals to that of the society at large. He described how he instituted savings of about 50% in the maintenance of government property in the Southern Region of the PSA. Here he was duplicating society's goals in his own organization. The trouble arose when politicians attempted to produced similar savings in other PSA regions.

The book tells how for nearly ten years senior staff in the other PSA regions resisted the improvements and cost reductions Chapman pioneered. And by 1976 he felt he had little option but to resign. In 1968 Lord Winterbottom minister of Public Buildings and Works demanded action to cut costs but nothing happened. Then John Silkin, the new minister attempted to obtain action. Chapman maintains his wishes were watered down by senior civil servants and little happened. The next minister, a Conservative, Paul Channon took an interest but met a similar fate. If one idea comes across clearly in Chapman's book it is the divergence between civil service and government aims. Efficiency benefits ministers but not bureaucrats.

In both examples we can see that neutral competence is being used to bolster unacceptable organizational goals. Politicians representing in these instances the public interest could not bring themselves to accept that a concept that their predecessors had conceived to protect the public good was being used against them. The FBI and PSA officials were deemed to be neutral, and therefore acting correctly and professionally. Neither of the governments involved in these episodes in the USA or Britain were prepared to act and make a serious attempt to solve the problems they appear to have perceived. The slogan of neutral competence was too great a talisman to threaten. Even in our earlier example of Kennedy's problems with the State Department the solution was not reform. Rather, Kennedy left the old organization intact and satisfied his wants using a new parallel system – 30 personal advisors.

But why do public organizations behave periodically in such an anti-social manner? The problem appears to be that senior civil servants are encouraged by neutral competence to represent an organization rather than the public at large. Their professional success is limited to their organization. This may work well if the organization works for the public good. But public organization can 'succeed' as we have seen by working diametrically against the public, the perceived political neutrality used as a very effective shield.

## *Summary*

During the last 100 years the doctrine of neutral competence has helped to build the vast public sectors we now have in all developed economies. In this context it must be seen as a substantial success. Public services are generally properly managed for the benefit of their 'clients' and society, this with limited waste and a near absence of corruption.

But the problems associated with the 'doctrine' are real. The extreme examples we have looked at illustrate the much more general problems of goal setting and motivation which apply to most public services to a greater or lesser extent. As we discuss later in the book more fully what is required is not rejection of neutral competence. This would be the equivalent of rejecting the idea of personal cleanliness because deep baths were wasteful of water. What is needed is an understanding that neutral competence requires additional sophistication concerning issues of goal congruence and motivation.

## The relationship between politicians and public servants

A review of the goal setting problems of the public sector is not complete unless we briefly investigate how politicians and public servants interact.

The relationship between politicians and public servants is complex. It takes the form of a game where the stakes vary from the insignificant to the very substantial. The politicans are theoretically strong when bold initiatives are required since they are potentially very powerful. The public servant has the advantage of knowing the ground much better than his opponent. He can lay traps, and bluff. And most importantly time is on his side. The politician needs to obtain quick results to succeed. Not so the public servant who knows he or she can wait for his or her chance.

In a magnificent passage at the beginning of his diaries, Richard Crossman, a Labour cabinet minister in the 1960s, describes day-by-day his total bewilderment as a minister in the hands of the civil service. Similarly, he describes his little victories over officialdom. They are hilarious in their pettiness and lack of consequence to the governing of the nation. The following is an exerpt from the diaries.

> *Thursday, October 22nd*
> I was appointed Minister of Housing on Saturday, October 17th, 1964. Now it is only the 22nd but, oh dear, it seems a long, long time. It also seems as though I had really transferred myself completely to this new life as a Cabinet Minister. In a way it's just the same as I had expected and predicted. The room in which I sit is the same in which I saw Nye Bevan for almost the first time when he was Minister of Health, and already I realize the tremendous effort it requires not to be taken over by the Civil Service. My Minister's room is like a padded cell, and in certain ways I am like a person who is suddenly certified a lunatic and put safely into this great, vast room, cut off from real life and surrounded by male and female trained nurses and attendants. When I am in a good mood they occasionally allow an ordinary human being to come and visit me; but they make sure that I behave right, and that the other person behaves right; and they know how to handle me. Of course, they don't behave *quite* like nurses because the Civil Service is profoundly, deferential – 'Yes, Minister! No, Minister! If you wish it, Minister!' – and combined with this there is a constant

> preoccupation to ensure that the Minister does what is correct. The Private Secretary's job is to make sure that when the Minister comes into Whitehall he doesn't let the side or himself down and behaves in accordance with the requirements of the institution.
>
> It's also profoundly true that one has only to do absolutely nothing whatsoever in order to be floated forward on the stream. I have forgotten what day it was – indeed, the whole of my life in the last four days has merged into one, curious, single day – when I turned to my Private Secretary, George Moseley, and said, 'Now, you must teach me how to handle all this correspondence.' And he sat opposite me with his owlish eyes and said to me, 'Well, Minister, you see there are three ways of handling it. A letter can either be answered by you personally, in your own handwriting; or we can draft a personal reply for you to sign; or, if the letter is not worth your answering personally, we can draft an official answer.' 'What's an official answer?' I asked. 'Well, it says the Minister has received your letter and then the Department replies. Anyway, we'll draft all three variants,' said Mr Moseley, 'and if you just tell us which you want . . .' 'How do I do that?' I asked. 'Well, you put all your in-tray into your out-tray,' he said, 'and if you put it in without a mark on it then we deal with it and you need never see it again.' (pp. 21–2)

In contrast public servants know that politicians can decide to disband or reorganize their department or organization at the drop of a hat. The evidence for this abounds. Local authorities in England cannot now employ manual staff except through the vehicle of a 'direct service organization', a semi-independent financially motivated body. The old civil service District Audit Service was replaced by the independent Audit Commission, British Gas was sold to the private sector, and Chatham Dockyard was closed with a loss of 8000 jobs. These are but a few changes out of many. So why do politicians of all persuasions get themselves into the difficulties Richard Crossman records?

The present relationship between public servants and politicians is not the result of chance. It is the result of years of evolution through trial and error. The position is in many ways ideal for the players involved. Richard Crossman knew from the very start of his period in office 'that one has only to do absolutely nothing whatever in order to be floated forward on the stream'. And if he does nothing, the public servant does the work of a cabinet minister. Both will be pleased with the situation.

Alternatively, if the minister or his local government equivalent takes it upon themselves to instigate change both he or she and the public servants will be heavily involved exercising power. Both again will be content. So what are the components of the relationship between politicians and the organization that is there to serve him? In short, they are as follows:

1. Political delegation of authority. The politician reduces his workload while the public servant's role increases to his advantage.
2. Political delegation of responsibility. The politician by delegation distances himself from responsibility for a government's actions.

   The public servant again increases his role to his advantage since his accountability is less than that of the elected politicians.
3. Electoral scheming. Politicians are well aware that they can increase their popularity by:

(a) Assisting the public with problems associated with officialdom – politicians 'clinics', etc;
(b) Appearing to reform the public sector to benefit electors.

The politicians benefit by giving assistance to known grievances. The public servant often benefits from increased funding as a result.

4. Political specialization. Politicians benefit from specializing in single issues, because this gives them the direct support of interest groups.

Specializing politicians require help from public servants. As a result both politician and public servant benefit.

This is not the place to discuss at length this fascinating subject. But one fundamental point should be clear by now. Politicians are usually more than happy to accept the stability that control by public servant brings to political life. After the work of democratic representation is over little energy is left to directly manage or reform what amounts to a substantial percentage of the nation's productive capacity.

As public servants what can we do? Obviously, the politician/public organization game is poor at formulating powerful motivating influences to control the management of the everyday. Norman Straus, a former adviser to Margaret Thatcher, suggested a new independent public body called 'NET', the 'Network for Exploration and Transformation', to give the public service a strong sense of direction. This idea has the benefit of recognizing the problem but it ignores the vital role of politicians in motivating bureaucracy.

# The way forward

Philanthropy and neutral competence represent much of the essence of public sector; similarly wrangling between public sector bodies and politicians is inevitable. But change is needed so that public sector organizations work more clearly for the public interest and so that the staff in those organizations place their efforts fully behind that same public interest.

The extraordinary anecdotes we have discussed throughout this chapter show a range of behaviour patterns, from the effective to the ineffective and from cunning to a rather limp foolishness. Yet in all but one of the examples we have looked at those acting against the public interest have got away with their actions. Polish building workers were very seldom charged for criminal damage, the State Department was not subject to closure or major reform, the FBI under Hoover continued unhindered by politicians in their work and the Property Services Agency was not forced to make drastic cuts. Only the doctors and social workers in the Cleveland affair received effective admonishment. What can we conclude from this? There are a number of conclusions, but the most important from our viewpoint is this: all the players in the examples acted rationally to promote there own self-interest at the expense of the interests of society as a whole. So successfully did they all manage this that despite the great publicity of many of these cases the choice of action for all but those in the Cleveland affair was vindicated when looked at from the individual's viewpoint.

The prime motive for the actions of public servants is self-interest. Put less emotively we can say that 'rational choice' determines many of the actions of the public servant whether he or she is supporting public goals or hindering them. Are we all to be horrified at this – public servants working for themselves rather than the public? No, not in the least. We should be greatly reassured. Most of the rest of the world works to better the individual rather than society as a whole. Why should civil servants be different? The problem arises because society does not expect 'public servants' to be primarily serving themselves. National Health Service doctors work for the nation, we believe. The welfare services are rooted in the philanthropic tradition as we have seen. Nowhere in the tradition of Western public services does the concept of self-interest ever raise itself. Electors, politicians and public servants themselves are constantly surprised by this elementary fact.

Public sector management methods need to recognize that reform must be people based. Any system that fails to fully incorporate the needs and aspirations of employees at all levels will be *abused*. Hard work is avoided by all if there is no reward; ambitious individuals will seek rewards that are against the public interest. Public sector organizations need to incorporate a clear system of personnel reward to encourage the best efforts of all to further public goals. At present few bureaucracies in the world have fully grasped this fact.

## Reader questionnaire

We have discussed goal setting and motivation for the whole of the public sector. But if you are to improve the performance of your organization a thorough analysis of its goal congruence is needed.

An analysis of your organization will look at two areas:

1. Motivation of operational staff
   Divided into:
   (a) personal motivation
       – are you motivated? (questionnaire 1)
       – what is the reason for your motivation? (questionnaire 2)
   (b) motivation of junior staff (questionnaire 3)
2. Organizational motivation (questionnaire 4).

Most of the ideas included in the questionnaire are not new. But it is useful to take the opportunity to examine your own organization's motivation and goal setting in the context of the problems we have discussed in the chapter.

## Personal motivation

1. Do you consider yourself motivated in your work?

ANSWERS

   (a) Are you actively concerned about the quality of service you provide?
   (b) Do you subject yourself to regular self-assessment concerning the quality of your work?

(c) Do you enquire from your clients (i.e. the public or other internal departments you service) what improvements or additions to the service they would like to see?
(d) Do you seek and obtain up-to-date training so that your work is of the highest quality?
(e) Do you ask for/obtain regular assessments of your work by superiors?
(f) Do your superiors actively attempt to motivate you in your work? i.e. by monitoring your performance against targets, recognizing achievements, encouraging ideas, etc.?
(g) Do you ensure that you motivate your staff so that your own aspirations are properly put into practice?
(h) Do you attempt to monitor the success of your staff motivation policies? i.e. by regular staff appraisals?
(i) Do you set challenging budgets for your department? Do you properly monitor the achievements recorded?

Positive answers to these questions will indicate a very high level of motivation. Later in the book we discuss how motivation and strong goal setting can be combined with good management information to give optimum results. If you score poorly the second questionnaire below should help you to find the reason for this.

2. What is the cause of your motivation?

ANSWERS

(a) Good/fair remuneration package.
(b) Fear of losing one's job if it is not done well.
(c) Loyalty to those who work with you.
(d) Strong support from superiors.
(e) Professional ethics.
(f) Concern for the real needs of clients who rely on you.
(g) Promotion prospects.
(h) A feeling of personal challenge in overcoming problems efficiently and effectively.

All of the above are important. In an organization that aims for a high quality service you should score well on all the above heads. If you are motivated you will want to motivate your staff. The next questionnaire is to assess your performance here.

## Motivation of junior staff

3. Are your staff motivated?

ANSWERS

(a) Do you objectively monitor the quality of your staff's collective and individual output on a regular basis (either personnally or through subordinates)?
(b) Do you recognize staff achievements by:
  (i) Regular personal assessments of a period's work?
  (ii) Congratulating individuals on their success?
  (iii) Explaining how their efforts fit in to wider organizational context?
(c) Do you promote the development of your staff by:
  (i) Providing training?
  (ii) Setting tasks that use individuals' skills to the fullest?
  (iii) Providing the necessary internal and external contracts to assist their work?
  (iv) Setting clear targets and enforcing them?
(d) Do you make sure that your staff know that you value them by:
  (i) Showing that you recognize their achievements, (b) above.
  (ii) Showing an interest in their interests and concerns.
(e) Do you give your staff challenges in their work by:
  (i) Setting clear objectives?
  (ii) Allowing scope for taking more responsibility?
  (iii) Encouraging ideas and the taking of incremental responsibility.

Unless you motivate your staff to share your goals your objectives will not be achieved.

Lastly you will not be reaching your full potential unless your organization's goals are similar to your own. The last questions allow you to investigate the motives of the public body you are part of.

## Organizational motivation

4. What do you consider motivates the organization you work for?

ANSWERS

(a) Does it monitor the service it gives to the public?
(b) Does it set minimum objective standards for the service it gives?
(c) Does your organization have effective methods of ensuring that weaknesses in service are corrected?
(d) If the service your organization provides were to be substandard would the public go elsewhere;
  (i) Readily?
  (ii) With some reluctance?
  (iii) Not at all?
(e) If your organization provides a first rate service what benefits does it derive?

# Part Two

## The Tools of Management Reform

# 4

# What makes an organization function?

This chapter seeks to analyse the context within which the management of public enterprise operates. The public sector is composed of predominantly large organizations. If we are to understand the needs of these organizations we have to start by looking at the general requirements of all organizations. The complex nature of public bodies can then be understood from a more solid basis. The types of requirements which we describe are work objectives, resources of labour and materials, and management information and accounting.

In the previous chapter we looked at one aspect of the behaviour of organizations, the importance of goals and objectives. We now go back one stage and ask what other requirements do organizations have? By answering this question we see that goal setting is closely linked to the provision of management information and the accounting needs of an organization.

## Organizations

Society is made up of a large number of interrelated organizations. People may work in a business, belong to the Womens Institute, bring up a family and sit as a school governor. Others may belong to a street gang or participate in a bridge club. Organizations of all sizes and complexities abound.

If we understand the idea of an organization almost innately, perhaps we can usefully define some of the common elements of all organizations that apply regardless of their complexity and size.

## Membership

All organizations have a **membership**. In some cases this is highly defined for instance in the traditional family – two parents plus children. But this need not be the case. School and college old boy and girl associations, for example, include all those who went to the same educational establishment and show some sort of interest in meeting from time to time their old school fellows. Membership is an essential element of an organization. Only once the membership has been defined can the other aspects of an organization become relevant. It is important to realize that we are not concerned with a legal but a behavioural view of membership here.

## Objectives

A membership can be obtained only if there is an **object** of membership. Normally, the objectives of the organization and the objectives of the member are similar but this need not be so. The object of a street gang may be to control or rule an area. This object will attract members who share that objective or who will benefit by subscribing to it – perhaps they want free passage through the gang land. Membership of the gang may be the easiest way of obtaining this. However if organizations are to hold together then there must be a set of organizational objectives which the members generally support.

## Materials

If the objects are to be obtained **materials** will be needed. The Womens Institute will need jars of jam for their stalls; a firm of accountants will need skilled staff; an army will need rifles. So far then, we have a set of objectives, a membership and the resources and materials necessary for accomplishing those objectives. But no organization stops there. Every organization has an **ethos**.

## Ethos

Whenever people gather together in common cause they are tied by a shared sentiment above the practical neccessity of shared objectives. Whereas the three other aspects of an organization we have mentioned are essentially objective in character, ethos is subjective. An organization may exist to sell Western cigarettes to Third World peasants in order to make money. You may or may not approve of the objects but it is an objective fact that a membership and the materials to realize the objects exist. But the ethos behind these will set the tone of the enterprise.

One tobacco company may have a very relaxed style based on confidence in a high quality set of products. Another may hold that success is not achieved by exuding a sense of style and class but rather by ruthless hard sell. Ethos, then sets an environment in which the membership and materials or resources attempt to achieve their objectives.

### Feedback

The last major aspect of all organizations is **feedback** on the success of their activities. No organization is oblivious to the effect of time. Every so often the membership will both individually and collectively consider the success it has actually enjoyed in comparison with the objects. If the object has been achieved the organization may terminate its existence. At the other extreme an organization may voluntarily liquidate if none of the objectives are realized. The Social Democratic Party under David Owen was perhaps an example of this. More usually, though, feedback is needed by the membership to plan future support and activities. A set of accounts may show that profits are down due to poor sales performance. The members (the managers and workforce, not the members in a legal sense) of the business organization effected will attempt to rectify this failing based on the accounts feedback received.

## Public sector organizations

Just like all other types of organization, public sector bodies exhibit the main components, that is, *membership, objectives, materials, ethos, feedback.* Because most public sector organizations are large they also tend to be complex. It is therefore worth considering the peculiar nature of public enterprise.

Who are the members of a public body? In law they are limited to elected politicians. But clearly an organization such as the Department of Social Security is not composed of just one member – the Secretary of State. Membership includes the employees as well. That is, civil servants. Senior staff members should hold to the objectives of the department, subject of course to the issues concerning goal congruence discussed in Chapter 3. The minister will find it difficult to work with them if goals conflict strongly. In fact all of the staff will be organizational members to an extent. In the crudest terms most social security clerks will consider payments of benefits to the needy to be an objective of theirs. But whereas the senior staff may well place this objective next to the personal objective of earning a living, the junior staff will tend not to. This takes us back to the issue of goal congruence discussed in the previous chapter.

### Public sector objectives

It is important to realize that not all members are equal. Some will take personal control of managing the organization's business. Others will assist as requested by their seniors. They will all to an extent support the objectives of the organization.

But the crucial point to recognize is that each group of members will do so for different reasons. Just as in our example of a street gang some will join because they wish to 'control' an area others will because they want free passage in that area. Some members of, say, the Department of Social Security join the DSS staff because they want to earn some money, others because they want a career and others still because they wish to assist the poor. All three will, however, be actively supporting the objectives of the organization; all will wish it success at least to an extent because their support will help further their own personal goals.

The objectives of a public body are in some instances quite clear; in others they are far less obvious. Normally an act of parliament lays down the duty of an organization. This duty will form part of an organization's objectives. As an example the Audit Commission was set up under section 11 Local Government Act 1982. Section 12 makes it clear that all local authority auditors will be appointed by this new body. No other guidance is given. In this respect the Audit Commission is typical. In most cases an act is not sufficient to fully lay down the objectives of a public body. The Audit Commission's duties given in the act are expanded in a 'Code of Audit Practice for England and Wales'. But other far more substantial public bodies have no complete set of written objectives. The average local authority will have no explicit objectives and similarly government departments have no written constitution. Taking an example that refers to both central and local government the Highways Act 1980 section 41 requires all highways authorities to maintain roads. Generally speaking that is the limit of parliamentary direction. In contrast private sector businesses have extremely straightforward objectives. A standard objective applicable to most private enterprises might be 'to generate financial gain from making and/or selling a product within the bounds of the law and common decency'. Limited companies are required by the Companies Act 1985 to state in a Memorandum of Association the objects for which the company is run. Things are far more complex when profit is not the main motive for an organization.

Because statute gives so little guidance to public bodies, wide ranges of possible objectives are found. Up until the early 1980s many people felt that one objective of public enterprise was to give people jobs. During the miners' strike in 1984 many felt that it was better to produce expensive coal and to protect miners' employment than to have an efficient coal industry. In 1925 Poplar Borough Council in the East End of London paid wages above the local average to benefit the populace – so-called 'popularism'. Even when a more business-like approach is taken to define the objectives of public bodies severe difficulties are found. The Highways Act we have mentioned requires roads to be 'maintained'. What is maintained? No potholes, silky smooth surfaces, best in Europe or just good enough stop the electors complaining? The same problems apply to the whole range of public services. The Housing Acts require housing authorities to build houses. But how many, and to what standard? Much of the recent rise in homelessness in Britain has arisen because it is not considered acceptable for young adults to live with their parents or step-parents. Fifty years ago this was not the case, and as a consequence house building continues apace while the population falls.

In response to the real problems of setting objectives in the public sector there are a range of practices. Some bodies, such as the Audit Commission, produce a concise but thorough written list of objectives covering all the organizations' activities. Another example is the Local Authority Ombudsman Service. Comprehensive treatment of this type is however rare. Other bodies partially define objectives. Many local authorities produce written standards covering substantial areas of this work. For example, one district I am familiar with requires all paperwork regarding housing improvement grants to be dealt with within specific time limits. But for the majority of public bodies and for the bulk of their activities politicians and senior public servants consider that unstated objectives are preferable to explicit written ones.

We need to look at both the **cause** of this decision and the **effects** it has on public administrations. Britain is a country that fears dogmatism. Politicians and public of all political persuasions dislike the idea of a list of objectives that might limit reasonable actions. Consequently, Britain has no written constitution as well as no written objectives for its public bodies. Lack of written objectives benefits both politicians and public servants. If an objective is never stated one can never fail to achieve it. When the media only ever recognize bad news this failure to set explicit objectives is a great help. In addition when politicians create new services they want all the electoral benefit they can get with the least use of public funds. It is far better to promise a lot and to provide less, than to promise a highly defined but rather mean service which even then may not be delivered. As an example, the National Health Service was created to provide treatment for all. By cleverly omitting details of timescale for this pledge governments of both parties have been able to advertise universal health care while terrible and largely unquantified waiting lists built up. Very recently this issue has been partially addressed in the 'Citizen's Charter' White Paper which suggested a two-year maximum wait.

But the effect of undefined objectives on the quality of management of public bodies is far more serious. While politicians are helped in spreading scarce resources thinly under the guise of stupendous but unmeasured achievement, those working in the public sector found that lack of clear objectives greatly hindered their work. Because objectives were ill-defined and changed at short intervals the public sector developed a lack lustre ethos of doing its best under poor conditions. The present plight of the teaching profession in local authority education is a straightforward example. Because educational objectives were never set down or measured – 'schools are not factories' – teachers have been unable to prove that they have been successful. Neither have they been able to rebut those critics whose disparage the educational achievement of the nation.

Poorly defined objectives have also damaged the ethos of much of the public sector. With the exception of the armed services very few public bodies can mirror the ethos of excellence shown by such diverse non-governmental organizations as Rolls Royce, the Salvation Army, the Red Cross, Harrods, ICI or accountants Arthur Anderson.

## The relationship between the components of an organization

It is useful to show diagrammatically the relationship between setting of objectives, ethos, membership, materials and feedback – the five fundamentals of an organization. Membership, objectives and ethos provide an intellectual and political input and materials, the physical resources needed for the organization to produce results. Feedback from those results then influences members and the other immaterial inputs in a dynamic system (see Fig. 4.1).

For an organization to have feedback to members there must be a system to provide it. A political party will get its most important feedback through election results. These are provided free by the state. Other organizations need to invest heavily if they are to get the information they need. A coal mine will need among other things a weigh bridge so that it can measure the amount of coal it produces. A company such as ICI has a vast array of product measuring, quantity testing and management accounting systems so that people at all levels can monitor the quality and quantity of results achieved. Some organizations obtain adequate feedback through non-accounting methods. Cricket club members will be happy if they are given a summary of match results that show more wins than losses. A Polish club in England will be pleased if membership increases and social activities profilerate. These measures will not be adequate for British Rail. A large complex and financially based organization needs feedback in the form of accounts. Schools, hospitals, administrative offices all fall into this category as does the majority of the rest of the public sector.

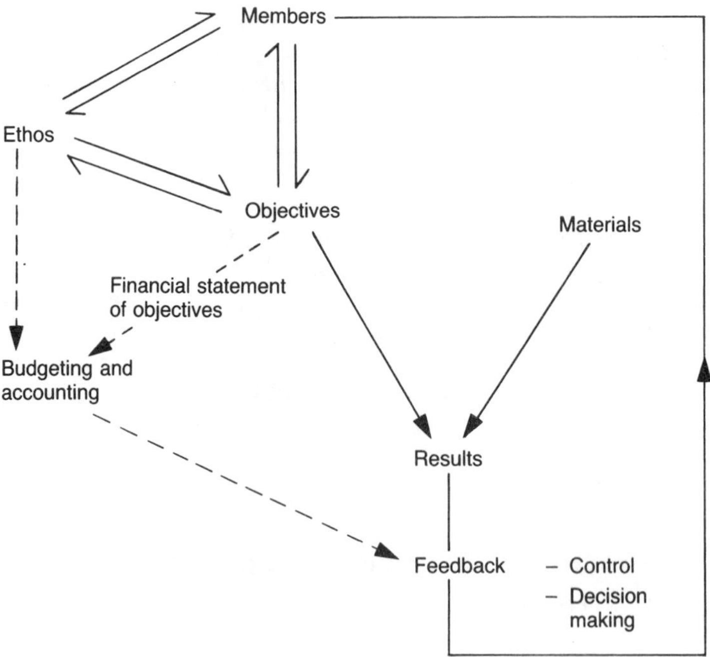


**Fig. 4.1** The relationship between the fundamental components of an organization.

# The role of accounting in organizations

Accounting falls into two distinct portions; anticipation of the future – budgeting, and recording the past – book-keeping and reporting. If one is to get the most from accounting then it is concerned with three major issues:

1. Explicit statement of **objectives**.
2. **Control** over an organization's operation.
3. Information for **decision taking**.

We can immediately see that accounting is very closely tied in with the five major components of an organization – particularly objectives, feedback and ethos as shown diagrammatically in Fig. 4.1.

Let us consider an organization that has been formed to build and let houses to the public. This is its main objective. Further clarification of the objective is needed so that the organization, perhaps a district council, can operate in this field. As we have already discussed the quality of houses needs to be agreed upon.

The market these houses are to be entered into also needs to be considered as will the rent to be charged. A good local authority will need to state in writing a whole series of these qualitative assumptions. But this written list will be of only partial assistance. It is no use deciding that rents will be at a level so the poorest can pay and then deciding that an enormous number of houses will be built a year. We live in a world of scarce resources and consequently money is always limiting.

The objectives for the short to medium term need to be set down in financial terms. A budget needs to be drawn up. It will link the housing authority's objectives to **constraints**, of which the first will be lack of money, and **opportunities** such as the use of government grants. At its very simplest a budget for building council houses might be as follows:

## *Budget for building council houses for one year*

| | £ |
|---|---|
| Maximum borrowing possible | 1 000 000 |
| Government grant available | 400 000 |
| Expected excess of rents over revenue expenditure | 250 000 |
| | 1 650 000 |
| 40 houses at £40 000 each | (1 600 000) |
| Funds carried forward for future years | 50 000 |

The budget then forms the goal of the organization for the period, in the example, a year. The budget is not a passive forecast by an individual finanacial man. Rather it is the financially formulated objective of the members of the organization. It is their manifesto.

Having set these objectives the organization must attempt to achieve them. In some enterprises the members will fight tooth and nail to meet or better the budget. In others a quiet confidence may pervade. 'I think you will find we are just about on target' would perhaps be the catch-phrase applicable. Other organizations will take a very different view. 'We always set over-optimistic budgets to keep the councillors happy. We never meet them but they don't want any of their pet programmes dropped.' Or the following is sometimes heard. 'Its very unlikely we will have funds for all this. But I should not worry; something is bound to slip.' Or again, 'I put in last year's, plus 5%. It won't be enough so we will have to dip into reserves at about Christmas time.' We can see that the ethos of an organization has a direct effect on the budgeting process.

Once the budget has been set actual achievement can be measured and compared to it. This process provides the organization with feedback, feedback of two distinct types, information concerning **control** of the operation and information for **decision making**. Using the example of the council houses discussed above control represents perhaps ensuring that building is well under way so that all 40 houses will be finished and paid for by the end of the year. It involves ensuring that the objectives are carried out as planned and budgeted for. Decision making is more complex. It relates to changes in plans or formulation of new objectives. For instance, the accounts may show that the council houses being built are going to cost not £40 000 each, but £50 000. A decision is now required. Do we try to raise money or do we build fewer houses?

Of course most of the work involved in carrying out objectives is not concerned with money or accounting. Doctors and nurses cure people of illness. They do not account all day long. But people can only be cured if there is money for it. It is therefore very much in everyone's interest to understand that effective budgeting and accounting directly relate to the number of people cured. Medical objectives need to be set down in financial terms. Once they are, financial control and decision making can take place so that of all the possible methods of running a medical service the one which allows the best use of scarce resources for the benefit of patients is chosen.

In practice agreeing and setting budgets can be very difficult. Often this is because poorly presented financial data cannot readily be related to the organization's objectives or its physical achievements. It is relatively easy to calculate that a house cost £40 000 to build; it is more difficult to calculate the cost of effective treatment for schizophrenia.

## Summary

This chapter aims to demonstrate the links between a number of characteristics within organizations. The most important relationship is that between members, objectives and feedback or management information. The objectives of organizations soon become diluted if management information is poor. Straightforward service objectives soon degenerate into a multitude of personal objectives if members cannot easily appreciate the success of their labours. In Chapter 2 we said that good value for money is based on goal congruence, management information and professional flair. Once we have looked at the structure of organizations the reasons for the importance of these three key attributes of VFM become more easily understood. In the next chapter we look at management information and accounting in more detail.

## Reader questionnaire

ANSWERS

1. Who are the 'member' groups in your organization?
   Members of public bodies normally include politicians, senior managers, and various levels of operational staff all with different interests in the organization.

2. What are the legally defined objects of your organization?
   Find the legislation that governs your work and isolate those parts that give organizational objectives.

Once you have answers to these questions your view of your organization and your role in it should have become explicit. You are in a position to look at more complex accounting issues discussed in the next chapter.

ANSWERS

3.
(a) In the context of Chapter 3 and the concept of goal congruence what do you consider to be the true objectives of the public body you work in?
(b) How do the various member groups of the organization view these objectives.
(c) To what extent are they compatible with their own?

4.
(a) What do you consider to be the major resources your organization uses? Your answer should include such items as skilled labour, computing capacity, adequate buildings.
(b) Which resources are the most difficult or costly to obtain? Place them in the order in which they become limiting.

5.
(a) What do you recognize as the 'ethos' of your organization?
(b) How does your ethos compare to that perceived in the leading organization in your field?
(c) Why is there a difference?
(d) Do you obtain adequate feedback to do your job optimally or are the results of your actions unknown to you?

By finding answers to these questions many of the unspoken motives of those who work in your organization should become clearer. In addition, the strengths and weaknesses in the public body you work for should become explicit.

# 5

# Accounting

This chapter looks at accounting from two diametrically opposed perspectives. First, we examine the popular view of accounting aims and achievements. We discuss how these opinions relate to the accounting needs of organizations. We then continue by discussing some of the problems that accountants and users of accounting information face in trying to explain the world in financial terms. In strong contrast, the second part of the chapter then takes an accounting view analysing the theoretical role of accounting within public bodies. This is followed by a series of examples illustrating the benefits of management accounting in situations of limited complexity.

## The popular view

Turn on the radio or television and you will quite often hear strong complaints about cost control and accounting performance measures. A policeman will complain that senior officers only care about satisfying value for money criteria not about proper policing. Others complain that in education we need school leavers who can write properly not more cost control. And in the health service doctors complain that patients deserve priority not ward statistics.

These people are concerned that the quality of service comes second to arcane management systems of which they know little. There is a further fear that the flair and inventiveness of dedicated people will be lost in a maze of statistics. We need to look at the problem so that we can see how much truth there is in the fears so often expressed.

We live in a world of scarce resources. Mineral resources are finite, space is limited as are labour and skills. Because we cannot ever have all we might want we have to make choices. 'If I buy the bigger car I cannot afford the Caribbean Cruise.' 'If we have a larger Navy, pensions will have to be lower.' 'If we invest in a new paint plant the plastics division will not get their new office block.' The eternal problem of scarcity and choice applies to all of us as individuals, governments or industry.

Because we can only afford so much we need good information on costs. Going to a shop to buy a loaf of bread we ask the price and can view or have experience of what we are buying. Price, quantity and quality are all known. Things become much more complex if we buy objects less well defined than a loaf of bread. Consider a production line making a new product for a year. At the start of the period we are unlikely to know precisely, the quality of the production, how much will be produced in the year or what in the end a year's production will cost. Skilled labour may be more expensive than we had hoped, production may be slower but the number of items rejected may be lower than our best estimates. We do not know with certainty prices, quality or quantity. It is the work of accountants to help control and monitor problems such as this.

For commercial organizations and governments most of the spending they are involved with falls into the complex category. A local authority may wish to commit itself to providing nursery education. Costings are required from accountants before the decision can be sensibly taken. Politicians need to be sure that by providing this new service they are not doubling the council tax. We can see then that accountants are needed to help control the use of scarce resources.

But accounting does have a cost. Accounting systems and accountants are expensive. Furthermore, there is a political cost. You have to convince the accountant before money is released. Within both private and public organizations the Finance Director or his or her equivalent are powerful people who have strong personal control over the policy of the enterprise. Within the British Government the Chancellor of the Exchequer is second only to the prime minister and the Treasury is the most powerful government department.

## Do accountants have souls?

Although accountants are clearly useful there are a number of examples of accountants destroying effective organizations. Perhaps one of the best-known cases is that of United States car manufacturing. By the mid-1980s a vast and once great industry was all but broke. Business school whizz kids controlled the managements of most of the various companies. They were extremely hot on accounting and control. What they utterly neglected was the quality of the product. A big old-fashioned gas-guzzler was useless in a market of neat economic Japanese or European models. Accountants are not engineers, designers or marketing men. While cost control was first rate, product design and marketing was neglected. Accountants do not seem to have a soul. They are quite happy, it appears, to take financial decisions that have the most terrible non-financial consequences. During the 1980s in Britain many traditional industries were ruthlessly axed as a result of accountants' calculations. No concern was shown for history, communities or aesthetics. Coal fields were closed, factories shut and office blocks were built using cheap industrialized building techniques. Of course change is always unpleasant and much of these accountant instituted changes were well over due. But the doubt remains, accountants will rationalize away both body and soul so that nothing of value is left.

So where do we draw the line? How much power do we give accountants? The problem is this. If the accountant is excluded from senior management his rational analysis of a problem will probably be ignored by engineers or marketing men. The result will be decisions based on whims or bias. On the other hand, too powerful an accountant may dominate senior management. Flair may be rationalized away, dedicated professionalism may be undermined, important non-financial issues such as quality or aesthetics may not receive due consideration.

## A new problem?

Why are we seeing this problem only now? The history of Victorian industry and imperial expansion is not dogged by a fear of accountancy. Neither the American post-war boom nor the NASA space programme suffered from an excess of regressive accountants obsessed with unit costs or performance indicators. I think there are two reasons for this. First the Victorian and American industrial booms took place at a time of little international competition. Profits were good; cost control could therefore take second place. The same applies to the activities of the British Empire and to NASA. Money was not short, so financial control could take second or third place. The second main reason for the prominence of accountants is that the world is getting more complex. Where as formally financial miscalculation resulted in still lower standards of living for a mainly disenfranchized poor, now we all expect first rate planning in public and private sectors so that public services, standards of 'customer care' and economic growth continue unabated. For instance it is no longer acceptable to mismanage the health service. We are all implicitly aware that greater efficiency will in fact benefit us all. In Britain a 20% increase in productivity in the NHS would release an additional 1% of GNP for other purposes. This would allow us to double expenditure on primary education. Efficiency and proper accounting consequently effects us all. A more responsible attitude to accounting has therefore become a necessity.

But the anti-innovation mentality of financial responsibility and control needs to be removed. In an extremely competitive world it does not serve us well. We all need people with precocious flair and ability to achieve. Visions of a new and better way of doing things are a necessity. How do we fit this in with the essentially rational need to control?

There are a number of ways in which this can be achieved. They can be listed as follows:

1. Multidisciplinary approach;
2. Development of more sophisticated accounting techniques;
3. Segregation of production from research;

In major organizations the different professions involved often align first with their profession, and second with the organization. A doctor will consider that nurses have a nursing viewpoint which it will be very difficult to dissuade them from on a given issue. Similarly, most professions will consider the accountants' viewpoint alien to their own. If there is to be effective innovation within an organization all parties need to understand the important aspects of the others skills. A doctor needs to have a working knowledge of the costing associated with his work and he needs to be conversant with basic accounting techniques so that he can usefully judge the financial consequences of medical innovations. Productive staff such as doctors or teachers need to be able to understand and appreciate the concerns of accountants so that they can work together for a common goal. To do this training is needed.

The second need is for more sophisticated accounting techniques. The problem often arises where physical actions cannot be properly reflected in financially based accounts. A topical example is the difficulty of accounting for environmental policies. An accountant may calculate that a scrubber plant removing sulphur dioxide may not be financially viable in an industrial chimney. The factory down the road does not have one so the chimney is built without. The cost in damage to local limestone buildings over the next 20 years is not considered. This accounting problem is likely to be solved as governments and individuals begin to realize that the indirect actions of others can affect their costs. Legislation covering the costs of pollution will slowly be introduced so that the worst problems are tackled. A more difficult problem relates to consideration of human values. If for instance the pollution we have mentioned above damages the medieval sculpture on a cathedral, what is the cost associated with this? Or if we set educational standards at a specific level what is the cost in the long run compared to spending, say, 25% more? People quite rightly fear that the inability of accountants to measure all the costs of an action, particularly the longer term costs, means that suboptimal decisions are constantly taken. The solution is to understand the limitations of the figures drawn up by accountants (point 1 again). But in the longer term better accounting techniques are needed.

## Revenue and capital activities

Some areas of activity are of a productive and repetitive nature while others are one-off achievements. We may call the first a *revenue* based activity, the latter a *capital* based one. Thus making toy soldiers on a production line is clearly of a revenue nature. Developing a method of making insulin for diabetics using bacteria is a typical **capital** project. Once the method is developed, making the insulin is a revenue activity.

Revenue activities can be easily associated with unit costs, that is, say, the cost of making one toy soldier. Traditionally accountants have been very successful in providing useful information on revenue activities. But capital work is more difficult to cost account for. This is because many aspects of the work will be done for the first time. Little cost data will be available for these activities. The lesson here is that excessive attempts to cost account in innovative capital projects may be destructive, damaging flair. However, estimates of the costs and benefits of development projects which are intended to produce a highly defined result can and should be measured. For pure research non-accounting measures of output and for control are needed. A very simple measure would be long-term monitoring of Nobel prizes won by British university research laboratories. But as we saw in Chapter 1 the vast majority of public sector work is of an everyday revenue nature. Children are educated; patients are healed; pensions are paid. Only a small percentage of the work of the public sector is concerned with developing new products and services.

It is important then to be certain of the nature of the activity being accounted for. Although pure research may not readily yield to costing, revenue activities and product development will. The latter two should be under strong control, and the benefits of accounting in those areas will help pay for the financing of more speculative capital research.

As this and the following chapters develop we will look at how flexible but useful accounting techniques can be provided to account for much of the public sector activities. But we start by looking at the basic types of accounting in the following section.

# Accounting techniques

Having discussed in general terms some of the benefits and problems associated with accounting we need to look more specifically at accounting theory and practice.

Accounting falls into two quite separate types – financial accounting and managment accounting. This book is primarily concerned with the latter. But because the techniques used by accountants can be used in both we need to discuss the difference between the two types of accounting here.

## Financial accounting

This is the form of accounting which most people are familiar with. Reports sent to shareholders contain financial accounts. Local newspapers often give the abbreviated financial accounts of local authorities. Somewhere deep in the HMSO, government financial accounts can be found. These accounts aim to give the reader information on the stewardship of the organization he or she has an interest in. The members of the public who bought British Telecom shares want to know if the company made a good profit. They may be interested how much of that profit will be paid as dividends. The company's capital investment will be of interest as will the methods by which it is being funded. Does the company have to borrow from the banks or are retained profits sufficient; perhaps a rights issue of shares will be needed? In short the reader wants to know the *solvency* or financial strength of the company. And this is what financial accounts show. When the Department of the Environment reads the accounts of local authorities the solvency of the enterprises are under scrutiny. Spending in excess of income will effect the economy; it will also cause financing problems for central government in future years.

Financial accounts may also give other information such as the earnings of company chairmen, how much of turnover was earned from Brazilian operations and the name of group companies. But they give very little information on the operation of an enterprise. The accounts of the furniture store Habitat do not tell you how many tables were sold. Local authority accounts give no information on the productivity of policemen. The financial accounts of central government do not tell you how many miles of trunk road were mended. Operational matters are the concern of management accounts.

But before we move on to management accounting it is important to realize that financial accounts are not only used to report to persons external to an organization, they are also essential within an enterprise. Senior managers are concerned with solvency too.

Consider a local authority which has set a budget only to find that its council tax has been capped. If spending were to occur at the originally approved rate the authority would be insolvent by the end of the year because of the short-fall in tax revenue. The treasurer of the authority has to consider what he or she can do to balance the budget. Almost instant action is required and services will have to be cut. It is not use looking for increased value for money. If good value for money could be switched on at such short notice it would surely have been obtained long ago. To balance the budget the treasurer will have to agree with councillors and senior staff that the authority will say, no longer provide evening classes in Swahili, shelve major repairs to council houses, and provide only half the number of meals on wheels.

The treasurer's aim is purely financial. If someone suggested it would be preferable operationally to cut evening classes in Thai rather the Swahili saving the same amount of money, he would show no preference. Traditionally local authority treasurers have been trained in this role.

## Management accounting

If financial accounting is essential to the survival of an enterprise, management accounting has not traditionally been considered important. In fact the history of management accounts is barely a hundred years old. But because public sector organizations can survive with little management accounting this does not mean that it is not important. It is essential to all organizations if they are to be well managed.

When in Chapter 4 we discussed the fundamentals of organizations we said that accounting provided three major benfits; explicit statement of objectives, control, and information for decision taking. But while all forms of accounting tend to provide control over an enterprise only management accounting helps define objectives and aids decisions. This is shown graphically in Fig. 5.1.

Figure 5.1 shows that only one aspect of management accounting is fully concerned with objectives and decisions making – that is management accounting for outputs. So we can understand this better we need to discuss in more detail the techniques of the management accountant.

Management accounting is concerned with making budgets and then monitoring actual performance in comparison to the budget originally set. In the previous chapter we discussed how a budget represented a statement of objectives, of intent. We also discussed how by monitoring budgets organizations could obtain much of the feedback they needed. But if we are to understand the importance of good management accounting we must look at how budgets are made and how they are reported upon.

If a housing authority built 30 houses in a year and each cost £53 300 we can say quite straightforwardly inputs of £1.6 million gave 30 houses as output. We could analyse this in more detail.

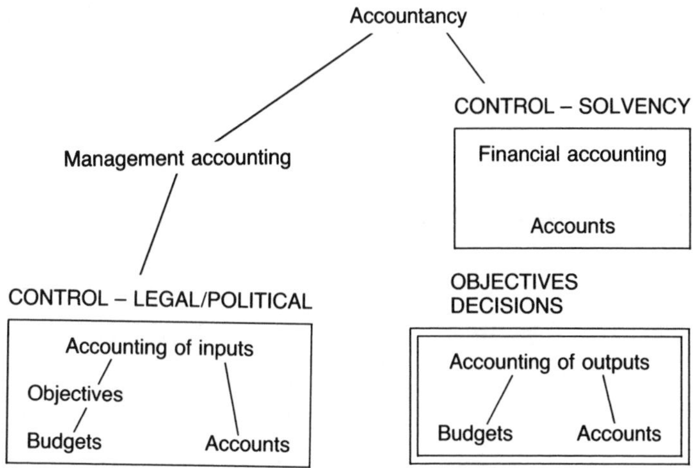


**Fig. 5.1** Accounting types.

## *House building costs*

| *Inputs* | £ |
|---|---|
| Land | 400 000 |
| Materials | 500 000 |
| Labour | 500 000 |
| Professional fees and sundry costs | 200 000 |
| | 1 600 000 |
| *Outputs* | |
| 30 houses | 1 600 000 |

We could go further:

## *Variance analysis of a budget*

| *Inputs* | *Original Budget (£)* | *Actual achieved (£)* | *Difference (£)* | |
|---|---|---|---|---|
| Land | 200 000 | 400 000 | 200 000 | A |
| Materials | 600 000 | 500 000 | (100 000) | F |
| Labour | 625 000 | 500 000 | (125 000) | F |
| Professional fees and sundry costs | 175 000 | 200 000 | 25 000 | A |
| | 1 600 000 | 1 600 000 | nil | |
| *Outputs* | | | | |
| TOTAL cost | 1 600 000 | 1 600 000 | nil | |
| No. houses built | 40 | 30 | 10 | A |

A = adverse variance  F = favourable variance

Looking at the figures we can see one reason fewer houses were built than budget was because the land cost twice that expected. Materials and labour also varied as follows:

## *Analysis of unit variances*

| | | *Cost per House* | | | % |
|---|---|---|---|---|---|
| | *Budget (£)* | *Actual (£)* | *Difference (£)* | | |
| Materials | 15 000 | 16 667 | 1667 | A | 11 |
| Labour | 15 625 | 16 667 | 1042 | A | 7 |
| Total | 30 625 | 33 333 | 2708 | A | 9 |

By looking at the materials and labour costs we can see that these too were well above budget. At the rate at which 30 houses were actually built 40 would have cost £1 333 000 (£33 333 × 40), £108 320 more than budget. So in fact not only did the land cost more but so did the building costs. Simple management accounting looking at the cost of outputs has told us much that we need to know if the objectives of house building are to be sustained.

Because of the high price of land we may decide to build flats next year or perhaps to renovate old property. Alternatively, we might increase rents so that we can continue building houses as originally planned.

But not all council and local government activities can be set down so easily. Consider a typical comprehensive school with 1000 pupils. The budget may be as follows:

## *A school budget*

| *Inputs* | £ |
|---|---|
| Teachers | 1 011 000 |
| Other employees | 134 000 |
| Premises costs | 261 000 |
| Stationery and other supplies | 27 000 |
| Total cost | £1 433 000 |

But what are the outputs? Because educational outputs are complex and often controversial, accountants for education authorities do not usually analyse them. Let us now look at the school budget in context of some actual costs.

### *Variance analysis of input costs*

| | *Budget (£)* | *Actual (£)* | *Difference (£)* |
|---|---|---|---|
| Teachers | 1 011 000 | 1 080 000 | 69 000 A |
| Other employees | 134 000 | 82 000 | (52 000) F |
| Premises costs | 261 000 | 157 000 | (104 000) F |
| Stationery | 27 000 | 32 000 | 5 000 A |
| TOTAL | 1 433 000 | 1 351 000 | (82 000) F |

What has been going on? Excluding teaching costs the school cost less to run. Perhaps we should all be pleased at this exemplory parsimoniousness. Teaching costs went up by £69 000 or nearly 7%. Not only was the school cheaper but the children got more tuition than previously. More good news.

But perhaps this is all wrong. Major teacher vacancies were suffered that could be rectified only with temporary supply staff costing 30% more than regular employees. Premises costs slumped not due to careful spending but because all maintenance to school buildings was halted until a financial crisis was weathered. The additional stationery costs represented paper given to children so they could amuse themselves in periods when there were no teachers to teach them.

But did the best teachers leave? Perhaps there was a policy of encouraging the less able to go. Probably both good and bad left. The accounts information we have does not tell us. It does not inform because outputs have not been **defined** and they have not been **measured**.

In the example of the council houses the output was defined as 'a house'. It was measured by counting the houses built. For the school output definitions are clearly more complex. But if it were considered a useful measure, teacher skills and experience could be defined as an output. (In Chapter 6 we discuss teaching outputs further and in Chapter 8 we give examples of how they could be measured.) You could grade teachers into categories of excellence and then measure for specific schools the grading mix actually achieved for a given input, for example:

### *Analysis of teacher costs*

| | *Budget* | | *Actual* | | *Difference* | |
|---|---|---|---|---|---|---|
| | *(£)* | *(No.)* | *(£)* | *(No.)* | *(£)* | *(No.)* |
| *Inputs* | | | | | | |
| Teachers' Costs | 1 011 000 | | 1 080 000 | | 69 000 | – |
| *Outputs* | | | | | | |
| Grade A | 456 250 | 25 | 288 750 | 15 | (167 500) | (10) |
| Grade B | 412 500 | 25 | 391 200 | 24 | (21 300) | (1) |
| Grade C (supply) | 142 250 | 10 | 400 050 | 20 | 257 800 | 10 |
| TOTALS | 1 011 000 | 60 | 1 080 000 | 59 | 69 000 | (1) |

Now we are beginning to get useful information from the accounts. We can see that rather than getting more teaching than the budget for our extra money we have probably got less. First, experienced and effective A grade teachers have been lost and replaced by C grade supply staff. Second, teacher retention is clearly a very major problem which is likely to lead to a teacher shortage in the near future. Third, supply staff cost more than A grade teachers. In the longer term they are poor value for money.

Of course there are problems in defining outputs for schools that are meaningful and are not devisive. Teachers may object to grading. Grades may be unfairly given either because of personal enmity or conversely so as to enhance a set of figures. Nevertheless, defining and measuring outputs is the only way of clearly defining material objectives and of providing the necessary data so that rational decisions can be made.

## Summary

So far we have seen how better accounting can assist in the management of the public sector. In particular we have looked at the issue of management accounting. We have seen that this form of accounting is needed if organizations are to define their objectives and to report back achievement. Regular management accounts allow for control of costs. But just as importantly they can allow decisions to be made based on solid material achievement rather than mere input costs. Output measurement, and the potential this gives for effective decision making, means that sophisticated management accounting is a necessity in any well-managed organization. In the next chapter we see how management information is used in practice.

## Reader questionnaire

The questionnaire seeks to encourage you to consider your views on the value of accountancy and management information. First you look at your reaction to simple questions concerning the value of accounts. Then you are asked to re-examine these views in the context of the scarcity of public resources. Next you review how you set your budget so as to maximize the use of resources and explicitly lay down objectives. Lastly, you are asked to consider briefly how your budget could be reorganized so that it would better define the expected needs of your department or organization.

1. Do you agree with the following views on the value of accountancy and managment information?

ANSWERS

(a) I consider that accountants care little for quality of service and make no attempt to understand my role as a professional.

(b) Much of the public sector is concerned with providing for the needs of individuals. Accountancy is quite at odds with this.

(c) Administration is a cost which needs to be reduced at all times so that professionals can be left to get on with the job.
(d) Management information is an expensive luxury that at present we cannot afford.
(e) Of course, I would like more data on the activities I carry out but that is something for the future. At the moment I need to get on with the job in hand.
(f) Managment information and accounts are always so out of date that they are useless.

If you generally agree with the statements above you are clearly weary of the value of a quantified approach to management. If this is the case you will discover more about your views in the next set of questions.

2. In a world of scarce resources what are your priorities?

ANSWERS

(a) It is essential that resources benefit the largest number of people possible.
(b) The maximum benefit for the most people requires low costs for the services provided. Do you agree?
(c) In the public services quality of provision is a necessity though it makes wide coverage of service expensive.
(d) The assets of public bodies should be built to last and benefit future generations in the way that, for example, Victorian sewers have.
(e) If people are willing to pay for a higher quality of service it is to the benefit of the public sector as a whole. Do you agree?

If you generally agree with these statements then you must necessarily consider that strong financial control over public services is an imperative. If this conclusion is inconsistent with your views in (1) above review those statements again before moving on to (3) below.

3. Your budget should should represent your departmental/organizational objectives for a period. Answer the following questions to find out whether your budget assists you in the management of your department.

ANSWERS

(a) Does your budget set down your objectives for the year ahead? Or does it only state the amount of money you have been allocated?
(b) If you do not have a set of written objectives how do you maximize your output?
    (i) Always work hard/work floods onto my desk.
    (ii) Long years of practice.
    (iii) This is my superior's problem.

(iv) At the beginning of the week I consider what needs to be done by Friday.

(c) Whether your objectives are explicit as in (a) or implicit as in (b) do you consider your objectives in the light of your budget?

(d) If your budget was increased by 10% would this:
   (i) Be of major benefit to your work.
   (ii) Increase your workload unbearably.
   (iii) Increase your output by 10%.
   (iv) Increase your output by 20%.

(e) Does your budget differentiate between costs that will not be affected by increased activity and those that will? For example, office rent and rates will not usually be affected by increased productivity but staff wages may increase as work levels are stepped up.

(f) Have you any idea how the provision of more of the same services that you provide at present (i.e. increased output) will affect your costs?

If you do not have clearly stated objectives and your budget is not clearly related to your expected achievements for the year, the last part of this questionnaire should start to help you think how you can improve your budget setting. However, the later chapters of this book will go into the subject in much greater detail.

This chapter discussed the bare structure of all organizations and followed this by discussions of the legal objectives of public sector organizations. Then the importance of accounting for feedback was discussed. At this stage it is useful to consider the structural aspects of *your* organization.

4. Your department spends money so as to provide a service. Review the following statements in the context of the activities your department is involved in.

ANSWERS

(a) What are your outputs? For example:
   (i) New council houses.
   (ii) Education of children.
   (iii) Payment of social security at the correct value and timing to members of the public.

(b) If you were to increase the output of your department what would you provide? For example:
   (i) More hernia operations a year.
   (ii) More training for soldiers.
   (iii) More sheets washed.
   (iv) More children educated/the same number of children with better exam results.

(c) If you can define increased service provision as in (ii) above what aspects of your service output can be measured? For example:

  - (i) Number of operations.
  - (ii) Number of classrooms cleaned to a defined standard.
- (d) If outputs cannot be reliably measured directly can other variables be measured that vary in proportion to outputs.

# 6

# The structure of output-based management

We are now in a position to start implementing some of the ideas and techniques we have discussed. The object is to measure achievement. This is then used as a tool to refine objectives, ensure value for money and to motivate staff. This chapter starts by defining typical public sector outputs and then demonstrates the use of output data in a management situation.

## Definitions and measurement of output

The key to much we have discussed is the measurement of output. But before we can measure we must define. The two key questions are:

1. What **is** our real output?
2. How can we measure it?

The majority of public sector outputs are relatively easy to define and measure. For instance a surgeon may have as outputs successful appendicitis operations. A benefits manager will have benefits claims processed as her definition of output. Education is generally considered to be more than good exam results but clearly a tangible output exists. Social work outputs are more complex still. However, there is always an output from every useful job – if there is not, the job is not useful.

Once you have defined what your output really is, you need to think of ways of measuring it. It is important to realize that your definition and your measurement procedures need to be highly practical. If you define your output as, for instance, 'an awareness amongst training course participants of the value of imagination in the consultative process', or some such abstract idea, you are immediately causing yourself problems. The correct way of covering this objective would be to say 'course participants are expected to reach grade C or above after the final course assessment'. This may sound limiting but if the assessment is affective so too will be the measurement process.

It is important to consider output measurement as a creative challenge not an administrative straightjacket. If it is not too far-fetched an analogy it may help to remember the struggles of the great scientists Rutherford, Madame Curie, and those who were trying to understand the nature of the matter around the turn of the century. By defining concrete objects very precisely they were able to use the simplest of equipment to obtain results beyond the limits of the imagination.

# Practical steps in defining outputs

Outputs need to be defined in terms of the nature of units of output and also in terms of their quality. Not every achievement will be perfect. Computational errors will occasionally be made in tax assessments, some patients will die as a result of normally safe procedures and some services may be delivered rather later than the recipient might have hoped. Any definitions of output thus fall into two categories which we can call 'quantity' and 'quality'. When we come to measuring output both aspects will require measurement.

Let us take an example. Planning applications are received by a local authority and are logged on a microcomputer. As each application is processed the computer is updated. At the end of a period the computer could be used to report:

1. Total number of applications processed;
2. The time taken to process applications giving:
   (a) the average processing time;
   (b) the percentage of applications exceeding the statutory deadline of eight weeks.

The computer is thus measuring the quantity of output and one aspect of the quality of output – timeliness.

To help understand the nature of outputs we will now look at seven categories that are fairly common to public sector organizations. Your work will probably fall into one of these categories.

## *Public sector outputs*

| *Nature of work* | *Output* |
|---|---|
| 1. Administration of application forms | One form processed. |
| 2. Maintenance work | Maintenance of assets to a quality over a period of time. |
| 3. Medical work | One successful medical procedure or 'cure'. |
| 4. Education | Moral and academic achievements of one pupil. |

| | |
|---|---|
| 5. Hotel services | Board and lodging for one person for a day to a given standard. |
| 6. Major construction works | Construction of one asset of a defined type. |
| 7. Service maintenance of military and civilian assets | Provision of a standard service for a period of time. |

# 1. Administration of grants, benefits, application forms, etc.

The public sector is said to communicate with the outside world via official forms. Benefit offices, tax offices, licencing offices and hospitals are just some of the public sector bodies that use a form as a first approach to their customers. Every form that is filled in must be processed. The act of processing thus provides a very natural unit of output. A member of the public applies for a car licence disc. The form is received, processed and a licence dispatched. This is clearly one unit of output. But we must also consider the quality of the processing undertaken. Not every form will be perfectly processed. There will be processing errors and some forms will be processed unacceptably slowly. We will look at the control of quality in Chapters 8 and 9.

# 2. Maintenance work

The public sector is responsible for billions of pounds worth of capital assets. The majority are buildings, roads and items of military hardware. Repair work is constantly needed and satisfactory maintenance of assets is a major output for highways authorities, health authorities, housing authorities, property services agencies and the armed forces.

Maintenance work falls into two main types: emergency repairs and planned maintenance. Neither of these methods of organizing work are in themselves outputs. What matters is the serviceability of the assets subject to maintenance. Thus outputs for repair work take the form of availability of an asset for use at a given quality of repair. Examples of maintenance outputs could be as follows:

1. Wiring in schools will always be maintained at electricity board approved standards.
2. Operating theatres will be maintained at such a level that usage is always safe.
3. Fifty per cent of the nuclear submarine fleet will be ready for sea at any one time.
4. Office space will maintained so that it will always provide a satisfactory working environment.

Maintenance is always to a quality level. A building can be maintained at a level adequate for office use or it can be maintained at a level adequate to ensure it remains structurally sound (i.e. weatherproof roof and waterproof windows). Vehicles can be maintained so that they last for ten or for 20 years. The quality level chosen depends on a number of factors. These include likely usage, social norms, availability of funding and requirements to promote value for money. When the cost of maintenance outputs are measured the concern is with costs per unit time of keeping an asset maintained.

## 3. Medical work

Medical work normally involves the short-term care of a patient who is ill or needs medical attention. The object of care is normally a 'cure'. Not all medicine is of this nature. Much geriatric and mental hospital work involves maintaining a patient who is incurable over a long period of time. We consider this type of care and the catering for short-term patients separately under 'Hotel Services' below.

For most medicine the output is a complete cure for an ailment. Some medical procedures allow for very easy definition of cures. Removal of tonsils leads prima facie to a cure for tonsilitis. But treatments for various cancers may be less clear-cut. At the end of the period of medical care the patient may still be alive, but for how long will he or she remain so? Five years? Three weeks? Or until the age of 80? What may appear to be a highly satisfactory output may be seen after a period of time to be less satisfactory. Other problems relate to the age and condition of the patient subject to treatment. For a given condition some patients may be otherwise fit 20 year olds while others may be diabetic 80 year olds with weak hearts. Lastly, many diseases cannot be cured, for instance eczema or muscular distrophy. Doctors in these cases promote valuable care but benefits will be hard to define in terms of cure. The output here should be effective patient care over a period of time.

Medical professionals will need to produce output measures that best fit their specializations. In a market system an output may well be a unit of care for which a charge is made, for instance a operation to remove a gall stone. Quality data should to be kept as well. Survival rates for serious diseases must be monitored. Data of this type will provide important feedback and will form useful marketing material when selling expertise. The second case studies in Chapters 8 and 9 look at the problems involved.

## 4. Education

Experts will argue for hours over what an educational output might be. To some extent we can avoid much of this by looking at the present structure of education in Britain based on the paper 'Local Management in Schools'. This system attempts to define outputs with regard to 'parent power' and to a lesser extent 'employer power'. Schools that will receive the most funding will be those that attract the most pupils. In theory, parents will send their children to the schools which give them what are perceived to be the greatest advantages. Parents may look for discipline, good exam results, a reputation for happy children or a school known to have a good name with local employers. These then will form the outputs of schools. Teacher dedication or the quality of playing fields are not outputs; these are inputs that may lead to the outputs listed.

Exam results are easily measured – they are designed to be. It is also possible to measure 'discipline' and 'happiness'. They are not nebulous concepts. They will be reflected in the behaviour of children, in absentee rates, the number of recorded disciplinary proceedings, the number of complaints by parents and those living near the school, the number of parents at parent evenings, teacher turnover, and so on. All these things can be defined, measured and monitored to give a sound basis on which to record achievement.

Of course a school in an inner city area will not be sending the majority of its pupils to university while a home counties grammar school might. The output is unavoidably related to the environment in which the pupils grow up: it is relative. Information is needed on the children going into the school before the measured outputs are meaningful. (We will address this further in the case studies at the end of Chapters 8 and 9.) In tertiary education, the emphasis is very much more on examination results and research achievement and output measurement is consequently that much easier.

## 5. Hotel services

The public sector is a major supplier of 'hotel services'. Prisoners are provided board and lodging in gaols, patients in hospitals, the aged in old peoples homes and the armed services in barracks and on ships. All these public sector establishments provide for very large numbers of people.

Output measurement is relatively straightforward. We are concerned with keeping one person for a given length of time at a given standard. The standard might vary from the need to slop out in prisons to the provision of personal servants for army officers.

## 6. Major construction works

We have already said that the public sector is responsible for very substantial capital assets. These assets are generally built specially for the public organizations that use them. Only a small percentage are purchased. Consequently, much public sector work is involved in constructing buildings and roads. These assets are clearly outputs of the departments that order them.

Public sector capital assets are usually built using private sector construction companies. The company employed will usually win the contract after a tendering procedure, thus one would hope that the best price has been obtained for the specified works. However, this does not mean that output measurement is not needed. The public body needs to measure the quantity and quality of buildings and other construction work over a period.

Optimal specifications can be worked out, the best tendering procedures used and the timing of projects carefully adjusted so that high productivity at set standards is achieved efficiently.

An interesting aspect of the purchase of capital assets is their associated running costs. Running costs include cleaning, staffing, heating and lighting as well as maintenance. High running costs add very substantially to the real cost of an asset. We look at these as outputs in their own right next.

### 7. Service maintenance of military and civilian assets

An increasingly large element of all organizations is the need to keep major assets ready for use. A computer will need an air-conditioned computer suite and a small retinue of computer personnel. A building will need janitors and security men and cleaning staff as well as heating, lighting and the payment of rates and possibly rent. An infantry regiment or a warship will need to be kept in a state of service readiness.

Output in these situations is the provision of a building, computer, operating theatre or fighting unit at a stated standard over a period of time. For instance one could measure operating theatre service output on the basis of an hour's availability for use. Office building service maintenance is best measured over a year to take into account the effects of the seasons on heat and light usage. Military units could be measured using costs per day.

Office space is a relatively standard commodity. Computer services are far less so. Poor programs or a change in requirements by computer users will make service provision more complex and the definitions of a standard of service difficult.

It is possible to subdivide output to take into account particular service irregularities. One output could be the provision of a computer together with day-to-day work such as back-up runs and maintenance programmes and equipment. Subsidiary outputs could be solving specific problems regarding specific one-off operating requirements, say the writing of a program to remove a bug. The effectiveness of the program run on the computer is not the output we are trying to define and measure. The availability of a tool for use is our output here. Choice of program falls upon computer users and is consequently a variable that will affect the outputs of those who use the computer rather than the productivity of the computer service itself.

## Use of output figures

We have seen that there are a number of typical public sector outputs. We have defined them and considered how we might measure them. At this stage many simplifications were made. We talked for instance about processing application forms and one form being a unit of output. We ignored the fact that forms from some applicants or customers will be straightforward to process while the same form submitted by others might take ten times longer to deal with. Problems of fitting the real world into the idealized situation we illustrated are discussed throughout the rest of the book.

Before we consider specific public sector situations we need to look at how output once defined and measured is used to manage and control the production of goods and services. Management data on output will be needed for effective management. In the worked case study that follows we look at a private sector company working in conditions that are not fully subject to market forces. By taking as an example a straightforward manufacturing process we can consider the technical issues involved and the management techniques used simply and objectively. We can then start to apply them to more complex public service situations. The details given in the case study are fictional but are based on a successful UK enterprise.

# Case study – Mon Products Ltd

## Background

Mon Products Ltd is a company within a multinational group involved in the chemicals and petroleum products sector. Its role is to process raw materials produced elsewhere by the multinational into components to be used by yet other group companies. It does not sell outside the confines of the group. The two main outputs of Mon Products Ltd are a special purpose thermosetting plastic and high quality colouring matter for use in pigmenting the raw plastic. The two outputs are produced in two different plants in one factory. They are known as the 'polymer line' and the 'dye plant'. The polymer line which makes the plastics is the major business of Mon Products Ltd.

Below we give an extract of the summarized profit and loss account of Mon Products for a recent year.

### *Summarized profit and loss for the year to 31 March 199X*

| | £'000 | £'000 |
|---|---|---|
| Sales (at standard price to group) | | 80 000 |
| Cost of sales (purchases) | | |
| Semi-cracked petroleum (at standard price to group) | 35 000 | |
| Other raw materials | 12 000 | |
| Dye plant input | 8 000 | |
| Labour | 12 000 | |
| | | (67 000) |
| Gross Surplus | | 13 000 |
| Depreciation of plant | 1 500 | |
| Administrative salaries | 1 200 | |
| Other overhead costs (rates, computer, stationery, insurance, canteen) | 1 300 | |
| | | (4 000) |
| Net operating surplus | | £ 9 000 |

From the accounts we should note the following points:

1. All sales are at a standard price to the group. They are effectively the group's method of financing the Mon Products operation.
   Sales in this case are analogous to Government Grants or Parliamentary Votes.
2. The main raw material is also at a standard price set by the group.
   As a consequence Mon Products do not know the true economic cost of their major non-labour inputs.
3. In the accounts the dye plant costs are grouped and shown as a single figure.
4. Group financing costs, bank interest, tax and dividends have been omitted.
5. The net operating profit has little real meaning to either:
   (a) the Mon Products Ltd management,
   (b) the owners of Mon Products in the holding company.

Mon Products is operating in the private sector within the plastics market. But it is important to note that due to its position within the multinational group and the specialized nature of its products, the Mon business and its management cannot use profits or surpluses as an indication of their success.

Within the private sector there are many companies in the same situation as Mon Products Ltd. In the public sector nearly the entire operation is in Mon's position. As Mon's sales figures are really a way of financing production in the same way as the council tax, government grant or general taxation finance education or hospitals.

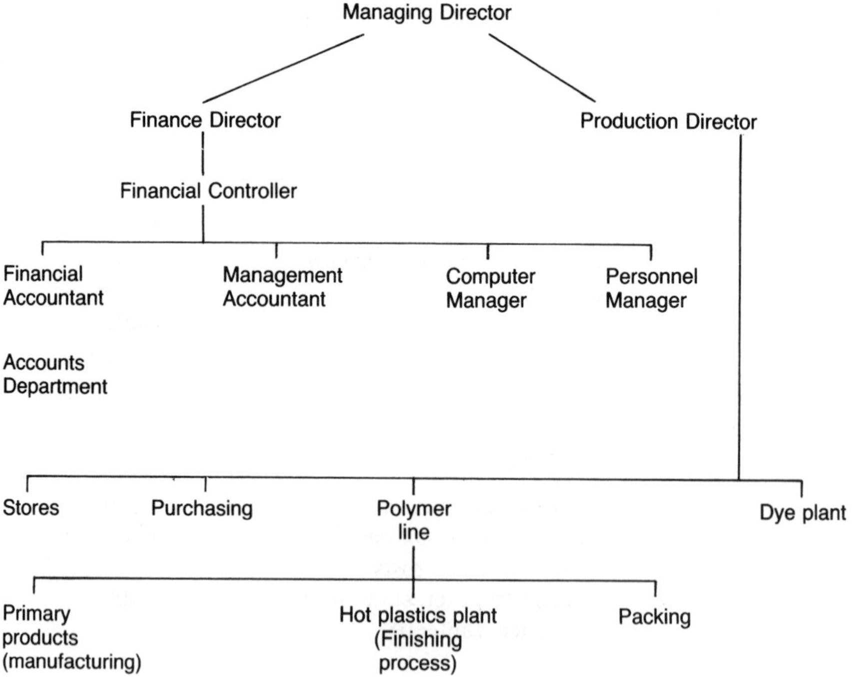


**Fig. 6.1** Management structure at Mon Products Ltd.

But now let us look at how Mon's management control their plastics production business.

## Management control at Mon Products Ltd

Mon Products management structure is shown in Fig. 6.1. The two major management areas are production and finance. Because Mon has a guaranteed market for all its output the company has no need for marketing or sales departments. Just as in the public sector, Mon's prime purpose is to produce high quality output at the lowest possible price. Value for money is everything. How then is it achieved?

## Monthly management accounts

The basis of all control at Mon Products is the monthly set of management accounts. This document shows the physical and financial achievement of the company every month. It also makes comparisons with previous months so that managers and production staff can see trends. The accounts have a number of sections as follows:

### *Contents of monthly management accounts at Mon Products*

1. Summary;
2. Polymer line summary
   (a) primary products accounts
   (b) hot plastics accounts
   (c) packing accounts;
3. Dye plant summary;
4. Production overheads summary;
5. Finance department overheads summary.

As we have said, for Mon profit is not a meaningful indicator of performance. The management accounts although they give a profit or surplus figure give much more useful information about output achieved in the period. Mon's role is to produce products for use within the group as efficiently as possible. It is therefore on outputs that the management accounts concentrate.

## Control on the factory floor

Table 6.1 shows an extract from the period 8 management accounts for the Primary Products Division. You will see that these accounts illustrate three key points concerning achievement of the Primary Products Division in the period.

**Table 6.1** Mon Products Ltd, primary products division – management accounts, period 8

| | *Average for previous 12 months* | | *Previous period* | | | *Period 8* | | | *Standard production* | | | | *Quantity variances* | | | *Price variance* |
|---|---|---|---|---|---|---|---|---|---|---|---|---|---|---|---|---|
| | *Quantity* | *£000* | *Quantity* | *£000* | *Price* | *Quantity* | *£000* | *Usage* | *Price* | *Quantity* | *£000* | *Usage* | *Quantity* | *Yield £000* | *Production £000* | *£000* |
| Output (at standard price) | 11 340 | 4536 | 10 437 | 4175 | 0.4 | 10 958 | 4383.20 | | 0.4 | 11 500 tonnes | 4600 | | −542.00 | | −216.80 | 0.00 |
| Less: Materials | | | | | | | | | | | | | | | | |
| Semi-cracked petroleum | 14 175 | 2693 | 13776 | 2617 | 0.19 | 14 202 | 2698.38 | 1.30 | 0.19 | 14 000 tonnes | 2660 | 1.22 | 202.00 | −163.75 | 125.37 | 0.00 |
| Catalyst replacement | 580 | 458 | 510 | 377 | 0.74 | 526 | 389.24 | 0.05 | 0.7826087 | 575 kg | 450 | 0.05 | 21.90 | 17.14 | 21.21 | 22.41 |
| Electricity | 7 002 | 343 | 6 312 | 322 | 0.051 | 6 421 | 327.47 | 0.59 | 0.0492754 | 6 900 MWh | 340 | 0.60 | 153.80 | 7.58 | 16.02 | −11.07 |
| | | 3494 | | 3316 | | | 3415.09 | | | | 3450 | | | −139.03 | −54.20 | 11.34 |
| Less: Labour | | | | | | | | | | | | | | | | |
| Chamber cleaners | 34 702 | 180 | 32 700 | 173 | 0.0053 | 33 860 | 179.46 | 3.09 | 0.0055804 | 35 840 hours | 200 | 3.12 | 290.85 | 1.62 | 9.43 | 9.49 |
| Process controllers | 11 901 | 82 | 11 626 | 80 | 0.0069 | 11 505 | 79.38 | 1.05 | 0.0068404 | 13 888 hours | 95 | 1.21 | 1728.45 | 11.82 | 4.48 | −0.69 |
| Production operatives | 30 270 | 148 | 30 300 | 148 | 0.0049 | 29 915 | 146.58 | 2.73 | 0.0049426 | 31 360 hours | 155 | 2.73 | −33.01 | −0.16 | 7.31 | 1.27 |
| | | 410 | | 401 | | | 405.43 | | | | 450 | | | 13.28 | 21.21 | 10.08 |
| Surplus for department for period | | 632 | | 458 | | | 562.68 | | | | 700 | | | −125.75 | −32.99 | 21.42 |

1. Absolute output of plastic in tonnes;
2. Total cost per tonne of output;
3. The usage of inputs to achieve one tonne of output.

As well as the period 8 figures standard or budgeted figures are given as well. In order to understand the structure of this large spreadsheet let us look first at the section headed 'Standard production'. Part of this has been duplicated below.

| | *Price per Unit £'000* | *Quantity* | *£'000* | *Usage* |
|---|---|---|---|---|
| Output – plastic | 0.4 | 11 500 tonnes | 4 600 | N/A |
| Semi-cracked petroleum | 0.19 | 14 000 tonnes | 2 660 | 1.22 |
| Catalyst replacement | 0.7826 | 575 kg | 450 | 0.05 |
| Electricity | 0.0492 | 6 900 MWh | 340 | 0.60 |
| | | | 3 450 | |

The aim of this section of the spreadsheet is to summarize expected production of plastic. Mon expects to produce 11 500 tonnes of plastics output from 14 000 tonnes of semi-cracked petroleum. Semi-cracked petroleum costs £190 a tonne, so 14 000 tonnes should cost £2 660 000. The agreed selling price of the plastic produced is £400. This is shown on the spreadsheet. 11 500 tonnes at £400 a tonne totals £4 600 000, the expected turnover for a period.

If 14 000 tonnes of semi-cracked petroleum are used to make 11 500 tonnes of plastic then 1.22 tonnes of input are required for every tonne of output. This then is the usage (14 000/11 500). The same applies to the catalyst. For every 11 500 tonnes of plastic made, 575 kg of catalyst needs replacing. The usage here is therefore 0.05 kg per tonne of output (575/11 500).

Standard production represents a budget. Actual production can be compared to this budget standard in a number of ways. The simplest involves straightforward comparison of columns of figures, for instance the figures for the most recent production period to the standard. More detailed comparison will involve the calculation of the variances shown in the right-hand columns of Table 6.1. These are discussed in some detail later.

Although these accounts are used by senior management they are particularly appropriate for use at the monthly 'shopfloor' meeting. At this meeting the achievement of the Primary Products Division is reviewed by managers, supervisors and shopfloor workers. If things are not going well – and they were not in period 8 at Mon – then the people who will change things are the operational staff. Managers do not control the running temperature of productive equipment, nor do they clean dirty equipment before re-use; the operators do. These people need to see the results of their actions in black and white.

The poor results in period 8 were caused by two main factors:

1. Production was down 542 tonnes or 5% from expected.
2. Usage of semi-cracked petroleum was inefficient. 1.30 tonnes was used per tonne of output compared to the standard of 1.22 tonnes. This represents a 6% loss.

The shopfloor meeting will be asked to discuss these two main causes of poor figures. This discussion will fall into two parts.

1. What were the causes of low productivity and low efficiency?
2. How can these be prevented in future?

The causes of poor productivity and yield were found to be problems in cleaning the production chambers. New cleaning materials were blamed by some operatives because although cleaning was more effective the safety gear needed slowed down proceedings. Parts of the plant are important to clean thoroughly and the reasons for this were reiterated by some technicians: dirty plant costs yields.

The other problem is that during the pre-Christmas period there is a reduction in the number of cleaners available. This year it was particularly difficult due to an unexpected rise in time taken off. Both problems led to attempts to run production longer before cleaning. This had resulted in reduced plastics yields.

The meeting then went on to discuss better ways of planning for holidays and how cover could be obtained at peak periods.

The key points to notice are that data provided is simple but pertinent. At the meeting only variables within the control of the staff of the Primary Products division are dealt with.

## Control by senior and middle management

Table 6.1 shows the figures with comparative data by way of variance analysis and figures from previous production periods; this allows the management to view production trends. Table 6.1 then further analyses of period 8 achievement by detailing the costs associated with the inputs and outputs of the period.

This data allows senior management to carry out two of its most important roles. That is:

1. Responsibility for medium and long-term control *within* the organization;
2. Responsibility for managing the effects of *external* changes.

Much of the medium-term control required within the organization can be obtained by monitoring the effect of output levels on financial results. One very useful tool for doing this is the 'quantity variance'; this is split into two other variances, the 'yield variance' and the 'price variance'.

External changes that might effect Mon Products are changes in the demand for plastics and the cost of inputs of materials and labour. In this case study we can ignore demand for the plastic produced because there is a guaranteed market. The effects of input costs are analysed using the 'price variance'.

All these different variances have been calculated on Table 6.1. Their calculation and uses are described next.

## Internal organization

### *Quantity variances*

The total quantity variance for inputs represents the standard cost of additional materials used. Thus in period 8, 202 tonnes of semi-cracked petroleum more than that budgeted for were used. The total cost of this is £190 × 202 which equals £38 380. However, this statistic is not very useful because although inefficiency resulted in increased usage of petroleum, low production meant that less material was actually used than might have been expected. To get round this problem the quantity variance is broken down into a 'yield' variance and a 'production' variance. The following paragraphs describe the calculation of both these variances. Normally they are calculated by accountants. As long as accounts users understand the relevance of the variances their calculation should not worry them. However they are given here for completeness.

We will look at the yield variance first. In Table 6.1 the yield variance is £163 750 adverse. This figure represents the cost of the inefficient production. This figure is useful because it places the scope of the 'chamber cleaning' problem in perspective. £163 750, a substantial sum is being lost each month as a result of infrequent cleaning work. Clearly, swift action as discussed above is required.

The yield variance is calculated as follows:

10 958 tonnes of output (actual output for period 8) would be expected to require 10 958 × 1.21739 rounded to 1.22 (standard usage) or 13 340 tonnes of semi-cracked petroleum input.

Actual input for 10 958 tonnes of plastics was 14 202 tonnes of petroleum. The excess used is 14 202–13 340 or 862 tonnes. At the standard price of £190 this wasted additional usage is worth £163 750. That is 862 × £190 to the nearest pound.

The production variance analyses the materials cost changes due to the difference in output in period 8 compared with the standard. The cause of the difference, in our case poor yields, is ignored because this has already been analysed in the yield variance. The production in period 8 was lower than the standard. If less output is produced then assuming standard usage, input consumption will also be lower than total standard input. The production variance shows the cost saving associated with producing less. In period 8 lower production resulted in a saving of £125 370 in semi-cracked petroleum usage.

The variance is calculated as follows:

10 958 tonnes of plastic were produced in period 8 compared with a standard production of 11 500 tonnes. This is a shortfall of 542 tonnes. This tonnage would be expected to require the use of 542 × 1.21739 (standard usage of 1.22 before rounding) or 660 tonnes of semi-cracked petroleum. At the standard price of £190 a tonne this is worth £125 370 (£190 × 660).

### *Other useful figures*

If they are to control the internal organization of the company managers need a simple and relatively accurate view of output trends. They need to know the average output per period for the year. They need to know whether output has been at budget levels in the recent past. If production is slowly declining then ultimately it is they who will take the decisions necessary to improve matters. The problem regarding 'Chamber Cleaning' at Mon will need acting upon. Output for both Periods 7 and 8 was very low and this was associated with low levels of chamber cleaning and poor yields. Managing director and products director together with the personnel manager and primary products manager and the management accountant will need to work out a method of obtaining the necessary chamber cleaning work during the Autumn and pre-Christmas period.

Clearly, there are a number of options. The personnel manager may advise that the rate paid to chamber cleaners is below the average for semi-skilled manual work in the area. The primary products managers might say that increased overtime is not feasible due to strict safety regulations. All five managers may then discuss the pros and cons of improving cleaning methods and of employing additional staff. Once concrete alternatives have been decided upon the management accountant will cost the options so that final decisions can be made.

## External factors effecting Mon Products

### *Price variance*

The effect of prices on results can be substantial and radically effect an organization. Mon is protected from price increases in its main raw material, 'semi-cracked' petroleum because the price is fixed. The same applies to sales prices for the finished product. However, the prices of other raw materials and of labour are subject to market fluctuation.

Price variances illustrate the financial effect of changing prices on a concern. They therefore allow managers to plan an organizational response to external changes. Production staff are only indirectly effected by changes in costs. Their responsibility is with quantities and usage as we saw earlier.

In period 8 at Mon Products price variances were relatively small. One variance of potential importance is the increasing cost of electricity. The variance for period 8 was £11 070 (see Table 6.1).

The variance is calculated as follows:

The increase in price of electricity was £51.00 less £49.27 or £1.73 per MWh. In period 8, 6421 MWhs of electricity were used. Thus the additional cost of electricity due to the price increase was £1.73 × 6421 MWhs or £11 070.

## Conclusions

By briefly reviewing the management data available for the Primary Products Department at Mon Products Ltd we have started to see how by measuring output and productivity we can manage a productive organization. The business of Mon has little in common with most public sector operations. However, the methods used to manage it are directly applicable to most productive organizations.

If we consider the output to be processed application forms instead of specialized plastic there will be little change in our reporting and control techniques. Our outputs could equally well be Hotel Services or the running of an office block. There will be differences but much will be similar.

By measuring outputs, and inputs, and by reporting to all levels of staff, the organization is under control. Each member appreciates the real affect of the work done in terms of measureable results. The 'chamber cleaners' can set themselves personal targets for achievement knowing that improved performance on their part will be reflected in the next periods' accounts. Managers can suitably motivate and reward staff based on measured performances. For instance production staff could be paid a bonus if yields are mentained at levels above budget for two consecutive periods.

# Comparison of Mon Products Ltd to a typical public sector department

Having looked at how Mon Products Ltd manages its activities in the Primary Products Department it may be worth comparing its management techniques to those in an average local authority housing benefits office.

Housing benefit administration has been chosen for comparision because:

1. It is a production process theoretically similar to the manufacturing process at Mon;
2. Many public services run departments processing similar forms for different purposes;
3. Most readers will be vaguely familiar with the processing of benefit applications. There are few conceptual difficulties in imagining how such a department functions.

# A brief outline of benefits processing

Housing benefit is a payment made to those on low incomes to assist them in paying their rent and council tax bills.

A typical benefits department works on the following lines:

1. Applicants for benefit initiate a claim by completing an application form on which they disclose their financial circumstances and the rent they are paying.
2. On receipt of the claim the benefits department carries out checks on the details given to ensure that they are accurate. The details on the form are then punched into a computer.
3. On the basis of data input, the computer calculates the benefit due to the applicant.

4. Benefit is paid to the applicant every fortnight. The application expires 60 weeks after the claim form was first received. At this point benefit ceases untill a new application is made.
5. District authorities may have an average caseload of about 10 000 and will pay about £7 million a year. Metropolitan boroughs may have 30 000 cases and pay approximately £20 million in benefits.
6. Administration costs are subsidized by central government in proportion to caseload. A district council will employ approximately 20 benefits staff whereas a metropolitan borough may have 60 full-time people.
7. Benefits paid are reimbursed by central government. When considering benefits admistration we will only consider administration costs. For simplicity we will assume that housing benefit itself is not to any extent a cost of the administering local authority.

A typical budget for a district council employing 20 staff will be as follows:

## *A typical local authority housing benefit administration budget*

| | *£'000* |
|---|---|
| Supplies and services | 30.6 |
| Establishment expenses | 25.0 |
| Computer costs | 45.2 |
| Salaries | 251.3 |
| | 352.1 |
| Grant from central government | 253.7 |
| Net cost to local authority | 98.4 |
| | 352.1 |

How then is this budget managed to provide the service of benefit administration in the typical authority?

## *Salaries*

The most important element of the budget relates to salaries. Once the annual pay agreement has been reached the budget holder can be relatively sure that salary rates are fixed. To ensure that the budget figure is not broken he must control recruitment and overtime. By keeping a regular check on the effects of both of these the largest budget figure can be managed.

## *Computer costs*

Computer costs represent the benefit department's proportion of total computer costs for the authority. The benefits manager may have a 'service level agreement' with the computer manager where by computer costs are fixed regardless of the final cost of computers at the year end. The other alternative is that the benefits department is charged for computer time. The more the computer is used the more the benefits department is charged. However the user department would have no control over total computer costs. They could only control their proportion of costs not their absolute amount. In many cases the benefits manager has almost no control over computer costs and consequently he is not able to effectively manage this part of his budget.

### *Supplier services and establishment expenses*

These figures relate to costs of stationery, postage, office equipment and bank charges. These figures will vary closely with caseload. Consequently the manager will be able to predict their costs based on previous years experience. Should caseload increase unexpectedly problems may arise. However, careful budgeting may allow some leeway by the inclusion of a contingency figure.

So we can see that by controlling staff numbers closely the benefits manager can keep to his budget as long as caseload remains stable. But so far we have only described control over inputs. What control is there over output, that is processed benefit claims?

### *Control over output*

The major control over output at most local authorities is the requirement to review all claims at least every 60 weeks. To assist over this benefit department computers produce lists of claims nearing their 60-week review date. The lists are often in the form of self-adhesive labels. These can be stuck onto claim forms and dispatched to claimants for them to complete prior to lapse of the original claim. It is difficult for departments to fall behind in this area of work because it is normally fully automated.

The next stage of output management relates to processing the forms returned from the 60-week review. Many claimants personal circumstances do not change for years – for instance pensioners on low incomes. Often a department may leave re-assessment of these individuals until the more risky re-applications have been assessed. Benefit payments to low risk 'customers' can be continued while re-assessment is in progress. Major problems would arise if benefit was stopped solely due to backlogs over re-assessment in the benefit department.

Best practice requires high risk applications to be re-assessed at more frequent intervals than 60 weeks. Benefit departments on top of their workload will flag claimants on unemployment benefit, those working on very low wages and others likely to be on a low incomes for short periods only. Regular re-assessments of these cases allows frequent checking of continued eligibility for benefit.

## Contrast with Mon Products Ltd

By now it must have become clear that housing benefits are not normally managed in the same way as we described for Mon Products Ltd. Let us briefly analyse the main differences between the two organizations' methods.

**Table 6.2** Comparison of management methods

| | *Benefits administration* | *Mon Products Ltd* |
|---|---|---|
| *Budgets* | | |
| 1. Budget set | Yes | Yes |
| 2. Budget controlled | Yes | Yes |
| *Inputs* | | |
| 3. Inputs analysed | In total | Per unit output |
| *Outputs* | | |
| 4. Outputs controlled | On an *ad hoc* basis | By periodic accounts |
| 5. Outputs defined | No | Yes |
| 6. Outputs measured | No | Yes |
| 7. Periodic analysis of productivity | No | Yes |
| 8. Performance Indication set and monitored (input/output ratio) | No | Yes |

Table 6.2 compares the management control methods of the two organizations. Where Mon relies on objective documenting of achievement in the form of periodic (4-weekly) management accounts, the housing benefit department tends to use more subjective methods of control. The housing benefit department is most concerned with total expenditure levels. In contrast Mon is interested in productivity. Mon measures what is achieved with inputs. The housing benefit department does not.

Why is there such a difference in the way two enterprises organize themselves? What does it reflect? In the first chapter of this book we discussed the cultural heritage of the public sector. It is this heritage that is the main cause of the difference in management style between the two concerns. In other respects the two are very similar. Neither operate in a market, both are paid by results, both produce an easily defined output, both have access to the accounting personnel required for financial reporting. Surely there are more similarities than differences?

# Summary

In this chapter we have started to discuss how to implement the management ideas formulated in the second chapter of the book. Public servants are paid to achieve public goals. In a fast changing world you will only be able to do this efficiently if your control is output based. The change this represents is enormous, but so are the benefits.

## Reader questionnaire

This chapter has been concerned with public sector service outputs. The questionnaire below seeks to help you analyse your own outputs.

ANSWERS

1. Is the concept of an output new to your department or organization?
2. If traditionally you have not considered that your service provided an output what did you believe were the achievements of your organization?
3. Does your work fall into any of the 7 categories listed on page 78?
4. If your output is complex then it may in fact consist of a number different outputs. Can you analyse your achievements in this way?
5. If you still cannot decide which output categories fit your organization then one of two situations has arisen.
   (a) Your outputs are highly specific.
   (b) You are involved in research or development work.
6. Are your outputs are highly specific? Define your own outputs and measure your achievement using these.
7. Are you are involved in research and development? Various aspects of your work can be measured. Do you carry out repetitive testing work? This may form a simple service output. Are you responsible for maintenance of the servicability of your laboratory? This will be another service output. However your major output – research achievement, will not readily be susceptible to the management accounting methods described in this chapter.
8. Lastly, if you really believe you produce no outputs that can be measured you are advised to think again. If you produce no outputs you are doing nothing useful. Does this describe your work?
9. If your organization or department produces clear outputs do you use them to manage and control the work of your organization? Or are you interested in total spending regardless of achievement?

# 7

# What do *you* get from output-based management?

## The concrete benefits of measuring output

We have talked at length about figures, about how important it is to measure and to have management accounts and to calculate ratios and variances. We are perhaps in danger of returning to the image of the accountant without a soul; an individual who would put a flat roof on St Paul's Cathedral to save money. To counter this view it would be useful briefly to rehearse the arguments for defining and measuring outputs.

Why are we trying to measure? We want to measure so that:

1. Managers can fully appreciate what has been achieved;
2. Politicians can see what their policies have achieved;
3. The public can:
   (a) appreciate what they are getting for their taxes;
   (b) check the results of the policies put forward by politicians.

Does this mean that the main beneficiaries of management information are politicians and public? What is the benefit to managers in laboriously measuring work that has already been done? There are a large number of benefits. This chapter looks at the many advantages you as a manager will obtain from using effective management information.

First the chapter looks at how better control over achievement assists managers in their everyday work and in the longer term with their careers. Next a worked example demonstrates management accounting in a typical public sector situation.

The last section of the chapter considers the benefits to managers of implementing management information systems so that they are well placed to implement the changes to the public sector that were discussed in Chapter 2.

## The benefits of management information in the office

Management information provides a substantial number of benefits to managers in their everyday office routines. These are:

1. Work can be better controlled;
2. Decisions can be taken more rationally;
3. Resources can be targeted more effectively to where they are most needed;
4. Excellence is rewarded rather than 'back biting';
5. Motivation to achieve is enhanced;
6. Objectives are set down unambiguously – you know your role as a manager;
7. The 'ethos' of the organization improves.

It is worth reviewing these benefits so that they can be fully comprehended in terms of the daily routine of work.

### Controlling and decision making

As we discussed in the case study in the previous chapter, management information is important to be able to control work and to take decisions. In the case study in Chapter 6 the management accounts highlighted the fact that productivity was falling. Because this was discovered relatively early control could be increased to prevent this continuing.

The case study also showed how decision making was made much more effective as a result of quantified details of the effects of low productivity. By knowing the cost of suboptional achievement the importance of finding a remedy could easily be judged.

In Chapter 4 we discussed the role of 'feedback' in organizations. Controlling and decision making are the two most important benefits of 'feedback' and they are best achieved through the use of high quality management information. We shall be considering them in greater detail in later chapters. But first let us look at the other benefits.

### Targeting resources

When there are a number of possible options decisions need to be made on how to target resources. As we discussed in Chapter 5 resources are always scarce. If information is available on past achievements then rational decisions can be made about where to spend public money.

### *Example 1*

Let us assume you are a doctor specializing in the treatment of Hodgkinson's Disease. It is a leukaemia-like cancer which if skilfully treated shows a recovery rate of up to 95%. Your work is based at a large general hospital that is having problems meeting its budgets. You are concerned that your specialty may be closed and your patients sent to London teaching hospitals. Another specialty in your hospital is a possible alternative choice to your department for closure. While your work is concerned with life-threatening conditions your rival's work is, in your opinion, trivial.

Working with your business manager and the management accountants you carefully isolate your costs. These are then used to calculate the cost structure for each patient you treat. Using your clinical records and with help from referring general practitioners you produce details of your success rates at treating the disease.

At the end of the exercise you are pleasantly satisfied with the results. What is more you think others will be as well. The cost per case works out at about the same as a trip to Disneyland and your recovery rate is close to that achieved in the hospital that pioneered the techniques you use. After a very useful meeting with the Trust Chief Executive your department appears secure.

The other specialty under threat had not produced a single figure to back their case. After this your hospital begins to actively sell your clinical expertise and patient numbers rise considerably.

It may look as if the above example is terribly simplistic. This is not in fact the case. Quite simple analysis of achievement can produce startling results. Remember the £30 Ministry of Agriculture laboratory rat in Chapter 2?

Senior managers need management information to run an organization. They need to target resources and to demonstrate success to their own superiors. Middle managers need management information to target resources within their budget head and to demonstrate to senior managers the success of their work. Junior managers likewise benefit from presenting satisfactory results objectively measured.

## Reward for excellence

In any organization some people are promoted while others remain in their old jobs. So often in the public service one gets the impression that people feel that some individuals work for promotion while others work to get the work done. The same applies in the private sector where some may feel that it is 'not what you know but who you know' that matters. Unfortunately, there will always be unfairness of this type in any organization. But when individuals can claim tangible quantified achievements the opportunity for bias is much reduced.

### *Example 2*

Consider a planning department in a local authority. For administrative purposes the department is split into sections covering three areas – a major town and two rural localities. Having worked in the authority for ten years you now head of one of the rural sections.

The other country section has just been taken over by a new recruit from a London borough. He is paid significantly more than you and it is an open secret that he was more or less promised the position of deputy to the Chief Planning Officer when the present incumbent retires next year.

After he has been at the authority for a few months you begin to notice that you are taking a surprising number of his telephone calls. Things are made worse because the conversations you are forced to have with his 'clients' are distinctly acrimonious. Why is the planning system so slow, they all demand? But like all upstarts the new planning officer is on good terms with the people that matter which in this case includes the Chief Planning Officer.

Recently the department purchased a computer to record planning applications. Staff grudgingly used the machine to the minimum possible extent. After a particularly disagreeable telephone conversation with one of your rivals' clients you have had enough. You push aside the work you are dealing with, cancel an afternoon meeting and in distraction find yourself looking through the user manual for the new computer. That evening you are still in the office at 9 pm testing sort routines on the PC. It is all suddenly becoming rather exciting.

You started by analysing the times taken to process individual applications. The following week you summon up your powers of persuasion and obtain the support of the old deputy planning officer in convincing the chief to introduce timesheets. After that it was not too difficult. On both quality of service and efficiency your section regularly turns out the best figures. What is more the Chief Planning Officer now enjoys selling his new productivity figures to councillors. The planning department will now be one of the first to occupy the new modern offices at present under construction.

Not everyone is in a position to prove objectively their individual abilities, but many are, especially in middle and junior management. At this level responsibilities are simple and success once measured is easily ascribed to the correct individuals. Middle managers benefit by having their true worths objectively measured. Senior managers can clearly see where good results are being achieved. The consequence is that excellence can be encouraged and recorded. This leads us on to the subject of motivation.

## Motivation

In Chapter 3 we discussed problems of motivation in the public sector. By looking at case histories we saw that individuals were normally either motivated by major goals shared by society at large, such as war or unacceptable poverty – or by specific personal goals. The everyday routine of work has seldom motivated public servants. We concluded that every public sector organization needs to incorporate a clear system of personal reward to encourage the attainment of mundane public sector goals. If we wish to reward, then we should only reward for achievement consistent with the public interest. This means that we must measure the quantity and quality of achievement to ensure that public goals are being met *before* we reward individuals. In practice this requires a management information system that measures outputs or achievements. Only once we have this can we reliably reward and motivate. Here is a simple example of what is meant.

## *Example 3*

Let us consider an organization which clerically processes documentation in vast quantities – a very common public sector task. Perhaps you are the new manager with overall responsibility for a land registry office. After you have taken up your post you begin to realize that less work is being done than you might hope. The offices are much noisier than they should be and boisterous chatter continues all day.

After some investigation you learn that motivation has been poor for the last year or so after a number of managers and supervisors retired more or less simultaneously. Clearly the situation has got to such a stage that you will need to do more than politely ask people to stop talking and get on with some work.

A number of options are open to you. You will probably choose more than one, but straightforward data on costs and achievement, combined with a simple method of rewarding hard work will be one of the best. Staff will very soon understand that their self-interest lies in work rather than chatter as it did before.

By categorizing the various types of registration you build up a number of cost models not dissimilar to those used at Mon Products Ltd (see Chapter 6). By doing this you are able to start monitoring the productivity of your staff.

By raising the issue with the staff union at an early stage and by explaining that improved and controlled productivity equated with a better public service (not an option open to your private sector colleagues) the support of key union personnel was achieved. After that productivity standards were worked out. These were then used to form the basis of a productivity based bonus system.

These changes have resulted in a motivated and productive workforce. Everyone knows what is required of them out of solidarity with their fellows and as a result of financial reward. People are now working to increase productivity. Whereas before the offices had an atmosphere of dejection, it now feels alive when you walk in every morning.

The effect on motivation of management information is one of its most important benefits. Good figures act as a 'pat on the back' to both managers and staff. Hard work is made much more enjoyable if the results of that work are objectively measured and reported. 'We all worked very hard' someone might say, 'but no one even said if what we had done was any good'. Will they work hard again? What do you think? But if the rest of the sentence was 'and the monthly figures were the best we have ever had', then things would be different. It is rather like the 'Space Invaders' computer games that challenge you and then record your score at the end. People become frantic to beat their previous best or that of colleagues. The feature that makes computer games so attractive is that they monitor achievement. 'Space Invaders' without a scoring mechanism would be like football without goals; just a boring way of killing time.

The rule is that motivation is based on evidence of success.

## Unambiguous objectives

In Chapter 4 we said that organizations set objectives and then monitored the attainment of these objectives using various forms of feedback. In Chapter 3 we discussed public sector objectives and concluded that for many organizations simple unambiguous objectives were lacking. But by setting up an effective management information system you are forced to define your objectives.

### *Example 4*

Perhaps you are a librarian in a public library. Your county council is genuinely concerned at the size of the library service budget for new books. So as to be able to defend your library's actions you are beginning to prepare your case. The key point must be that your library is economically upholding the objectives of library legislation.

You could say in you defence that the people who wanted the books you are ordering are all good and sweet and that it would be mean and nasty to turn them down. Many people could produce quite a good piece of rhetoric along those lines illustrated with individual examples of genuine need for the books requested. That is not your style. You want to demonstrate that your actions were and are consistent with the objectives for which public libraries were created. Using public library legislation and the vague policy statements the council once drew up, you produce a set of objectives which you intend to use as the basis of a management information system. Using the figures produced by this you will concentrate your work on important areas and justify your actions.

The Public Libraries and Museum Act 1964 requires that services are 'promoted' and 'improved'. (s1). The Act also requires that the service is 'comprehensive and efficient' (s7(1)) and that there is stock 'sufficient in number, range and quantity to meet general and specific requirements of adults and children' (s7(2)). Based on these general statutory requirements you set amongst others the following criteria for measurement.

1. 75% of the budget will be spent on 'general requirement books';
2. 25% of the budget will be spent on 'specific requirement books';
3. General requirement books will be expected to be borrowed at least six times a year for the first five years;
4. Specific requirement books will be expected to be borrowed at least three times a year for the first three years.

Having set these criteria you begin to measure your results. When you receive sales literature, or representatives, or a public request for you to order new books, you consider your budget and whether the title is likely to be 'general' or 'specific'. Having made this decision you then judge whether you think the book will be borrowed at least six or three times a year. If you have room within the relevant budget and you judge the book will be borrowed the required number of times, the purchase is made.

After the first nine months of enforcing this policy and measuring the lending achieved, you are surprised to find that your general category books do not appear to be as popular as you had anticipated; an average of six borrowings a year looks unlikely. By looking back over the figures you note a tendency towards artistic modern novels. Unfortunately, these are not making the six lendings figure but they are achieving three. As a consequence you buy less of these books and re-categorize them as 'specific'. A number of similar adjustments are also made. At last the dreaded budget showdown comes. Senior libraries staff are preparing their case. It needs to be a good one because social services are claiming more cash for 'care in the community'. Everyone is a bit worried. The Chief Libraries officer is having a series of individual meetings with a selection of librarians from local libraries; you have been asked to give your viewpoint.

At the meeting you state your achievement and how it meets the objectives you set based on the legislation. You demonstrate how you were forced to modify your purchasing policy to meet your objectives, and how having made adjustments you are meeting your targets. You are providing the Chief Libraries Officer with the information he has lacked all his working life – objective proof of his, or at least his services', usefulness. The requirements of legislation are being met successfully and economically with the proof readily available. Who is going to damage such a success story?

By setting strong objectives and maintaining attainment you are demonstrably achieving. Nor need you worry about **which areas** need your full effort; there is no uncertainty because you know. The job of a library is to lend books. Set that as an objective and measure your success. The job of a university lecturer is to teach students. Or it is to carry out research or perhaps to arrange funding for research? At present many public servants are not quite sure what they should be putting their efforts into. Is a highways engineer meant to build super new roads, save public money or to prevent pollution? Probably all three will be objectives but not all are of equal importance. By setting targets and priorities in the form of objectives to be measured the doubt and attendant vascillation and half-heartedness are dispelled. Real efforts can be input to reach a whole series of attainments.

## Improving ethos

In Chapter 3 we described the 'ethos' of an organization as the environment in which it attempts to achieve its objectives. We went on to say that for many public sector organizations the ethos is not that of 'excellence' but often that of 'getting by'.

At one of the first public sector clients with which I became involved I expressed concern to the chief accountant about the quality of the accounts he had given me. He looked at me as if I had come to work without a shirt on. He then uttered the few words needed to sum up his world view, 'We are not trying to win prizes you know.' It was the first but not the last time I was to hear this depressing belief so unashamedly expressed.

There are plenty of good reasons for changing this state of affairs. Clearly, we should aim for excellence and believe in it. If we do not hold this view our organization will be seen as second rate by those it is meant to serve or 'service'. It will not be getting the best out of its staff. Nor will it be obtaining good value for money.

## *Measurement and panache*

During the first few weeks of the Gulf War, General Schwartzkopf explained to world's media 'we set our objectives; we measure our results and then we reset our objectives'. He was describing how he was going to win. Substantial numbers of British public servants were instrumental in that victory. There is nothing boring or lacking in dash or unimaginative in measuring achievement of objectives.

The opposite is the case. Many of the most imaginative people in history set objectives and measured achievement showing the most extraordinary human qualities. Madame Curie is a good example; one of her objectives was to find the radioactive element in pitch blend and she monitored her results in the most unpleasant conditions until she achieved success. This is the ethos of excellence at its very best and most dramatic. But there are many examples nearer to everyday life where measurement of achievement and the ideal of excellence go hand in hand. Parker pens used to advertise that unless their ballpoint pens achieved a perfect line ten yards long the batch would be discarded. No one would check that their own pen was up to this standard but Parker could successfully promote themselves based on a reputation for quality goods backed by the ethos of excellence. A sulphuric acid factory at which I once carried out audit work was very careful to measure the quality of its raw materials and the purity of the resulting acid. The management of the holding company, which owned the factory, wished to close it to reduce the over-supply of acid to the market. But before the closure it was found that no other plant in the country could make such pure acid; the closure plans were rapidly halted. There was nothing smart or clever about the factory but it did have a dogged determination to do the job well. Measurement and excellence saved it from closure.

Another very different example of belief in excellence comes from the City of London discount market. Discount houses are rather select organizations that play a specific role in the control of interest rates by the Bank of England. The business involves lending money for a period of a few months by purchasing bills of exchange and the borrowing of money 'overnight' as banks balance their books every afternoon. The difference in interest rates between borrowing and lending is very slim at perhaps 1/16%. Traditionally dealings are recorded in the 'Money Book', a large leather bound ledger, using a stub of pencil. But if the business is to prosper information is required on the interest rates being paid as a result of lending – the purchase of bills of exchange. What might have been a good deal the day the bill was brought may be a poor one in a week's time if the interest rate paid to borrowers in the overnight market increases. The solution to the problem is the 'cost of money report' which a computer calculates every morning.

The skill of the dealers working at very fine margins is superb, and the quality of discount house lunches is a legend in the City. Professionalism and even a sense of devil-may-care flamboyance are quite compatible with clear objectives and sound measurement; in fact one is only possible with the other. In some areas of the public sector we instinctively know this. Nurses note a number of measurements every day on the board at the base of every hospital bed. It is this form of professionalism that gives the medical profession the high social status that survey after survey on public attitudes records. But in other areas the public sector is conspicuously lagging. Unmeasured poorly formulated objectives are one of the reasons for waiting lists for many simple medical procedures. A child may wait 25% of its young life before grommets to prevent ear infection and partial deafness are fitted, while in contrast enormous over-exposure of patients to X-rays has been found recently to be the major source of harmful radiation in society. This inconsistency in quality is quickly noticed by the public who could be said to view much of the health service as an odd cross between Steptoe & Son and Rolls Royce. The ethos of excellence needs to be consistently and rigorously upheld if it is to survive.

# Implementation of measurement systems

Now we have examined the theoretical and practical benefits of a 'measured' approach to management how do we start to implement change? The next section of this chapter looks at this.

## Setting performance standards

A recent letter in the *Independent* newspaper said reactive management or 'fire fighting', is 'a tacit admission that the management does not really expect to get standards up in the first place'. What then are we to do to remove a 'tacit admission' of failure.

We already have discussed much of the preliminary work. We have pointed out the need to define output and then to measure it. We have mentioned the need to be practical. There are in fact a number of procedures that should be carried out one after the other so that active measurement of outputs can be achieved. The following list flowcharts the process.

### *Setting up performance management systems in practice*

1. **Departmental objectives**
   – analyse and record in order of priority the objectives of your department or section.
2. **Definition of output**
   – from your objectives define your outputs.
3. **Measurement of outputs**
   – decide which aspects of your outputs are best measured to provide evidence of compliance with your objectives in 1. above.
4. **Systems to record output**
   – systems must
   (a) be simple,
   (b) provide information when required,
   (c) be reliable.
5. **Interaction with financial systems**.
   – your system should if possible be compatible with the financial information available from the main accounts department.

6. **Liaison with accounts department**
   – accountancy personnel should become involved in helping analyse the financial significance of the figures from your system.

## *Departmental objectives*

Most managers have a general feel for what constitutes the important aspects of their work. A housing benefit manager knows that he or she must arrange for processing of claims for benefit in compliance with statute and regulations. But comprehension of departmental objectives at this simple level is not enough.

One manager in a social security office might feel that accuracy of the computation of a claim is more important then speed of response to claimants. Another might consider that his major concern was the welfare and safety of his staff. Spending on plate glass protection at the benefits counter would for this manager take precedence over extra staff to facilitate quicker more regular reviews of entitlement. A third manager might consider claimant fraud her main concern; accuracy of computation, response time and staff welfare would all take second place to an efficient team of inspectors.

So we need clearly to state our objectives and then place them in order of priority. It is also important that we are sure that these objectives are consistent with our legal powers; that is that we have the legal authority to spend public money in the way we expect to. Conversely, we must make sure that our objectives do in fact cover our obligations under statute and regulations.

Much legislation is deliberately vague regarding the extent and priority of objectives. The reasons for this were discussed in Chapter 5. In these situations subjective judgement must be made taking into account professional best practice considerations.

A simplified set of departmental objectives for a meat inspection department in a local authority might be as follows:

1. To ensure that only licensed slaughterhouses and knackers' yards slaughter animals;
2. To ensure that all licensed premises only use licensed slaughtermen;
3. To ensure that methods of slaughter in use at slaughter houses and knackers' yards are in compliance with statute and regulations;
4. To ensure that only meat fit for human consumption is sold for that purpose.

All four objectives are important and can be simply stated. But the objectives are not all necessarily compatible. An inspector can enter a slaughterhouse under the Slaughterhouses Act 1974 s20, check the licences of the premises and its workforce, but this will not further the first objective. Spot checks will need to be made on shops and restaurants to ensure that animals were slaughtered in licensed establishments. Similarly, it is easy to check that licences are held, but expertise is needed to check that licences are properly held by 'fit persons'. All this means that choices need to be made. The relative importance of each objective must be decided upon and recorded.

Using the example of the slaughterhouse we could place the objectives in order of importance, namely:

1. Primary objective: safe meat (4).
2. Secondary objective: properly licensed slaughtermen (2) and (3).
3. Tertiary objective: animals only slaughtered in licensed premises (1).

Having placed objectives in a rough order of priority it is possible to consider outputs to measure. You cannot measure everything so you will try to measure those achievements that are the most important. By analysing your objectives into an order of priority, decisions are more easily and rationally made.

## *Defining and measuring outputs*

Now we need to define and measure the likely outputs we would produce in achieving our objectives. It is useful to consider definitions and measurement of outputs together because they are inextricably linked. An output of a brewery would be 'beer'. The measured output would be 'a bottle of beer'. We naturally tend to think in terms of quantities because by doing so ideas become more concrete. It is the practical aspects of measuring achievements that we are concerned with.

Clearly, in defining and measuring outputs we should start with our primary objective – safe meat. What is the output here? It is the 'guarantee' of safe meat to the public. Meat inspectors in conjunction with regulations will need to define what attributes a safe carcass should have.

An output has been defined. What is the measure? Clearly, the measure is the number of carcasses to which the 'guarantee' applies. At first this may seem odd because the number of carcasses produced by slaughterhouses are quite outside the meat inspection control – the inspectors do not produce the output. But control is not really the issue. Meat inspectors must guarantee that meat produced is safe. If one assumes that they are part of the slaughterhouse staff rather than local authority personnel then the concept of their output is probably easier to comprehend. For our two secondary objectives we are concerned with licensing of individual workers – slaughtermen.

In many ways this is a similar objective to that of 'guaranteeing' safe meat. We are 'guaranteeing' that slaughtermen, slaughterhouses and knacker's yards are all licensed. This also involves regulatory work. The question is not just 'do they hold a licence?' but also 'are they fit do hold a licence?'. Let us consider the first question.

To ensure that persons hold the necessary licences, checks need to be carried out. We are not concerned with the cost of each checking procedure – a check is not an output. The public pays meat inspectors to ensure slaughtermen do in fact hold licences. How this is achieved is essentially up to the meat inspectors themselves, but they must be able to demonstrate that their methods are effective.

Inspectors need to devise a checking routine and then monitor the cost of the scheme on a unit basis – a unit being one licence held for a year.

The second aspect of the secondary objectives is the fitness of licence holders to hold a licence. To ensure that holders are fit and proper persons checks are required on:

1. The working practices of current holders;
2. The training of those applying for slaughtermen's certificates for the first time while they work a probationary period.

These checks are not in themselves outputs. This is a crucial point to understand. Work is an input not an output. The output we want is a 'guarantee' of good working practice from slaughtermen consistent with holding a licence. Our measured output is the number of licences 'guaranteed'.

## *Systems of measurement and accounting information*

We now need to consider how having defined an output which can be measured we can start to monitor and control our work. In the next chapter case studies are given for three typical public sector activities. The purpose now is to discuss the problems associated with such a change in management emphasis before we start to look at the details available in the case studies.

Let us consider the primary objective of the meat inspectors. The measured output is a 'guarantee' of safety for each carcass from slaughterhouses in a local authority district. How do we set up systems to measure output and how do we report achievement? At its simplest we want to look at meat safety checking costs per carcass. Perhaps 5000 beasts were slaughtered in a week and perhaps our checking costs were £1500. We could then say that one unit of output – the 'guarantee' on one carcass – cost £0.30. This is useful information but major queries now arise.

1. If the number of beasts slaughtered fell would our unit costs rise?
2. Are we sure that we have accurately divided our costs between meat safety and other activities?

Let us consider a fictional department with costs as follows:

## *Costs of the meat inspection department at a district council for the year to 31 March 1991*

| | £ |
|---|---|
| Salaries | 151 133 |
| Vets' bills | 37 950 |
| Supplies | 3 910 |
| Total direct costs | 192 993 |
| Central administration costs | 7 431 |
| | 200 424 |

We need to split these costs between our outputs with some care. If we do not, spurious and misleading figures result. The best method of splitting salary costs is by using timesheets. Below we show the costs at our district council which were produced after timesheets were analysed.

| | *Safe meat* | *Licensing* | *All slaughtering (legal)* | *Management of department* | *Total* |
|---|---|---|---|---|---|
| Salaries | 90 680 | 35 198 | 5 713 | 19 542 | 151 133 |
| Vets' bills | 37 950 | — | — | — | 37 950 |
| Supplies | 2 346 | 754 | 264 | 546 | 3 910 |
| Total direct costs | 130 976 | 35 952 | 5 977 | 20 088 | 192 993 |

Of our costs we now know the cost of checking meat safety – £130 976. But the vets' bills only relate to meat which is for export. Clearly we do not want these costs to be attributed to all our outputs – only those which are for export. We must divide our costs again. Timesheets are still the best methods of achieving this.

| | Safe meat | | |
|---|---|---|---|
| | *Home* | *Export* | *Total* |
| Salaries | 71 637 | 19 043 | 90 680 |
| Vets' bills | — | 37 950 | 37 950 |
| Supplies | 1 384 | 962 | 2 346 |
| Total direct costs | 73 021 | 57 955 | 130 976 |

We need to know the total number of home and export carcasses. These figures can only be obtained from the records of the slaughterhouse. We must look at the statutory returns made to the Ministery of Agriculture Fisheries and Food that give the figures we need. Figures for our district council are given below. For simplicity in this next example no split has been given between cattle, pigs and sheep.

## *Number of beasts slaughtered in the year to 31 March 1991*

| | *Home* | *Export* | *Total* |
|---|---|---|---|
| No. of carcasses | 243 101 | 79 301 | 322 402 |
| Direct costs | £73 021 | £57 955 | £130 976 |
| Cost per beast | £0.30 | £0.73 | N/A |

Remember we are relying on the professional competence of the meat inspectors to carry out sufficient testing to be able to demonstrably 'guarantee' the quality of the meat produced. This means that the amount of testing done is related to the number of carcasses being processed in a period. So what happens when the number of carcasses increases? More testing will be necessary. But if the meat inspectors have a full time staff, salary costs will remain static. Or again numbers of carcass may fall. Let us look at some figures for meat killed for the home market.

| | *Month 1* | *Month 2* | *Month 3* |
|---|---|---|---|
| No. of carcasses | 20 258 | 23 297 | 17 361 |
| Direct costs | £6 085 | £6 385* | £6 085 |
| Unit costs | £0.30 | £0.27 | £0.35 |

* £300 of overtime paid

Surely, normal fluctuations in slaughterhouses usage are making our figures meaningless. Let us look at the implications of varying unit costs.

## *Management lessons*

Once we can see the effects of varying workloads on unit costs we can manage to optimize efficiency. For instance, if costs continue to vary from £0.27 to £0.35 then we should consider using part-time staff to cover peak periods. Or perhaps a more flexible workforce could be used to do other useful environmental health work when carcass numbers are down. If we are serious about optimizing output from scarce resources we need to consider these options.

## *Management data*

Whatever course of action is best we could try for management purposes to remove the heavy fluctuation in figures due to different operational levels. When not testing then staff could charge their time to other work or to 'non-productive' time. This might result in figures as follows:

| | *Month 1* | *Month 2* | *Month 3* |
|---|---|---|---|
| Direct costs | 6 085 | 6 385 | 6 085 |
| Less 'non-productive' time | (447) | – | (981) |
| | £5 638 | £6 385 | £5 104 |
| No. of carcasses | 20 258 | 23 297 | 17 361 |
| | £0.28 | £0.27 | £0.29 |

Now the figures begin to look meaningful for management purposes; productivity is nearly constant. We can also see the cost of 'non-productive' time. This was £981 in Month 3 – a significant sum.

## *Summary*

In this example we have shown how a manager of a public sector body could analyse his or her department's achievements. First, objectives were set. They were then placed in an order of importance. Having done this the true outputs of the department could be properly comprehended or defined, prior to measurement.

The next stage required an analysis of the input costs associated with different outputs. This then allows the calculation of unit costs. Only at this stage is it possible to analyse the productivity and efficiency of the department in carrying out its functions. The meat inspector manager at our district council is now in a position to introduce the high level of management control that we saw illustrated in the example in Chapter 6 from Mon Products Ltd.

A key point to remember, if you have not managed using outputs before, is that substantial changes will be needed in your organization. You should expect this because unless there was substantial change the new management techniques you are using would clearly be having little effect. Second, do not expect to be able to fully anticipate the affects that output based management will have on how you use your newly set up management information systems. You will need to fine tune your system after you start to begin measurement. Similarly, it will be some time – perhaps six months to a year before the full benefits of your new systems are seen. Do not expect to see instant improvements.

Last, good management information systems and output measurement do not lead to a quiet life. The manager is forced to manage. By motivating his or her staff and monitoring their real achievement the manager's life becomes active. You will be working with your staff even more than you do now, helping, explaining, listening and cajoling the best out of them. Your life will be active but you will certainly see the results of your endeavours, a reward your predecessors never had!

# Markets and charters

In this part of the chapter we seek to place the management systems we have talked about into the context of the changes that are taking place in the way the public sector is being organized.

In Chapter 2 we mentioned the popularity of the concept of 'Citizen's Charters' among political parties. A consequence is that there will be a requirement for much more information about public service outputs. The other main change in public service management is the use of 'internal markets'. These too can only function on the basis of solid measurement of achievement.

Both these changes in the public sector have the same effect in that they make analysis and control of outputs of prime importance. They both force suppliers of public sector goods and services to actively analyse, control and manage their operations in a much more thorough way than ever before.

## The effects on management techniques of markets and charters

Internal markets can be used where the public have an element of choice. University education is a classic example of this. A student may go to Exeter or Aberdeen making the decision based on the qualities of the two universities. In contrast the same element of choice is not available regarding water supply. The consumer has to use the local water company; it is impossible to change supplier. Many public services fall between these two extremes. If you live on the Kent/Sussex border and someone steals your car, the Kent police might be assigned to look into your case. If, however, the Sussex CID had a very good reputation for clearing up crime you might wish to be under the care of the police force with the better performance; but it would clearly be impractical to expect the West Midlands force to take charge of your case. Where an internal market is not possible or is considered undesirable for technical or political reasons a 'Charter' is a sensible way forward.

The theories of 'Markets' and 'Charters' are entirely different. A market works on the basis of competition; a charter is an honest statement of aspiration, success and

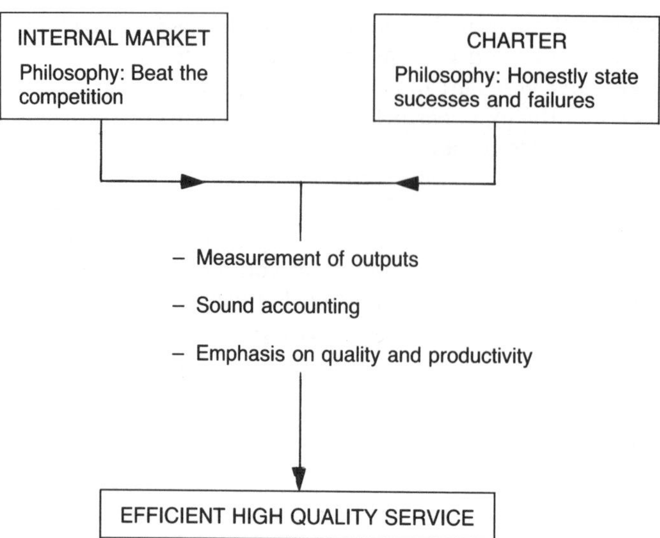


**Fig. 7.1** The relationship between internal markets and charters.

failures. But both will involve many of the same management techniques. Both will require measurement of output and clear measurement of performance. This relationship is shown in Fig. 7.1.

An element of competition is present in the charter concept. By publishing achievement you are open to comparison with other similar organizations. This aspect of a charter system varies in emphasis between commentators. The other aspect of a charter is its contractual element. It can be seen as a pledge between politicians and public servants on the one hand, and electors on the other. The idea is that the promise should not be broken. One problem is that there may be a tendency to promise little so that failure is unlikely.

An aspect of charters that does not arise with internal markets is the potential for conflicting viewpoints between politicians and staff. Under the charter the politician will contract with the electors. He or she agrees say, a set standard of social services at a reasonable price. But can the politician convince the public servants that it is possible? He will also need a contract with the managers and staff who provide the service. Markets and charters need to be looked at bearing in mind the points made in Chapter 3 regarding motivation and goal congruence in the public sector. But here we consider the management information needs of both systems.

## Management information requirements

In a market you need to know enough information about your unit costs to be able to ensure that your selling price will recoup expenditure. Under a charter you need to know enough information about your unit costs to be able to report achievement to the public. In both systems unit costs are vital.

Consider a hospital which has an expertise in providing hernia operations. It may have invested in day surgery facilities and patient management systems so that doctors, nurses and facilities can all be used with the minimum of waste. Clearly it will wish to sell this hernia service on the internal market. But what price should it charge? It must on average charge at a level above the total cost of providing the service and at or below that price of competitors. The only way such a hospital can ensure it obtains the income it needs to cover its expenditure is to measure and cost its output.

Now let us look at a local authority environmental health department. A 'Citizens Charter' would require information to be published on costs for this service in such a way that comparisons could be made. This means that the costs of outputs needs stating. For instance the costs per type of restaurant of implementing the new regulations on food premises might require publishing. This can only be done if outputs are measured for a given input. In other words just as for the hospital, unit costs would be calculated.

## Compulsory competitive tendering

For many services outputs will be measured by both a 'client' and a 'contractor'. Under legislation requiring compulsory competition tendering (CCT) much of the output measurement will be done by contractors. For instance in a refuse collection service the contractor will almost certainly have to calculate unit costs for emptying dustbins so that he can calculate a realistic tender price.

What though is the client's management accounting need? He will have to calculate the unit costs of administration outputs for the service – that is the unit costs of checks on the contractor's work, producing tender documents and liaising with the public, politicians and other local authorities involved in the collection and disposal arrangements. But the client's responsibilities are greater than this. It is the client who is responsible ultimately for the service, not the contractor. If dustbins are not emptied the public blame the council, although certainly the contractor will be brought to task.

Because they are ultimately responsible client departments need to be able to calculate the costs of total outputs – both for their own work and the contractor. If a tender document is poorly drafted contractor charges will be unreasonably high. Electors need to know that this is the case. So, too, do managers. This information is only available if the cost of total outputs are calculated. The contractors unit prices will need to be analysed so that total figures are known.

## Unit costs and profit

In the public sector there is a considerable amount of confusion regarding the concept of making a profit. The whole idea of profit is alien to the culture of the public servant; it is associated with uncouth men with fast cars, and moonlighting and a disregard for poverty. These views are closely tied in with the concepts of philanthropy and neutral competence that were discussed in Chapter 3. Now that markets are being introduced into public sector management it will be useful to discuss how business people view productivity and performance. Some ideas used in business will be useful, others less so. The first point to understand is that both public services and businesses need to measure their performance. In the two examples given below the businesses are trying to measure the costs of the goods they are selling to ensure that money is being made on the transactions they enter into. Clearly public services also need to measure the cost of the goods and services they produce, but the immediate reason for measuring is somewhat different. We then look at the idea of profit, its importance, and how ultimately public and private enterprises need to record the wealth created by their activities.

## *A second-hand car dealer*

Let us start with a second-hand car salesman with a small forecourt on the Old Kent Road. He has all the brash orange day-glow posters you could imagine; these promise reliability and great value. He also has ten cars, one of which is an M registration Jaguar. And he has a few hundred yards of cheap plastic bunting to bedeck his patch. How does he make sure his business prospers?

He has two main concerns. His first is that he has enough money in the bank to buy new stock; he wants to make sure he is solvent. His second thought is that when he sells a car he does so with sufficient profit to cover his small overhead costs and to provide enough money to keep his wife in the style she has become accustomed. He is concerned with margins. As long as a second-hand car salesman can judge his cash flow so as to keep money in the bank and cars on the forecourt which he can sell, life is alright.

Businesses do not consider profit to be nearly as important as one might imagine. This is because profit is a theoretical concept. Most business people are more concerned with the concrete here and now. Many highly profitable businesses are very short of cash, and cash matters. In the short-term profits do not to nearly the same extent, because high living, investment in new equipment or bankruptcy are all a function of cash availability rather than profit.

Our car salesman does not regularly calculate his profit; this is done nine months after the year end by a local accountant. Success is a continuing, or if he is ambitious, a growing business and a comfortable domestic life. He does, however, know what is in the bank and what his margins are at any time of the day or night. As businesses expand the complexities of solvency and margins become more complex. The type and number of creditors expand, a range of liquid assets are held and stock exceeds ten old cars one of which is an M registration Jaguar. Moreover, margins become difficult to compute once there is any element of work carried out on inputs whether as a result of a manufacturing process or in the provision of a service. When this happens the business person's view becomes hazier and the employment of accountants is needed to keep the business in contact with reality. Measurement of outputs using the management accounting methods we have described becomes crucial.

### *The toy manufacturer*

Consider a simple manufacturing process. A range of toys are made in moulds out of plastic and are then assembled. In total about 100 people are employed. The business management will wish it to remain solvent. Accounting for solvency was discussed when we considered financial accounting in Chapter 5. Little more needs to be said on this topic. The management also want to keep up margins. The price a particular line of toys is sold for must exceed its cost of manufacturing by enough to cover overheads, interest and the costs of share capital and if possible to provide enough for future investment. Management accounts will be needed to ensure that adequate margins are being obtained to achieve that goal. These accounts might be similar in format to those produced by Mon Products Ltd in our example in Chapter 6.

At this stage we can draw a useful conclusion. As businesses become more complex, measurement of outputs in order to calculate margins becomes more difficult, but more important. The business starts to depend slightly less on the flair for trade of a business person and more on the technocratic expertise of accountants and computer people. So if the public sector starts to realize the importance of measuring outputs in a business-like way this has little to do with diluting public service values but a lot to do with sound organization of affairs.

## The significance of profit

We can learn a lot more from looking at how businesses operate. When a business publishes its yearly accounts economic commentators are interested in the level of profits or surplus. To the economist profit is a measure of wealth creation. In a perfect market profits equate to the creation of wealth. In the medium term these can be invested in capital assets that can be seen and felt and enjoyed. In Victorian Britain the profits from the Industrial Revolution were invested in the capital infrastructure of the country. As a result we obtained among other things, the public utilities we discussed in Chapter 1.

But if there is no market or there is a monopoly which renders the market imperfect what does profit equate to then? Clearly, some of it will still represent created wealth. Britain had a near monopoly on building railways in the middle of the last century. Profits were high but wealth was still created – but not as much as in a perfect market. In the worst situation a monopolist might hold the right to sell all water. Water although abundant might be sold at £1 a pint. The monopolist would show excellent profits but the wealth created would be minimal because people would be paying for a near worthless commodity.

How does this effect public sector enterprises? First, it means that profit or excess of income over expenditure cannot be used as a measure of achievement or wealth creation where there is a form of public monopoly. That is a hardly surprising but clearly important point. Second, it brings into light the value of a profit figure at the bottom of the set of accounts.

Profit = Achievement = Value added in outputs = Created wealth

The relationships may not be exact but in a near perfect market it is a useful assumption. It explains why businesses publish accounts showing a profit rather than a list of outputs and unit costs.

Most present-day public sector organizations cannot show a profit because either they do not trade or because they operate in an imperfect market. A business, because it does usually trade in a near perfect market can reduce its accounts to a profit figure. Both a list of outputs and the profit figure share one concept – they are an attempt to measure created wealth. In contrast the profit of a monopoly or the surplus on a set of local authority accounts means almost nothing – they just record the transfer of monies from one organization to another. In Chapter 10 we consider further how to report in public sector organizations and a worked example is given.

## Summary

Charters and internal markets are both attempts by politicians to move the public sector away from its philanthropic past towards a view of the public sector based on economics. This change means that public bodies need to measure achievement and to report it, because they are to be considered *producers* of goods and services. That is the major change. A vital by-product of the view that the public sector is a major source of economic outputs is that it becomes easier to manage to optimise output levels for a given input of taxpayers money. The political change leads to a management change that will effect us all.

# Conclusion

In this chapter we have tried to draw together the implications of output measurement. First we looked at how measurement benefited individual organizations and the people that work in them. This aspect of any change in management methods is important because unless those who implement change benefit, no management revolution will take place. Then we gave a framework for setting up output based management systems. This forms the first step in transforming the theoretical material in the previous chapter into the concrete steps a manager can take to benefit his or herself and the organization he or she works in. The last part of the chapter attempted to place the management concepts of this book in the context of the political initiatives that are at present current, in particular the ideas of a 'Citizens' Charter' and the 'internal market'. The individual manager by initiating change from within an organization is taking part in a radical reassessment of the public sector and its role within society.

## Reader questionnaire

This questionnaire seeks to demonstrate how performance measurement can be used to enhance the quality of the workplace environment for the benefit of individuals and the organization as a whole. Far from being a threat to staff performance measurement generally invigorates organizations because it tends to replace weak subjective assessments with objective facts.

The first part of this questionnaire is concerned with the benefits to individual managers. It attempts to demonstrate the benefits to individual development of performance measurement.

The second part of the questionnaire helps you to try to place the concept of measurement into your own department.

The last part of the questionnaire is designed to help you consider the idea of measurement in the context of other related concepts such as 'profit' and professional 'flair'.

## How would you benefit from performance measurement?

1. Does measurement make life misery or does it encourage excellence?

ANSWERS

- (a) Do you work hard?
- (b) Do you receive thanks for your efforts?
- (c) Do you do a better job than your colleagues?
- (d) How do you know that this is the case?
- (e) Are you colleagues motivated to work effectively?
- (f) How do you know that when you work hard that your work is effective?
- (g) Are the best people promoted in your organization or is it the best liked that receive reward?
- (h) Are you proud of the organization you work for?
- (i) What objective facts do you have to support your pride or its lack?

## How would your own organization benefit from performance measurement?

2. If you could measure accurately your department's achievements would it better serve the public?

ANSWERS

- (a) Have you defined your department's objectives?
- (b) Do you measure the attainment of those objectives?
- (c) If you do not measure the attainment of your objectives how do you know that you are meeting your objectives and are making good use of available resources?
- (d) Do you think that measurement of your achievements would damage the service you provide?

## Do you consider flair and genius the antithesis of objective measurement?

3. Do believe that only boring mechanical jobs can be objectively measured?

ANSWERS

(a) Output measurement is for factories only. Do you agree?
(b) In the caring services objective measurement has no place. Do you believe this to be true?
(c) If we introduce ideas of measurement into the welfare services we reduce human existence to simple profit or loss. True or false?
(d) If money is short the people who should benefit from the public services receive a mean and inhuman service. The worst hurt are the weakest and most in need. Do you agree?
(e) Objective measurement of public sector achievement particularly in the welfare services is essentially evil. It seeks to eliminate the human qualities of love and respect purely because they are 'messy' and do not fit easily onto accountants' balance sheets. Like it or not we must be prepared to pay a little bit extra to avoid turning schools and hospitals into factories. Is this right?
(f) Florence Nightingale, the inventor of modern nursing replaced amateurism with an objective reasoned approach based on ordered efficient wards and cleanliness. Do you think that in all other respects, including performance measurement, an objective approach is damaging in the caring services?

# Part Three

## The Application of New Management Techniques

# 8

# High quality public services

## Measuring quality as well as quantity

So far within this book we have spoken mainly about quantity. At Mon Products Ltd the concern was with costs per unit of plastic produced. No mention was made of the quality of the product. And in Chapter 7 the meat inspectors were deemed to provide a consistently high standard of service. Again we were concerned with cost per unit of output assuming all output was of the same quality.

But as the 1991 'Citizens' Charter' White Paper highlighted quality of public service is in fact the area of greatest concern with electors. People object to slow responses to their claims for housing benefits. They dislike hospital waiting lists and many spurn local authority education for their children. Why then is it only in Chapter 8 that this issue is raised?

## The link between funding and value for money

In the early chapters of the book we discussed the history and culture of public services. Within those discussions we stressed the lack of accountability of public services to electors. Because in many cases accountability within public services is poor, the temptation is to explain the scarcity and low quality of services only in terms of insufficient funding. Of course many services are under-funded but if lack of money is ostensibly the only reason for poor services then resources need to be used more efficiently. Our initial concern with quantity of production and productivity therefore mirrored the strongly held concern that more money was required for public services.

It is not only within this book that concern for efficiency and productivity have taken initial precedence over the issue of quality. Much of the work of the Audit Commission and the National Audit Office has been directed at efficiency issues. Recent Audit Commission studies on local authorities have been on subjects such as housing maintenance, refuse collections and management of cash resources. These types of project are concerned with getting more for the same cost or the same, cheaper. The National Audit Office carries out work in the same vein. An example would be their work on the Royal Mint.

Much of this concern with efficiency has been successful. After Audit Commission work on polytechnics, staff productivity at many establishments nearly doubled; this was in part achieved by more efficient time-tabling of lectures leading to improved use of staff time. The Commission's work on refuse collection stimulated many local authorities to cut costs by nearly 30%. But other projects have been less successful. In the main this has been because effective management information systems needed to control the use of resources were absent. An example in this category is the NAO's report on maternity services which concluded that 'due to the lack of reliable data, the National Audit Office could not form any firm conclusions as to whether these services were being provided in the most efficient way.' (Maternity Services, 16 March 1990, HMSO). The issue of the lack of management information is an abiding issue that returns again and again.

Poor productivity, then, is clearly a major concern in the public sector. So many of the problems that public bodies face are based on the public's foreboding that after the taxpayer has parted with his or her money, too little of concrete value will materialize. As we discussed in Chapter 2, low productivity in the public sector is an issue that is certain to remain until productivity increases more in line with the economy as a whole.

## Quality control

But while lack of productivity is theoretically the new political issue in the reform of public sector management because of the horrendous cost implications of failure, quality of service has become the political obsession in the early 1990s. Why is this? There are a number of reasons. The list below includes some of the more important issues relevant to the United Kingdom.

### *Reasons for the political demand for high quality public services*

1. The 1980s were the decade of the service industry. The quality of retail, banking and financial services all rose rapidly.
2. Increasing wealth within much of the country gave rise to increased demands and expectations.
3. Increased fundings of major public services were seen to produce negligible increases in quality of service, e.g. police and health.
4. The community charge or 'Poll Tax' increased the public awareness of public sector issues.

5. Quality control became a key issue in the stream lining of British Industry after the recession of 1980–81.

The key point is that throughout Western society standards are improving. The public sector cannot therefore lag too far behind changes elsewhere in the economy. It is worth looking at some of the innovations that are ensuring that quality is improving in the economy as a whole. We can then begin to see how quality can be improved in specific public sector concerns.

## Standards in industry

Nearly every industry has its own club or association. Examples are the Furniture Industries Research Association, the Society of Motor Manufacturers and Traders and the Cement and Concrete Association. These associations act as spokesmen for the industries they represent; they also sponsor the setting of standards for their products. In Britain the British Standards Institute sets British Standards to govern the quality of a vast range of products. These vary from glass, glassware, and glazing to cinematography, and from aerospace materials to heating, ventilating, air conditioning and ventilators.

The British Standards Institute does not produce these standards itself; it coordinates efforts by industries and trade associations who wish to strengthen their businesses by setting dependable quality control standards. There are also international standards under the ISO (International Organization for Standardization) and a multitude of foreign equivalents to the British Standards Institute.

## Legal status of standards

Because standards are set by industries, they are voluntary in the way that club rules are always voluntary – if you want to carry on breaking them you may be asked to leave. However because industry standards can be so effective some have become set in statute. Where a legal standard is required, say on a safety matter, it is often easier to use the British Standard than to redefine new legal criteria. An example of this, which was topical in the late 1980s, concerned the fire risk from foam plastic furniture filling materials. Under the Consumer Protection Act 1987, Statutory Instrument 1988 No. 1324 was drafted which required compliance with British Standards 3379, 5651, 5852 Part I, 5852 Part II and BS6807!

## Standards and service industries

Strict quality standards for goods have a long history. Hallmarks for precious metals are particularly well known. But quality standards for services are a much newer phenomenon. Only 20 years ago the service sector was almost devoid of quality standards. Even today most services continue without a guarantee or even a statement explaining the quality of service provided. Accountants, surveyors, solicitors, teachers, retailing companies and doctors give no guarantee of service quality.

This laxity on the part of some of the best trained people in our society appears extraordinary. While factory workers produce goods conforming to strict quality requirements, top barristers, accountants and bankers are under no obligation to perform. While this anomaly can in part be put down to an unwillingness on the part of powerful interest groups to set themselves performance targets which others could monitor, this is not the whole explanation. Shop workers and office cleaners normally operate under the same loose regime.

Recently things have changed a little. After the secondary banking crash in the mid-1970s, private sector auditors set up the Auditing Practices Committee to draft Approved Auditing Standards. The first standard was published in April 1980. The financial services industry works to standards set down by the various self-regulating bodies. For instance the pension business is controlled by Lautro. This body sets standards for its members to follow; periodic checks are then made to ensure members comply with the rules. FIMBRA is the body regulating financial advisors. Again a code of practice has been laid down which members must follow.

But in areas where major financial loss in unlikely few such standards are at present in force. Neither private nor public sector doctors use quality standards. The same applies to teachers and the vast majority of solicitors.

It is important to realize that when we talk about standards we do not mean that service industries necessarily are run poorly or that professional people are not subject to adequate training. Rather what we are saying is that there is a lack of quality assurance to the customer. If you need a component for a machine which complies to a British Standard then any such component bearing to the British Standard Kitemark will satisfy. When choosing a solicitor or dentist such a simple approach is not at present possible. You are forced to enquire from others whether they know a good practitioner who is effective and who provides a good customer service. There is no universal agreed standard upon which you can rely.

## The International and British Standard on quality systems

The standard setting organizations have been aware of the lack of quality standards covering management systems for both manufacturing and service sectors. Various attempts were made to remedy the omission but until recently there has been little support among the intended users of standards. However in 1987 the International Organization for Standardization revised ISO 9000, 9001, 9002, 9003, 9004 on 'Quality Systems'. The English Translation of these became BS 5750 Parts 0 to 4. These standards were vigorously taken up by some of Britains' industrial competitors, particularly in Germany. This is turn has lead to a strong interest in setting quality standards in Britain.

There are certainly benefits for enterprises that obtain a certification showing compliance with the standard. After the bovine spongiform encephalopathy (BSE) scare concerning the safety of beef, providers of animal feeds came under public and government criticism. Just a year after this Dalgety, one the largest farm suppliers, prominently advertised its compliance with BS5750 on the front cover of the widely read trade magazine *Farmers Weekly*. The implication was clear; they were superior and they were trustworthy.

### *BS5750 in the public sector*

Outside industry a number of solicitors' firms have adopted the standard. This appears to be one of the first uses of quality standards for non-financial services. Many other service industries are at present reluctant to set quality standards of their own or to seek compliance and certification under the British Standard. However it is difficult to see how they can avoid the active use of standards for very long. In response to this need central government is sponsoring the use of BS5750 in Sandwell College of Further and Higher Education. The results as publicly reported in the *Times Educational Supplement* (12 April 1991, p. 10) suggest that education is surprisingly well-suited to a quality systems approach.

BS5750 attempts to ensure that management quality is high by standardizing the procedures an organization uses in its work. This involves the recording of all procedures used by producing a procedures manual. Once this has been done British Standards Association inspectors test check the implementation of the procedures manual in the organization applying for the standard before the standard is granted.

The standard is therefore specific to each applying organization. Much of the benefit of applying for the standard comes from thinking about and then defining the procedures an organization carries out. Sandwell College soon realized that their job was 'student enhancement' not courses provided. This was a major step forward which could only have resulted from an attempt to define standards. The first solicitors who applied for the standard, Panoni's in Manchester underwent a similar revelation. They soon discovered that they needed to agree the extent of their service very precisely with their clients before work began and then keep their clients informed about proceedings. Traditionally many solicitors have done neither of these things and perplexed clients are often unaware of the work being done for them as any one who has purchased a house will know!

## Over standardization

People do not enjoy having no assurance over service standards. The cost, time wasting and uncertainty this involves is quite incompatible with many mainstream areas of modern life. A doormat is subject to a number of British Standards but a doctor does not comply with any quality standards. This state of affairs is clearly crazy.

There are of course areas of human existence that are unsuited to standardization. Creative thought cannot be standardized – to some extent this was attempted in the Middle Ages in the old universities. The result was first the ossification of society and then the explosion of the renaissance. The renaissance removed most of the standards used under the scholastic system and weakened the hold of the

universities. Other areas unsuited to standardization are certain aspects of art and scientific research. This does not mean that nothing can be standard in these areas. Clearly rules have assisted artistic achievement; for instance the requirement of rhyme and rhythm in a sonnet has been a cause of masterly creation. And in modern science standard units of measurement, for example, are essential.

It is clear that we can make a general rule regarding the use of standards. Whenever two or more groups of people interact with one another some form of standardization may be useful. Standards increase trust, prevent waste and encourage people to produce the best they can consistently.

# Measurement of quality

At present the issue of quality is being widely debated by management consultants and by public and private sector managers. The concept of 'total quality management' is particularly fashionable – at least to talk about. BS5750 is also much discussed. Little catch phrases like, 'one bite at a time' and 'win-win relationships' and the Japanese idea of 'quality circles' are becoming increasingly popular. In Chapter 9 we discuss some of these current management theories. But the thrust of this chapter is that whatever management concept you subscribe to one aspect is critical – you must measure the quality you achieve and reward the people responsible for what they have done.

In the previous Chapters we have discussed measurement of output volumes or quantities so that we can monitor productivity. But from now on we need to measure *quality* as well as quantity.

## Quality outputs

When we were looking at quantities we saw how important it was to define outputs. Outputs for quality measurement purposes will be the same as for quantities. An illustration will make this clear. A unit of output might be one breakfast. To measure productivity we would have to measure the cost per breakfast; to measure quality we would have to sample the breakfasts! Two different measurements are needed but both are concerned with breakfasts.

How do we measure quality? This depends on the service provided. All services will have a number of common attributes which need measuring. These are success or failure, timeliness and customer relations.

### *Success*

The first attribute is clearly success or its opposite, failure. If you use a service you want it to be successful. You may catch a bus to get to the railway station. Most buses will get there but a few will not because of breakdown accident or staff sickness. It is therefore important to monitor success rates. For most public sector services there is a reasonably clear concept of success or failure so that measurement presents few problems.

In a minority of situations success might be more difficult to measure. Consider a solicitor approached regarding a legal issue. He or she advises that the chances of winning in court are low so the case is dropped. Was this a successful outcome? One will never know. The same applies to doctors who advise that treatment for a disease considered terminal is useless. It is very difficult to judge crude success rates in these sorts of situations.

But success is important in many other areas. It matters for trains and buses and getting water to houses. It matters for commonly curable diseases and for education and for hotel services, application form processing, maintenance work and many of the other typical public sector outputs discussed in Chapter 6; and if it matters we must measure.

## *Timeliness*

A service can be provided successfully, but that success can be achieved on time or rather later. To renew the bus analogy, we can catch the bus to the station, but miss the train. The bus got there, but late. We cannot catch the train we wished to, but we can catch the next. The result is that the consumer of the service suffers needlessly.

Take another example – the hospital waiting list. You have a hernia it is uncomfortable, slightly unpleasant and you are understandably worried about it and the operation. A long waiting list probably does not in this case reduce the success of the operation when it is done. But the wait does cause the client to endure the concern for longer. For nearly every public service timeliness is important because late provision reduces the quality of service given.

But there are some services where poor timeliness can mean that the service fails. The obvious example is death while on a hospital waiting list. But other examples would be late provision of teaching – the pupil would have passed the exam, but only if it had been postponed until the full course had been taught. Or again breakfast might be late. No one in the college was able to eat it because lectures had already started.

No more examples are needed to show how important timeliness can be. The rule then, is that you must measure achievement of timeliness.

## *Customer relations and care*

A service can be successfully provided on time but the customer may be jumping up and down with fury. You go to a supermarket checkout desk. You are just beginning to unload your basket when the cashier drearily whines 'Can you go to the next desk please' since she makes no attempt to look at you while she speaks, unwittingly you carry on. She repeats the statement in an identical fashion and you begin to realize all is not well. By the time you get to the checkout that is operating you have sworn that you will never buy anything again from that supermarket. Or in another scenario perhaps you go to collect a state benefit. The process of collection is not unduly difficult but the staff look at you as if you were a cheat and fraud, the office is unpainted and the furniture beaten to death. You ask a simple question. It does not penetrate a dirty bullet-proof glass screen so you end up shouting, bent double, through a crack one-inch wide just above the counter.

Clearly customer relations and customer care are more than just a few frills on top of the basic service. In a decent society they are crucial. But there are other arguments in favour of good customer relations – even in a monopoly situation. A satisfied customer will assist in the provision of the service, increasing productivity and quality success rates. Your staff will be happy and helpful if your customers are helpful. The atmosphere in the workplace will be conducive to achievement.

But you cannot expect good customer care to be produced by a few *ad hoc* words from senior managers. It must be actively managed for. And that means you must measure the quality of your service as it affects the customer.

## Measuring success, timeliness and customer care

Having defined outputs we need to measure their success, timeliness and how they affect the customer. When we discussed measurement of quantity there were a number of stages to consider. These were set out in the list under the leading 'Setting up performance measurement systems in practice' in Chapter 7 page 105. When considering quality, stages 1 to 4 in this list apply. Stages 5 and 6 do not. This is because we do not normally try to measure the costs of different levels of quality; we only measure its achievement. We will discuss this further a little later.

Stages 1 and 2 in the list – 'Departmental Objectives' and 'Definition of Outputs' will be identical processes to those used for quantity measurement. Clearly, at these stages you will consider quantity and quality together. It is at stage 3 that the split comes. Stage 3 is concerned with the aspects of output you wish to measure. For quantity these will be units of output – one application form, one bed for the night, one effective operation (one cure), and so on. For quality you will measure the quality of outputs. For instance the failure to assess an application made, the time on a waiting list and the satisfaction of a customer. The overall process of setting up performance measurement systems in practice is shown in Fig. 8.1.

Let us look at a simple example of setting quality standards. Consider a library ordering books on the request of readers from other libraries in the same library authority. The librarian at one of the towns in the area wishes to measure the quality of the ordering service being provided. The output is 'the notification to the reader that an ordered book is now available'. It is no use obtaining books from other libraries but then failing to notifying the reader of its arrival. So what do we measure? Figure 8.2 outlines the measurement of quality. We need to look at each aspect of quality separately.

Success is easy to measure. If the ordered book arrives a success has been achieved. We need to measure how often books do not arrive. Out of 100 orders for books known to be held by the library authority we would hope all 100 would be sent to the ordering library. But remember it is not good enough that the book arrives, the reader must be informed as well. Success is therefore the receipt of the

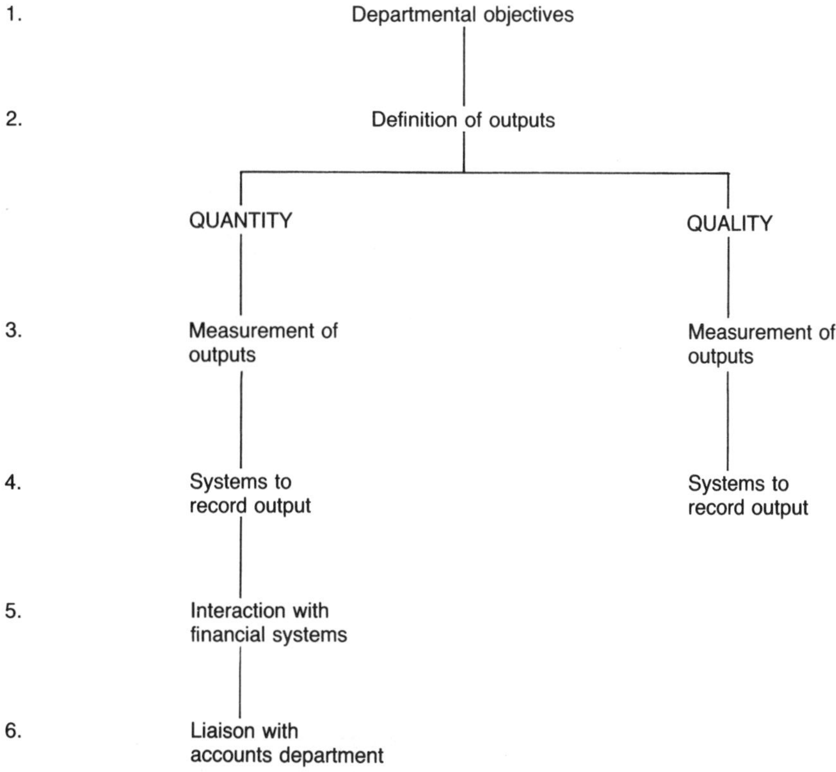


**Fig. 8.1** Setting up quantity and quality measurement systems in practice.

book and notification to the reader. If books are received and notified for all 100 orders then the system is completely successful.

But if a reader wants a book it is best provided instantly. A slow ordering service is clearly not as good as a rapid one. I once ordered a book from a library. It arrived nine months later and it was an out-of-date edition. We need to measure the time in days between the date of the order and the date the notification of receipt of the book is sent the reader. If all our books are taking nine months between these two dates then this is clearly of interest!

Last, what about customer care? Success and timeliness will effect this issue. Other factors will be of importance too. The items we will measure fall into different groups. First, you can measure things that the library does. How long do you have to queue to make an order; are there effective catalogues allowing readers to locate books in other libraries; how long does it take to fill in the order form? Then there are things which the readers do; they may complain about the service; they may thank the library for the high quality of service and they may use the ordering system more or they may cease to use it. Both aspects of customer care will need measuring. Some will be best measured on the basis of individual units of outputs – complaints per order, average queuing time per order – others will best be considered for the library as a whole – increase or decrease in service usage.

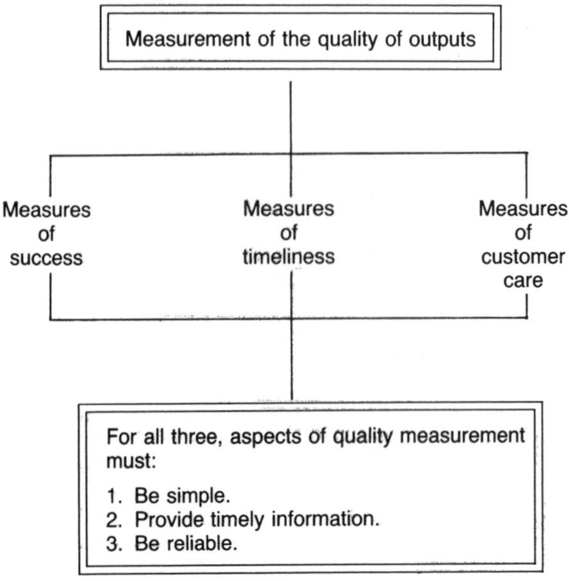


**Fig. 8.2** Measurement of quality.

# Measurement in practice

Quality of service is often very straightforward to measure, especially when services are computerized. There are three main methods of measuring quality. These are:

1. Transaction recording analysis.
2. Inspection and test check.
3. Customer questionnaire.

The processing stages that transactions undergo can be recorded on a computer to record the quality achieved. This is a relatively new method of controlling quality. This is transaction recording analysis. The traditional methods of quality measurement and control involve inspection and test checking. We deal with this method next. Last, customer care can be measured using customer questionnaires. This form of quality control is little discussed in this chapter because it is relatively straightforward, but it is well-illustrated in the case studies that follow. Table 8.1 shows the main methods of measuring quality and the applicability of each to major public sector outputs.

## *Transaction records*

One of the most useful ways of measuring and recording quality is a transaction record. If a transaction is initiated, worked on and then completed all this can be recorded.

**Table 8.1** Methods of measuring quality

| *Method of measuring* | *Output per list on page 105* | *Quality attributes that could be tested* | *Notes* |
|---|---|---|---|
| S = Success<br>T = Timeliness<br>C = Customer care | | | |
| 1. Transaction recording analysis | – Administration of forms | S, T, C | Only suitable for some aspects of customer care. |
| | – Maintenance work | T, C | Recording customer feedback over time. |
| | – Medical work | S, T, C | Most acute and many chronic cases. |
| | – Education | S, T, C | Recording and analysis of the education of individual pupils. |
| | – Hotel services | C | |
| | – Capital works | S, T, C | Except for timeliness this is not the main method of measuring quality. |
| | – Service maintenance | C | See Inspection and Test Check below. |
| 2. Inspection and test check | – Administration of forms | S | Periodic test check of success will be needed for some activities, e.g. social security benefit. |
| | – Maintenance work | S | Periodic inspection to ensure good order. |
| | – Medical | S | Tests are required to ensure success of treatment. |
| | – Education | S | Examinations, course work, assessments. |
| | – Hotel services | S, T | Periodic inspection to check standards. |
| | – Capital works | S | Periodic inspection to check quality. |
| | – Service maintenance | S, T | As for maintenance work. |
| | – All Output types | C | Some test checks will overlap with customer questionnaires. |
| 3. Customer questionnaire | – All outputs | C | Certain questionnaires are necessary for all output types. |
| | | T | The timeliness for certain outputs is best measured using questionnaires, e.g. arrival of an ambulance. |

Consider the library order system we discussed earlier. Dates for ordering by the reader, actioning of the order, receipt of book and reader notification could all be recorded on a transaction record. Analysis of the computer population of transactions records could then provide useful data concerning the quality of the service regarding success and timeliness. Customer care information could also be included. For instance the number of times the reader enquired whether a book had arrived could be noted on the record.

Traditionally record cards have been used to note the processing stages of a transaction. This system is effective for monitoring individual operations. But it provides no overall analysis on the quality of a total service. This has been radically changed with the introduction of computers.

When using a computerized record, details are recorded in just the same way as for a card system. The date a patient enters hospital is recorded, so are the results of tests carried out. The nature of treatment given is included on the record together with the dates it is administered. Lastly, details of the recovery or demise of the patient can be punched in. Even simplified to this extent an individual record is useful. But the beauty of a computer record is that data for whole departments can be analysed. Information on this scale was never possible to achieve until computers became relatively inexpensive. And the data they provide can be surprising to staff, managers and public.

As an auditor I have often selected random or statistical samples of transactions for testing. On showing these samples to client staff it is quite usual for staff to be surprised by the items chosen. Staff in a housing benefit department consider most of their 'clients' to be young people in and out of work and constantly changing houses, and boy or girl friends. But a statistical sample of their caseload will show a predominance of impecunious pensioners interspersed with a few stable one-parent families. Probably only 2% of cases conform to the stereotype held by staff.

Why is this? The vast majority of cases are straightforward to process and are unmemorable. The small percentage of difficult cases are time-consuming and interesting or at least colourful. It is easier to remember abuse from a mother with eight children, all on income support than the 50 pensioners who never have a query. For 50 successes there may be one problem case, but it is the problem that is remembered.

For everyone involved in productive work there are similar distortions. It is for this reason that measurement is so important. At one large local authority I was once asked to review an insurance section run by three staff. Each claim had a record card recording the stage in the claim process. But it was not possible to discover how many claims had reached each stage nor was it possible to quantify the value of outstanding work. Documentation was perfect but information on the quality and quantity was almost non-existent. If, however, each claim has been recorded on a computer with a reasonable program vital quality and efficiency statistics would have been available whenever desired. All that is needed is the capacity to sort information and then to add up the figures for each chosen parameter. It is this type of job that computers do best and a PC is often all that is needed.

In the case studies in this chapter the use of a computer for transaction recordings and analysis is demonstrated.

## *Inspection and test check*

Where specific checking is needed to control the quality of output test checks or inspection techniques are required. Often a management system does not automatically provide details on the quality of output. When this is the case output must be specifically checked to ensure it is of the right quality. Sometimes it is possible and desirable to test check every item of output. An example would be school examinations where every child would be expected to take part. In other situations it is not possible to obtain data on the quality of every item. An example of this would be the processing of application forms. Not every form processed would need checking.

These methods of measuring quality are the traditional techniques of the quality control inspector. Items would be taken at random from a production line, tested and on the basis of the results batches of goods would be accepted or rejected. In service industries the equivalent is a review of paperwork by more senior staff or a visual inspection of such services as office cleaning or maintenance work by a superior or clerk of works.

The test check of quality is as relevant today as it ever was. But whereas until recently test checking was the only true form of quality control now it forms just one aspect of quality measurement. In addition, nowadays the information gained from test checks can be put to much greater use. At one time a rejected batch of goods would be seen as no more than a limited failure. Now with modern ideas on management, that same rejected batch would be seen to affect all levels of productive and managerial staff. An enterprise exists to produce high quality goods and services to further its objectives. If production is of poor quality then this reflects on everyone since they are all there to help produce the service.

## *Methods*

There is a clear distinction between testing and inspecting. Testing is mechanical and dispassionate; inspection is more subjective and involves a less structured approach. It follows then that where possible, technically and financially, testing of output is preferable. We can define them both as follows:

1. Testing: *Reperformance* or *Performance* of a *routine* by a specialized member of staff to ensure that procedures, goods or services are at the necessary standard to give the correct result or output.
2. Inspection: *Review* of a *routine or complete service* by a senior member of staff to check that procedures or service standards are fully and correctly implemented or maintained to give the result or output of the necessary standard.

A typical test on a service would be the reperformance of the assessment of a claim for unemployment benefit to ensure that decisions to pay benefit had been correctly taken. Tests tend to be intense and small scale. One claim for unemployment is negligible when an office might pay thousands. It follows then that tests need to be part of a larger programme. This programme should normally be statistically controlled.

An inspection could involve a review of the state of repair of an army barracks to ensure that repair work being carried out is to the specified standard. The person carrying out the inspection will look at a relatively large quantity of work. Comparison will be made to specifications but a majority of the inspection will be in the form of a general review. Reviews are not insignificant to the total quantity of work done. In some services all work will be reviewed. The majority of building work is subject to review or inspection. The same applies to audit work where review is a requirement under the Auditing Standards and Guidelines. Review then, need not be part of a statistical programme in the same way that tests must be to be effective. Never the less inspection should not be on an *ad hoc* basis; it must be planned and controlled.

Inspection and test checks are not audit. This is an important point because quality control and measurement is an internal managerial responsibility of a department. Audit is an external assessment of a service. This is the case for work done by either internal or external auditors.

## *Work programme*

All inspection and testing work needs to be controlled by a programme. This will state the following:

1. The objectives of the inspection/testing;
2. The methods to be used for;
   (a) carrying out the inspection/testing;
   (b) considering the result;
   (c) ensuring improvement to working practices are made where required.

For instance, in a school the academic capabilities of pupils might be tested every three weeks using a substantial piece of work in each main subject. Perhaps an essay is required in English, exercises in French and a 40-minute written test in mathematics. If these three-weekly pieces of work are to be used to monitor teaching success then they must be part of a programme. The results will be near useless if a sporadic approach is taken. First, the objective of the tests must be understood by the staff involved. Second, the test material must match that being taught; if this elementary precaution is not taken the test will clearly not reflect current teaching success. Third, there must be consistency in the standard of the work set for monitoring purposes. Fourth, the testing must be carried out regularly. Last, the results of the testing would need to be available for discussions by individual teachers and the headmistress. She would need to control the whole process so that she could use the results to help manage the school more effectively. One week's results in a situation like this are meaningless. Trends and discontinuities would be the main sources of information from this testing work. Perhaps it is possible to see that the less able children are falling behind more and more. Teaching quality is clearly below standard for those individuals. Perhaps results always dip when a certain teacher takes over a class; action is going to needed to prevent this happening. Perhaps a teacher the headmistress loathes always produces excellent test results from his classes. Obviously he has some virtues!

The example above of testing in a school involved a 100% check. All pupils were tested, not just a sample. But often when the numbers of items to test are very large – perhaps running to many hundreds or thousands of items, then a statistical sampling method is necessary.

## *Statistical test checking*

A typical situation where statistical test checking would be useful might involve a computerized system recording details of tax assessments. Each time a new tax return is received it is punched onto the computer which then calculates the tax due. If returns are incorrectly punched onto the computer then incorrect tax assessments will be made.

Part of a quality testing programme for the tax office would therefore include test checks on the accuracy of assessment and punching. Assessments on the computer would be agreed to the original returns on a sample basis.

Most managers in charge of such an operation would recognize this procedure as important in checking the quality of a tax collection system. But most would not fully understand the importance of a planned approach. The number of assessments will be enormous. The amount of checking that can be afforded is small – perhaps 5% of transactions. In this situation the planning of quality testing is paramount. We can see why.

Where very small samples are taken – and ideally we should keep the labour of quality measurement to a minimum – small numbers of errors found in testing will have major effects on the conclusions derived from test results. The key aspects to control are the following:

1. Completeness of population sampled.
2. Random selection of sample.
3. Number of items sampled.

Every tax assessment on the computer should have an equal chance of being chosen for testing. This means that sampling must be from a list of all assessments. If all assessments for taxpayers with names beginning with A, B or C are omitted then the testing will give no evidence regarding these assessments. Second, the assessments must be chosen randomly. Judgemental selection of interesting assessments is not adequate. Ideally sampling should be carried out by the computer on which the records are held. Last, the number of items is critical, particularly if errors are found as a result of the testing work.

The following section shows how testing of tax returns could be practically achieved using a statistical method.

## *An example of statistically controlled quality control*

This example shows quality control over the input of details off a tax form into a computer. The computer then processes the data to give output. This type of procedure would apply to the processing of many other government forms. The theory involved could also be applied to measuring the quality of many service industry outputs.

### Attribute sampling

This example uses the statistical method known as attribute sampling. The method uses the following formula:

$$\text{Sample size} = \frac{\text{Poisson distribution reliability factor for the expected no. of errors}}{\text{\% Error rate}}$$

Poisson distribution reliability factors can be obtained from mathematical tables. The most useful values are given below:

| *Errors found in sample* | *Chosen confidence level (%)* | | |
|---|---|---|---|
| | *90* | *95* | *99* |
| 0 | 2.31 | 3.00 | 4.61 |
| 1 | 3.89 | 4.75 | 6.64 |
| 2 | 5.33 | 6.30 | 8.41 |

Let us assume there are five processes that we wish to check for accurate input into the computer. For each process input is either 'Correct' or 'Incorrect'. We are not concerned with partially correct input since this obviously involves an element of error. We wish to be: '90% confident that no more than 1% of processes are mispunched into the computer'.

We also expect to find no errors in our test samples. The reliability factor we require is thus 2.31. This is taken from the above table.

Now we insert this into the formula to find our sample size.

$$\text{Sample size} = \frac{2.31}{1\%}$$
$$= 231 \text{ items}$$

Regardless of the number of forms processed by the department we need only check 231 items.

### Sampling

How do we select the items we wish to test? It is vital that each item has an equal chance of being selected. This means that selection must be *random*. Since the forms have been input onto a computer we can use this to select the 231 forms we need to check using a random number generating program. In a computer age we let the computer do most of the work for us!

Each form selected will include the five input processes we need to quality test. Testing will involve checking the input form, the tax return, to the data held on the computer. This checking will be done manually by a member of staff more senior than the person who did the original input work. On the facing page we give the results from the 231 forms the computer selected randomly for us.

| *Input process* | *No. tested* | *No. errors found* |
|---|---|---|
| A | 231 | Nil |
| B | 231 | 1 |
| C | 231 | Nil |
| D | 231 | Nil |
| E | 231 | 5 |

**Results**

For the input processes where we have no errors we can say that we are 90% certain that for the entire population of forms, probably many thousand in number, only one in 100 items were input in error. The actual error rate may in fact be lower. At this level of errors we are satisfied that the quality of the service is acceptable.

For process E five errors were found. At this level of errors we can be sure that the quality of service is unsatisfactory. Error rates in the total population are almost certainly above one in 100. The reasons for this will need to be investigated. Perhaps staff training regarding process E is inadequate.

Process B gave one error in the sample. Error rates may be higher than one in 100. To find out we can increase the sample size using the Reliability Factor formula as follows:

$$\text{Sample size} = \frac{3.89}{1\%}$$
$$= 389$$

The reliability factor of 3.89 represents 90% confidence for one error in a sample. In our first testing sample we took the figure for zero errors. See the table above to see how it was arrived at.

We have already tested 116 items, so we now need to test another 158 for process B only. Results were as follows:

| *Input process* | *No. tested* | *No. errors* |
|---|---|---|
| B | 389 | 1 |

No further errors were found in the additional 158 forms tested.

**Conclusion**

We are now in a position to conclude that for process B as well as for processes A, C and D we are 90% confident that only one form in 100 is in error in the entire population of tax returns processed. Process E, however, is not under adequate control.

If a total of 5000 tax returns were processed by the office we are testing our sampling was able to give a useful result by checking about 5% of the total.

There are a number of different types of statistical methods of quality control. Some methods may be more suited to your work than others.

In this book we only demonstrate the statistical method known as attribute sampling. This statistical method is concerned with whether an attribute or quality is present or not. It is a 'Yes/No' test. For instance a patient might be considered 'cured' or 'not cured'. Attribute sampling cannot handle situations where a patient is considered say, 75% cured. For this type of statistical testing 'variables testing' is required. Using this type of testing, average or mean results can be calculated and standard deviations from averages can be used as measures of success or failure.

For quality testing in the service industries that make up much of the public sector, attribute sampling is normally quite adequate. This is especially the case when error levels are expected to be low. It also has the benefit that it requires small sample sizes to give meaningful results. In the example in Table 8.1 about 5% of the total workload was tested. Variables sampling requires more testing work and this all represents time that could have been used to boost productivity. But for those that require some measurement of variables the author suggests that the reader consults a simple volume on industrial quality control techniques. (Some useful works are given in the Bibliography at the end of the book.) If you work in a school the mathematics teacher should be able to help you analyse your assessment results!

There is one other point that it is important to understand. It is essential to comprehend the full significance of errors found in quality testing. In the example above one error required a 40% increase in testing to enable the conclusion that errors were at acceptable levels to be sustained. If you find errors when you are using attribute sampling you cannot use simple extrapolation to calculate total error rates. This is because the sample sizes you are using are far too small to make this statistically valid. One error in an attribute sample is highly significant. There is no reason for the attitude that by checking a few items we can be happy everything is all right. The world does not work like that.

## *Summary*

Test checking is a necessary but costly element of quality measurement. Without test checking the quality of many services can only be guessed at. This is not an adequate response to a legitimate management need. Uncontrolled and poorly planned checking may give no assurance of quality or the extent of its omissions. All testing is by its nature is non-productive. It needs to be cut to a minimum, be well planned, and make full use of statistics.

## *Inspection*

Inspection is generally less satisfactory than test checking. It follows that where both techniques are applicable testing should normally be used in preference.

The weaknesses of inspection of quality are:

1. The results are not quantifiable.
2. The results are often subjective in nature.

If we are trying to measure quality for management and reporting purposes, then both these weaknesses strongly tip the balance in favour of quality testing if this is possible.

Inspection as a means of quality measurement does have benefits.

1. Inspection is likely to cover a larger proportion of work done than testing;
2. Inspection is easier to plan and control;
3. The control and supervisor functions of management can be combined with inspection work.

Consider the maintenance of council houses. Perhaps there are 7500 to keep in good repair. As we discussed in Chapter 6 maintenance outputs are not individual jobs but a constantly maintained asset – a council dwelling.

Maintenance work for houses is based on a programme of planned work supplemented with emergency repairs where necessary. At any one time planned repairs of some sort are in progress. How do we control the quality of the output.

Quality measurement will fall into two distinct elements.

1. Inspection of individual maintenance jobs while they are in progress;
2. Regular inspections of buildings to ensure they are up to standard.

We can call the first type of inspections, specific since it is specific to a maintenance activity. The second type of inspection is general in nature. It relates to the general condition of the buildings.

Below we illustrate how both specific and general maintenance inspections can be controlled using the example of council houses.

In Fig. 8.3 we can see that the quality of the upkeep of council houses is under cyclical inspection using a detailed planned programme. The level of maintenance of houses is kept under constant review using five-yearly surveys. However, individual items of maintenance will take place. Inspection of the quality of this work will be necessary as it is done. In the example the kitchen units were shown as needing replacement in the year of survey – 1992. In Fig. 8.4, we show how this specific item of maintenance was quality controlled.

The replacement of kitchen units is a substantial job. All work of this size will need inspecting. Cyclical roof repair is expected to cost only £55 per Fig. 8.3. This size of job could be test checked only. Typically test checking for this type of work would involve inspecting between 25% and 75% of all work. A statistical sample would not be used because inspection would normally include an element of supervision.

Even a very simple quality control checklist such as this helps provide strong control. Results from checklists can be input onto a computer to give an overall assessment of the maintenance programme. If the new seal around the sink unit was found to be defective on 30% of houses inspected then clearly there is a problem. The contractor should be notified so that his people will take more care on the remaining work. Alternatively, there may be a design fault that is being highlighted. Another benefit of recording inspections is the column for rectification of substandard work. This helps to ensure that where substandard work is found it will be chased until it is put right.

## *Summary*

Inspection is a major source of quality control over many public sector outputs. Just as for testing work, inspection must be planned and controlled so that a high quality of public service can be guaranteed.

Condition Schedule

Property Code: az/162

Address: 53 Runworth Close

Year Built: 1954

DATE OF INSPECTION: 8 June 1992

Next Inspection: June 1997

| *Items of maintenance* | *Cycle (years)* | *Year due* | *Expected cost* |
|---|---|---|---|
| Re-tile roof | 60 | 2054 | 770 |
| Roof cyclical repair | 5 | 1996 | 55 |
| Pointing | 40 | 2013 | 825 |
| Windows replacement | 25 | 2016 | 2750 |
| Replace kitchen units | 15 | 1992 | 550 |
| Rewire lighting circuits, etc. | 30 | 2016 | 660 |

**Fig. 8.3** General inspection maintenance report for a single council house.

| | *Yes/no* | *Date rectified* |
|---|---|---|
| 1. Units supplied as specified | | |
| 2. Layout as sketch plan | | |
| 3. Old units removed | | |
| 4. Seal round sink affective | | |
| 5. Paintwork made good | | |
| 6. All units operate well | | |
| 7. Tenant finds work acceptable | | |

**Fig. 8.4** Inspection control sheet for installation of kitchen fittings.

# Conclusion

This chapter has looked as the issue of quality in the public sector. Quality is being forced on public sector managers by the increases in quality being experienced in the economy as a whole. If the building society in the high street is well designed, provides a pleasant professional service at an affordable price then so must government offices. All government services need to *measure* the quality of the service they provide. If necessary, statistical methods should be used to provide assurance that quality is up to a defined standard.

Quality involves provision of a service to a defined standard, on time, in a way that the public finds pleasing. All three aspects of quality need measuring and controlling. Ideally quality services should be provided to a published standard. British Standard 5750 is available to the public sector and its general use would help give the public the high standards of service they are rapidly coming to expect.

## Reader questionnaire

This is a short questionnaire that is designed to help you consider how quality measurement could be beneficially introduced into your own department.

ANSWERS

(a) Do you set quality standards for the goods and services your department provides?
(b) If you do not why is this?
(c) Do you periodically check the quality of the goods and services you provide?
(d) Is the checking you do carried out systematically or does it take the form of spot checking when there is time to do this?
(e) Are you happy with the quality of your departments output?
(f) Do you think the public would substantially benefit from a higher quality more reliable service? Is the present service good enough for them?
(g) What factors prevent you from instituting a thorough quality control system.
(h) Have other organizations similar to yours introduced British Standard 5750?
(i) Have you contacted them to discover the benefits and pitfalls of implementation?

In the next chapter we look at the benefits to the organization, as distinct from the consumer, of a quality control system. Low quality is extremely expensive to produce! In the words of the old proverb, 'a stitch in time saves nine'. If you can produce high quality goods and services at the first attempt the very substantial costs of putting errors right has been saved.

# Case study I – housing benefit administration

This case study continues the example of a housing benefit department used in Chapter 6.

Housing benefit departments in London boroughs, metropolitan districts and district councils are required to pay housing benefit to entitled persons under the Social Security Act 1986. The Act only gives outline detail of the nature of housing benefit payments. A large number of circulars and regulations provide the detail concerning who is entitled and the levels of payment due.

The department we are looking at is part of Senforth District Council. This is in the North of England in an industrial area not very far from the Scottish Border. The housing benefit department has just obtained a new manager. She is Abigail MacGovern.

Abigail MacGovern is an interesting individual with a colourful past. Everyone was surprised when she was promoted after old Ron Haworth retired. She had always been so rude to him and most of the other managers in the finance department. She had spent her childhood in South America; her father had been a Scottish missionary. When her parents died she was brought up by a distant cousin in Uruguay until she had run away at the age of 15. After working in some of the poorer areas of various large cities, she had decided to settle down.

At the age of 30, her childhood English still intact, she had saved the money required for the fare to Scotland. Although she had no idea what it would be like she had set her heart on 'return'. And now at the age of 44 she was the housing benefit manager of Senforth District Council. It had a Scottish sounding name and was about 60 miles South of the border. But it was the best she could do.

If Abigail lacked modest charm she made up for it with a self-educated intelligence. Once the reality of her promotion became clear to her she started to reorganize the office with a savage intensity.

She had always told Ron that the department was not managed but just left to rot. Even the more seedy establishments of São Paulo were better run, she used to shout at him. It was not an allegation that Ron was able to dispute.

# Housing benefit objectives

Abigail was very certain that a department under her control should carry out all its duties in an orderly and controlled manner. She was not going to be flooded with a workload she could not control. She knew that her role was to stand above the humdrum and direct with a cool head. She therefore defined the duties of her department, beginning with the legislation.

One of her first actions therefore was to summarize the objectives of the department as given in the Social Security Act 1986. These are given below.

### *The statutory requirements of housing benefit departments*

1. To pay housing benefit to those making valid claims for assistance with council house rents, private rents and council tax (Social Security Act 1986 s20(7) and s28);
2. To notify claimants of their entitlement subsequent to the receipt of the claims (SSA 1986 s29(1));
3. Overpayments of benefit must be recovered if subsidy is to be obtained from Central Government (s29(5));
4. To take steps to ensure that persons who may be entitled become aware of their entitlements (s31(4)).

# Quality and productivity

Abigail MacGovern knew that she must control the achievements of the department as well as its costs. She wanted to define a standard of output which could be measured.

'If someone ever bothered to ask you, "what do you do for living?", what the hell would you tell them?' she would demand of Ron in her rasping Scots-Portuguese hybrid of an accent. 'You'd just have to say "I spend public money"'.

'I don't know what you mean Abigail', Ron would grunt.

'You haven't the first idea what you get for the money you spend. You just make sure that you spend it and stay out of trouble. That's all you do.'

'Come on Abigail, we do the best we can with the resources we are given.'

'I could tell you a story about when I worked the bars of Montevideo...' Somehow at this stage Ron would get rid of her. He knew what she was going to say. Unlike his department, 'in the bars of Montevideo you only got paid for performance'. He had heard it a thousand times before. He had never dared ask what forms of performance you did get paid for. But the slur always hurt.

Now she was in charge Abigail set out the objectives of the department on a large sheet of paper. Beside each objective she placed details of what to her appeared to be the real outputs that matched the objectives. She was going to measure those outputs so that she could control her department and take proper decisions on the basis of real evidence.

Table 8.2 shows the output measures applicable to housing benefit that Abigail wrote down. She defined productiviy for the housing benefit department as the cost of properly processing a known number of each type of claim. For instance productivity could be, 'the unit cost of accurately processing one claim by a council house tenant on income support within 14 days of receipt. The chart defines possible housing benefit outputs and describes some quantity and quality measurements that would be need to be taken. It covers definitions of output, and output measurements – Stages 2 and 3, in Fig. 8.1. Next Abigail MacGovern needed to consider the systems required to measure output.

# Systems

If she was going to measure the outputs described in Table 8.2 then she was going to need a system to do this quickly and simply. The results she obtained from the system would also have to tie in with the financial systems which gave details of input costs. Let us first consider the practicalities of measuring housing benefit outputs.

# Quantities

Her major output was **one claim** duly processed. It is obvious then that she needed to be able to count the number of claims assessed (objective A), paid (objective A)

**Table 8.2** Houring benefits depantrent – objectives

| *Objectives* | *Output definition* | *Output measurement quantity* | *Quality* |
|---|---|---|---|
| A. To pay housing benefits to those making valid claims. | Correctly assessed claims falling into one of the following categories:<br>(a) Council house tenant on Income Support.<br>(b) Council tax-payer on Income Support (and not in other categories as well).<br>(c) Council house tenant not on Income Support.<br>(d) Council tax-payer not on Income Support (and not in the other categories as well).<br>(e) Private tenant on Income Support.<br>(f) Private tenant not on Income Support. | Assessment and initial processing of ONE claim in each of the defined categories. | Quantity will be measured under the following headings for each category of claim defined:<br>(a) Timeliness<br>– time taken to assess form from receipt of claim and any necessary additional information.<br>(b) Customer relations<br>– time taken to ask claimant for addition information after receipt of incomplete claim.<br>– number of customer complaints received for each claim assessment.<br>(c) Success rate<br>– error rate due to faulty assessment. Error rate due to faulty input to the computer and faulty processing. |
| | Payment of claims falling into the following categories.<br>(a) Council house rent (no cheque required).<br>(b) Council tax (no cheque required).<br>(c) Payment by cheque. | Payment of ONE claim in the categories defined. | Quality will be measured as follows for each category:<br>(a) Timeliness<br>– time between due dates for payment and that achieved.<br>(b) Customer relations<br>– as for 'timeliness'.<br>(c) Success Rate<br>– payment errors per payment made. |
| B. To notify claimants of their entitlement. | Correctly assessed claims of all types of categories. | Notification of ONE claim. | (a) Timeliness<br>– the time between assessment and notification to the claimant. |

| | | | |
|---|---|---|---|
| | | | (b) Customer relations<br>– as above.<br>– number of customers complaints received for each claim.<br>(c) Sucess rate<br>– the number of assessments never notified to claimants. |
| C. To reclaim over-payments of benefit from claimants. | Proportions of over-paid benefit reclaimed. | ONE claim recovered. | (a) Timeliness<br>– the time between the dates the over-payments commenced and the date the money was recovered.<br>– the time between the dates the over-payment was discovered and the date the money was recovered<br>– the time between the date the over-payment commenced and the date it was discovered.<br>(b) Customer relations<br>– as above.<br>– number of complaints.<br>(c) Success rate<br>– as for quantity. |
| D. To ensure persons who may be entitled become aware of their entitlement. | Number of new claimants. | ONE new claimant. | (a) Timeliness<br>– the length of time between the start of entitlement and the date of claim.<br>(b) Customer relations.<br>– as above.<br>(c) Success rate<br>– estimate of those claiming as a proportion of an expected total number of potential claimants. |

and notified (objective B) (see Table 8.2). How was she going to obtain these figures? The simplest method was to count the claims concerned, perhaps every week. New assessments could be listed on a clipboard by staff as each assessment was completed. Every week the total on this list could be totted up. This, however, was likely to be a tedious and inaccurate method, since items could be left off the list by mistake or added improperly to boost productivity figures.

The best method of recording assessments was likely to be on the housing benefits computer. This could be programmed to count first time assessments of new claims and re-assessments of old claims.

The number of payments made to claimants could be easily computed from cheque lists or similar computer listings. Similarly, the computer could count the number of notification letters sent to claimants (objective B).

# Quality

Although the regulations covering housing benefit give a number of time limits for various parts of the process of assessing and paying benefit, neither they nor the Act set down meaningful levels of service. It is therefore up to the authority to decide the quality of service it wishes to provide claimants. It is also up to the authority to measure standards achieved regarding the incidents of fraudulent payments, the accuracy and reliability of assessment and calculations of benefit and the frequency at which it requires claimants to re-apply.

For a form processing activity such as benefits the majority of quality measurements will be obtained by recording transactions and analysising the results. The use of this technique was described in Table 8.1. Again the computer used to record and process claims will be a major tool in measuring achievement. So that we can understand what is involved it will be useful to illustrate the processing stages in a housing benefit claim.

From Fig. 8.5 it is possible to see how the computer can be used to record the key

| | No. days |
|---|---|
| INITIATION<br>1. Claim form received from claimant.<br>PROCESSING<br>2. Claim form is assessed to discover whether there is an entitlement to benefit.<br>(a) Completeness of form is checked.<br>(i) if incomplete claimant is asked for missing information.<br>(ii) if more data is required to corroborate details given on the form claimant is asked to provide additional evidence as required.<br>(b) Date of receipt of last piece of information needed before assessment can start is recorded.<br>3. Details on the now complete claim form are input to the computer so that entitlement to benefit can be assessed.<br>NOTIFICATION<br>4. Date of notification to claimant of entitlement.<br>PAYMENT<br>5. Due date of first payment.<br>6. Actual date of first payment. | |

**Fig. 8.5** Processing stages for a housing benefit claim.

times and dates which will be important in measuring the quality of much of the service.

# Costs

The third area that needs measuring, after quantities and quality, is costs. Abigail will need to know the total costs of her department. She will also have to be able to divide these costs up between each different output. Before we get into too much detail let us look at how Abigail can use the information she has. The costs of the department are as follows for one year (as per Chapter 6).

| | *£'000s* |
|---|---|
| Supplies – services | 30.6 |
| Establishment expenses | 25.0 |
| Computer costs | 45.2 |
| Salaries | 251.3 |
| | 352.1 |

Abigail needs to divide these costs up between the year's output. This means that £352 100 is to be divided amongst all the output the department produced in the year. It is a large task, of that there is no doubt. But it is a task performed by countless enterprises across the world.

Table 8.2 shows that we have a large number of different outputs. Let us look at one output type first by itself. We will look at assessment of claims (objective 1A).

We need to be sure what she is trying to achieve. What she wants is the cost associated with outputs 1A (i) to (vi) (Table 8.2). But remember not all the £352 100 spent on benefits administration will produce these outputs. Other outputs will be payment of claims (objective 2A) notification (objective B), overpaid benefits reclaimed (objective C) and entitlement publicity (objective D). So how do we apportion the £352 100 between outputs?

## Salaries

Benefit administration is a predominantly labour intensive activity. Seventy-one per cent of expenditure is on staff costs. Abigail MacGovern must start apportionment here. Now whenever staff costs need analysis some form of time recording system is needed. The simplest time recording is carried out using timesheets. The timesheet splits available staff time over the different activities the employee has been engaged in. Since the cost of labour is known the labour cost of the activity can be calculated. But how is she going to use the timesheet to apportion salary costs over outputs? Abigail will need timesheets which require staff to split their time over the outputs listed in column 2 of Table 8.2. The timesheet she has produced to do this is shown in Fig. 8.6.

Each staff member must divide his or her time each day between the outputs. No other analysis is possible except for 'wasted time'. We will consider this in the next chapter. In practice staff will find completion of such a timesheet too complex for easy use if they become involved in a large number of different outputs for short periods. This problem would be overcome by streamlining duties. Staff where possible could assess council house tenants on income support (1A[1], Fig. 8.6) for most of one day before administering payments of benefit (1B[3]) in the late afternoon, for instance. Abigail considers such changes in work pattern would in many cases improve productivity. She did not view this as counter productive.

At the end of a week the timesheet will need processing in a time recording system. The time for each grade of employee will be added up for each output type and multiplied by the hourly cost of that grade. The total cost of recorded time as derived from the time recording system will agree with the total payroll costs actually incurred for the week.

At the end of this exercise Abigail McGovern had analysed salary costs between outputs. Next she had to consider the other expenditure on inputs of which the largest is 'computer costs'.

## Computer costs

Most computers automatically record the time they spend working on different activities or programmes on a computer log. This will form the basis of Abigail's apportionment of costs. But it will probably be difficult to split actual computer time on assessment of claims between the output categories we have defined. In this situation estimates will be necessary. For instance a relatively complex assessment of a private tenant not on income support (output 1A[6] Fig. 8.6) might be found on a test basis to take twice the computer processing time of council house tenant on income support (output 1A[1] Fig. 8.6). Using these types of assumptions based on test cases, Abigail could apportion computer costs to output.

## Supplies and services

Supplies and services and establishment expenses together represent 16% of total costs. Some of this expense will vary with the workload of the department. For instance the cost of stationery, which is included in supplies, will clearly increase if more claims are processed because more paper will be used. But other costs, such as rates on the office used by the department will not vary with workload. Abigail needed to carefully divide costs between those that vary with workload such as stationery usage, and those that do not. The first type are know as 'variable costs' and the second 'fixed costs' or 'fixed overheads'. When she measures productivity she is not concerned with fixed overheads. They must be removed from total costs before we can analyse achievement.

The majority of 'establishment expenses' will be fixed overheads. We can ignore these for the present and concentrate on 'supplies and services'. These may contain

TIME SHEET

Name: Date:
Period:

| OUTPUTS | Hours charged to each day of a four-week period | | | | | | |
|---|---|---|---|---|---|---|---|
| | 1 | 2 | 3 | 4 . . . 18 | 19 | 20 | Total |
| 1. Assessments<br>A1) Council tenant on income support<br>2) Council tax-payer on income support<br>3) Council tenant not on income support<br>6) Private tenant not on income support<br>Payments<br>B1) Council house rents<br>2) Council tax<br>3) Cheques<br>2. Notifications<br>3. Overpayments<br>4. Entitlements | | | | | | | |
| TOTAL HOURS | | | | | | | |

**Fig. 8.6** Staff timesheet.

fixed overheads but the majority will be variable costs. How did Abigail analyse these over outputs? Telephone costs will vary with output but how do we allocate costs to each output category. Theoretically it would be possible to log the calls and charge them to individual claims. At present the technology is not available to make this process viable. Abigail therefore made reasonable estimates and charged costs to the different outputs using a rational and defensible method just as she did for computer costs. Since supplies were just 8.7% of total costs slight inaccuracies were not a major worry.

## Unit costs

To be able to explain to her staff the importance of accurate completion of timesheets Abigail produced Fig. 8.7.

# Accounting

Let us recapitulate on what Abigail MacGovern has done. She has:

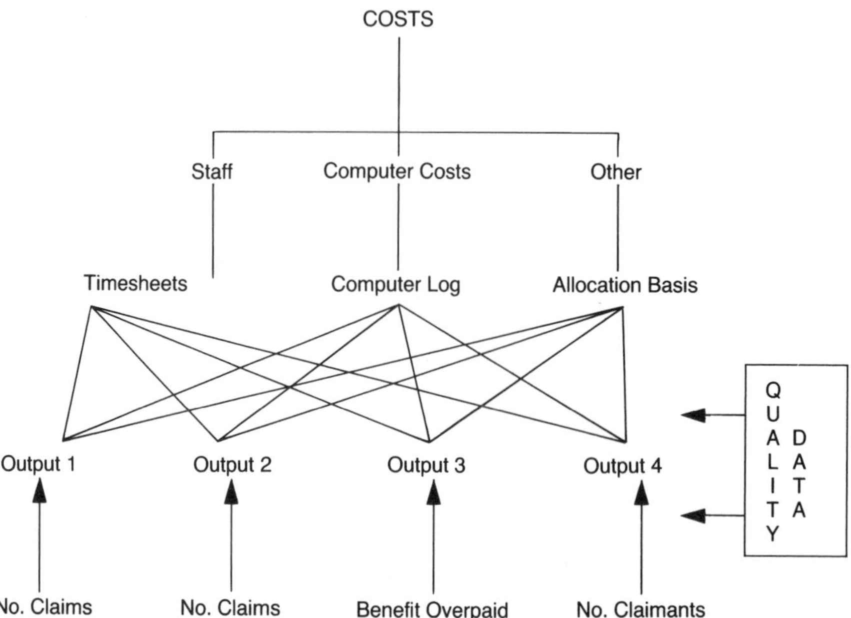


**Fig. 8.7** Abigail MacGovern's measurement system.

1. Defined her outputs;
2. Set up systems to measure or count how much of each her department is producing;
3. Set up a system to measure the quality of her outputs;
4. Set up a cost accounting system, based on timesheets, to allocate costs to outputs.

Having done all this what will she do with the information? So as to be able to monitor the achievements of the housing benefit department she produces every four weeks, that is 13 times a year, a management accounts package.

In this document she verbally reviews the department's performance. But the core of the document is the 'unit costing spreadsheet'. The period 6 spreadsheet is given in Table 8.3. This table shows the unit costs in period 6 for each output. This information is useful, but it is even more useful when it is compared to budget figures and previous months achievements. Abigail shows these comparisons in her management accounts package separately for each output. The figures for private tenants on income support are given in Table 8.4.

These figures are in exactly the same format as those for the Primary Products division of Mon Products Ltd (see Table 6.1).

Just as managers at Mon Products discussed their results with the shop floor staff every month, Abigail does the same at Senforth District Council. The results for Period 6 appear in total reasonably good. Period 6 total budgeted costs per Table 8.3 were £27 085. Actual costs were significantly less at £25 927. However, Table 8.3 only gives a partial view. It does not show how much work was expected for the budget cost. Much more detailed information is given about this on Table 8.4 for a

**Table 8.3** Housing benefit – monthly summary, period 6

| *Output types* | *Budget for year* | *Budget for period* | *Actual costs for period* | *Assessment of claims* | | | *C.T.* | *Private on I.S.* | *Private* | *Payment of claims* | | | *Notification* | *Overpayments* | *Entitlement* | *TOTAL* |
|---|---|---|---|---|---|---|---|---|---|---|---|---|---|---|---|---|
| | | | | *Tenants on I.S.* | *C.T. on I.S.* | *Tenant* | | | | *Tenant* | *C.T.* | *Cheque* | | | | |
| Units of output – number of assessments | | | | 103 | 61 | 41 | 67 | 131 | 58 | 2174 | 6418 | 1582 | 431 | 28 | 599 | |
| Salaries – managers | 43 000 | 3 308 | 3 205 | 160 | 175 | 307 | 612 | 469 | 772 | 159 | 178 | 241 | 25 | 25 | 82 | 3 205 |
| – supervisors | 68 000 | 5 231 | 5 171 | 504 | 210 | 510 | 798 | 1201 | 1006 | 277 | 168 | 301 | 105 | 91 | | 5 171 |
| – Grade A | 83 500 | 6 423 | 6 315 | 151 | 210 | 54 | 783 | 2002 | 974 | 357 | 218 | 501 | 104 | 902 | 59 | 6 315 |
| – Grade B | 56 800 | 4 369 | 3 998 | 847 | 831 | 799 | 473 | 401 | | | | 215 | 125 | | 307 | 3 998 |
| | 251 300 | 19 331 | 18 689 | 1662 | 1426 | 1670 | 2666 | 4073 | 2752 | 793 | 564 | 1258 | 359 | 1018 | 448 | 18 689 |
| Computer costs | 45 200 | 3 477 | 3 306 | 294 | 252 | 295 | 472 | 720 | 487 | 140 | 100 | 223 | 64 | 180 | 79 | 3306 |
| Direct supply costs | 30 600 | 2 354 | 1 927 | 171 | 147 | 172 | 275 | 420 | 284 | 82 | 58 | 130 | 37 | 105 | 46 | 1927 |
| | 327 100 | 25 162 | 23 922 | 2127 | 1825 | 2138 | 3412 | 5213 | 3523 | 1015 | 722 | 1610 | 460 | 1303 | 573 | 23 922 |
| Establishment expenses | 25 000 | 1 923 | 2 005 | 178 | 153 | 179 | 286 | 437 | 295 | 85 | 61 | 135 | 39 | 109 | 48 | 2 005 |
| | 352 100 | 27 085 | 25 927 | 2305 | 1978 | 2317 | 3699 | 5650 | 3818 | 1100 | 782 | 1745 | 498 | 1412 | 622 | 25 927 |
| UNIT COSTS – Total costs/No. units of output | | | | 22.38 | 32.43 | 56.51 | 55.20 | 43.13 | 65.82 | 0.51 | 0.12 | 1.10 | 1.16 | 50.44 | 1.04 | N/A |

**Table 8.4** Housing benefit – monthly summary, period 6: private tenants on income support

| | *Average for previous 12 months* | | *Previous period* | | | *Period 6* | | | | *Standard production* | | | | *Quantity variances* | | *Price variance* |
|---|---|---|---|---|---|---|---|---|---|---|---|---|---|---|---|---|
| | *Quantity* | *000* | *Quantity* | *000* | *Price* | *Quantity* | *000* | *Usage* | *Price* | *Quantity* | *000* | *Usage* | *Quantity* | *Yield 000* | *Production 000* | *000* |
| Output – number of assessments | 115 | | 121 | | | 131 | | | | 100 claims | | | 31.00 | | | |
| Salaries – managers | 24 | 350 | 29 | 421 | 14.84 | 32 | 469 | 0.24 | 14 | 28 hours | 392 | 0.28 | 3.60 | 71.07 | −121.52 | −26.55 |
| – supervisors | 104 | 1104 | 105 | 1111 | 10.6 | 113 | 1201 | 0.86 | 10 | 75 hours | 750 | 0.75 | 38.30 | −150.52 | −232.50 | −67.98 |
| – Grade A | 287 | 1811 | 300 | 1980 | 6.63 | 302 | 2002 | 2.31 | 6 | 240 hours | 1440 | 2.40 | 61.96 | 74.64 | −446.40 | −190.24 |
| – Grade B | 30 | 153 | 39 | 207 | 5.3 | 76 | 401 | 0.58 | 5 | 0 hours | 0 | 0.00 | 75.66 | −378.30 | 0.00 | −22.70 |
| | | 3418 | | 3719 | | | 4073 | | | | 2582 | | | −383.12 | −800.42 | −307.46 |
| Computer costs | 24 | 675 | 28 | 690 | 27.5 | 26 | 720 | 0.20 | 30 | 20 hours | 600 | 0.20 | 6.18 | 0.55 | −186.00 | 65.45 |
| Direct supply costs | 126 | 367 | 136 | 396 | 2.85 | 147 | 420 | 1.12 | 3 | 106 units | 318 | 1.06 | 41.37 | −25.53 | −98.58 | 22.11 |
| Total direct costs | | 1042 | | 1086 | | | 1140 | | | | 918 | | | −24.98 | −284.58 | 87.56 |
| Establishment expenses | | 382 | | 403 | | | 437 | | | | 333 | | | | −104.00 | |
| Total cost of output for period | | 4842 | | 5208 | | | 5650 | | | | 3833 | | | −408.10 | −1189.00 | −219.90 |
| UNIT COSTS | | 42.10 | | 43.04 | | | 43.13 | | | | 38.33 | | | | | |

single output only – assessment of private tenants on income support. A single output is shown for simplicity. Abigail also has another spread sheet which aggregates all outputs to show overall performance.

Table 8.4 shows that for that output chosen, figures are poor. Abigail MacGovern will find out why and what can be done about it at the meeting. But first she analyses the results shown on the spreadsheet. One hundred claims of this type were expected per the budget in each period. In period 6 there were in fact 131 claims. The expected unit cost is £38.33 whereas the actual for the period was £43.13. Not only were unit costs up but so were total costs from the £3833 expected to an actual cost for the period of £5650.

This difference in cost is highlighted by the adverse variances shown in the variances section of the spreadsheet. The 31 additional claims have cost an extra £1189 – the production variance. Inefficient processing has cost an extra £408. This is shown as an adverse yield variance. Price increases for inputs have cost £219. This is shown by the adverse price variance. For this particular output nothing seems to have been right in period 6. Luckily, some other outputs have shown much better variances.

In a service such as housing benefits production variances cannot be controlled very easily because they represent the effect of external demand. Since total costs are in budget Abigail does not need to worry too much about the adverse variance in this instance. In addition, central government payments for housing benefits administration are based on caseload. Even if total costs exceeded budget due to volume of work more finance should be forthcoming in the following year. For many other public services a restriction on the availability of the service is the only way to reduce demand and hence production variances.

Abigail had expected that much of the work on private tenant on income support claims should be done by grade A staff who would spend 2.40 hours on average per claim. In fact a significant amount of additional supervisor time was spent. See how the yield variance for supervisors is £150 adverse. Worst still abortive grade B time cost £378. Supervisors have been spending too much time on these claims because grade B staff have been used to assess them. In the budget grade B staff were not allocated to this work because it was considered too complex. The excessive involvement of supervisors shows this view was correct. The other cause of poor figures was a 6% pay rise above budget – look at the price variance figures!

What other issues will Abigail MacGovern be raising at the meeting?

# Summary

Abigail McGovern has revolutionized the management of the Housing Benefits Department at Senforth District Council. Whereas Ron Haworth used his judgement to ensure that total costs were kept within budget, Abigail has started to objectively measure real achievement. This is not a just a mathematical exercise. Abigail has analysed the work of the department and set clear objectives. She knows the problems of processing different types of claims not just subjectively but analytically. If it takes a grade A staff member longer than 2.40 hours to process the average private tenant on income support claim then Abigail knows from experience and measurement that something is wrong and the department is not working to its potential. To sum up, under the Abigail McGovern school of management managers become involved, know their subject, and objectively check that achievement matches potential. Under the old system a manager did none of these things. He just kept out of trouble!

## Reader questionnaire

ANSWERS

1. What are the statutory duties of your organization or department?
2. Have you ever systematically matched your work to these duties and objectives?
3. Do you record your output? Do you have an existing system that could be adjusted to record useful output data?
4. How much do you know about your costs?
5. Do you have a personal computer? Why don't you start to use it to analyse costs and output on spreadsheets?
6. Are you prepared to analyse your department to the same extent that Abigail McGovern was, or is it just too much trouble?
7. Are you really in control of your department or organization?

# Case study II – a health service budget: general surgery department

This case study looks at how a general surgery department in a large hospital might be managed to maximize achievement of both the quantity of work done and its quality. The consultant surgeon in charge of the department is a Frederick Asherton.

Under the NHS internal market Parkinson Hospital has contracts with purchasers. But these contracts give little detail of the nature of the work to be done. Most are block contracts which define treatment in terms of 'patient episodes' assuming a standard case mix.

Fred Asherton is rather worried by the changes taking place in the health service. All the new emphasis on money he finds both disconcerting and unpleasant. He had rather hoped that at his age – somewhere in his late fifties – he could ignore the reforms. He was just settling into pretending that nothing had changed in the NHS and was, he thought doing rather well when two things happened. First, he had a visit from an irate unit manager asking to know why the general surgery budget was heavily in deficit. The man had even had the impudence to demand whether Asherton thought he could carry on as if the health service reforms never existed. The second incident had involved his son, John. He had rung up two nights ago and had announced that he was engaged. The rather surprised father had asked who the bride was to be. In fact she was a chartered accountant in the City. When the happy couple came down that weekend Mr Asherton took the chance to question his prospective daughter in law on the mysteries of accounting practice.

# Quality and productivity

Having been assaulted both at home and at work by demanding news both involving accountancy, Frederick Asherton decided that a change in policy might be advantageous. Rather than running away from the reforms in the health service he now thought he would pioneer some modern management at Parkinson Hospital and show up a few of his colleagues. He had a brief meeting with the unit manager, found out what the whole charade was about and agreed a time to see the unit accountant. It all seemed much easier than anticipated. Everything hinged around finding out how much clinical work was costing so that more could be achieved with only limited increases in funding. In this way the hospitals in the area could be kept solvent. The other aspect the unit manager mentioned was his hopes to start measuring the quality of treatment and service provided by Parkinson Hospital so that this could be used as a method of enticing more work off fund holding GPs. The Resource Management Initiative, a government sponsored programme to analyse the work of hospitals was not very advanced at Parkinson Hospital so Fred would have to do much of the pioneering work himself.

The term 'productivity' sticks in the throats of most medical practitioners. Quite rightly doctors and the other caring professions dislike the idea that their work is mechanistic or that their patients are machines. However it is not uncommon for patients to be considered as 'clinical material'. Clearly, some middle road is required between the excessively individualistic and the unpleasantly mechanistic. Frederick Asherton developed the phrase 'clinical output' to refer to productivity – the amount of work done for a given sum of money.

The other main achievement of a hospital is the quality of its work. As we have said quality is composed of, success, timeliness, and customer or patient care and satisfaction.

Medical people tend to consider that they do the best they can under the conditions pertaining. This does not, however, equate to quality. Quality as a measure is in a sense absolute since it does not vary with conditions. A waiting list time of nine months is a wait of nine months regardless of the reasons for it. In contrast, doing the best you can do is relative to the conditions you work in.

In this case study we will use the word 'quality' in the sense explained in Chapter 8. If not commonly used in health service circles at least it is unambiguous and easily understood by lay people.

# General surgery objectives

Fred Asherton thought that if he was going to become a reformer then he had better start at the beginning of the problem and work methodically through. So he started by looking up the health service legislation.

Objectives of the National Health Service are quite straightforward. They are given by the National Health Service Act 1977. They are as follows:

1. To secure improvement in the physical health of the population (s1(a));
2. To prevent, diagnose and treat illness (s1(b));
3. To provide appropriate services for ensuring the above (s2(a));
4. To provide for those suffering from illness (s3(1e));
5. To provide aftercare of those who have suffered from illness (s3(1e));
6. To provide services as are required to diagnose illness (s3(1f)).

In short there are few statutory objectives. None of them relate to the quality of services provided. Much is left to the Secretary of State for Health – and hence effectively to practitioners.

Fred Asherton summarized the above for his own benefit by saying that the health service must: diagnose illness appropriately, treat illness appropriately, and provide aftercare for those recovering from illness appropriately.

The objectives of appropriate diagnosis, treatment and aftercare need to be achieved successfully making the best use of available resources. We are back to the issue of scarcity discussed in Chapters 3, 4 and 5.

# Objectives and clinical and quality outputs

The next stage that Frederick Asherton had to consider was how to define outputs and how to measure them. He needed to consider both quantity, clinical outputs, and quality. The concept of an output in medicine did not come naturally to him. He had mused about it for some time before he rang up his son's fiancée, Alice.

# Clinical outputs

She had suggested that clinical outputs were the 'cures' he achieved. Her reasoning for this was that discussed at the beginning of Chapter 6. The outputs of a general surgery department are cures for specific complaints such as hernias, appendicitis, ulcers and cancers. For most hospitals there will be a number of commonly repeated operations and many other less common complaints. Each attempted 'cure' is a potential clinical output.

On the basis of this telephone call Mr Asherton decided to divide output between the three major objectives he had set himself. Thus the output of the diagnosis objective was to be correct diagnosis, of the treatment objective, effective treatment and the aftercare objective, long-term cure. Naturally the likelihood of a long-term cure will depend on correct diagnosis and effective treatment as well as proper aftercare but by breaking down the work of the department into separate elements causes of problems are more easily isolated and corrected.

So that he could get the whole idea of objectives and output clear in his mind Frederick Asherton set out the three objectives and their outputs in a matrix (see Table 8.5).

**Table 8.5** General surgery – objectives

| *Objectives* | *Output definition* | *Output measurement clinical* | *Quality* |
|---|---|---|---|
| A. Appropriate Diagnosis is made. | Diagnosis of a disease of each type as follows:<br>(i) Hernia<br>(ii) Appendicitis<br>(iii) Duodenal ulcer<br>(iv) Cancer of the gut<br>(v) Other | Testing and diagnosis of ONE case in the categories defined. | Quality will be measured under the following headings for each output.<br>Timeliness<br>– the time taken to diagnose a disease from referral date by GP<br>Patient satisfaction<br>– as above<br>– number of queries and complaints received during the diagnosis<br>Success<br>– the rate of correct diagnosis expressed as a percentage of the total |
| B. Appropriate patient treatment is provided. | Treatment of a disease of each type as follows:<br>(i) Hernia<br>(ii) Appendicitis<br>(iii) Duodenal ulcer<br>(iv) Cancer of the gut<br>(v) Other | Treatment of ONE case in the categories defined. | Quality will be measured under the following headings for each output.<br>Timeliness<br>– the time taken to commence treatment of a disease after diagnosis<br>– the time taken between the start and completion of treatment<br>Patient satisfaction<br>– as above for Timeliness<br>– the number of queries and complaints received between diagnosis and completion of treatment<br>Success<br>– the rate of successful treatment as a percentage of the total |
| C. Appropriate after treatment care. | After treatment care of a disease of a disease of each type as follows:<br>(i) Hernia<br>(ii) Appendicitis<br>(iii) Duodenal ulcer<br>(iv) Cancer of the gut<br>(v) Other | After treatment care of ONE case in the categories defined. | Quality will be measured under the following headings for each output.<br>Timeliness<br>– the time from the completion of treatment to complete recovery<br>Patient satisfaction<br>– as above under Timeliness<br>– the number of queries and complaints received concerning after treatment care<br>Success<br>– the long-term success rate of the treatment, e.g. five-year mortality rates |

## Quality

Next he had to consider how to measure output quality. In the health service timeliness is clearly one of the most important measures of quality because waiting lists are a concern to politicians and the public. The success of the medical procedure carried out is another fairly obvious measure of quality. If an operation is done but the patient dies of the original complaint, then there is a lapse of quality. For many diseases a high success rate is unlikely but nevertheless the object of treatment is usually a 'cure'. In these circumstances then, a death must be considered a lack of success. Last, there is patient satisfaction. A recent unofficial study at St Bartholomew's hospital in London showed that many doctors never knew whether their patients were satisfied with the service they received. Many never knew whether their patients even survived. In fact considerable numbers of patients when traced for the study said they felt worse or no better after treatment. In a more sophisticated world the satisfaction of the patient with all aspects of the service is important. This lesson is being learnt by GPs under their new contract arrangements. Those that do not give acceptable service are beginning to lose patients.

Fred Asherton had few conceptual problems with the concept of service quality in the medical profession. He added some quality measurements to his objectives and output chart as shown in Table 8.5.

## Timeliness

For a general surgery department the timespan for each case starts with referral of the patient by a GP. Some tests may already have been done but many others may not have been. The first objective of the department is therefore diagnosis. At the end of the diagnosis stage the treatment stage follows if this is necessary. And after treatment comes aftercare. Asherton had always been interested in the time it took to diagnose and treat a patient so he viewed this aspect of his measurement system with particular interest. He set down these time periods in a diagram (see Fig. 8.8).

The days between each stage of the process will normally be best kept to a minimum. To measure this aspect of the quality of the service each time period will

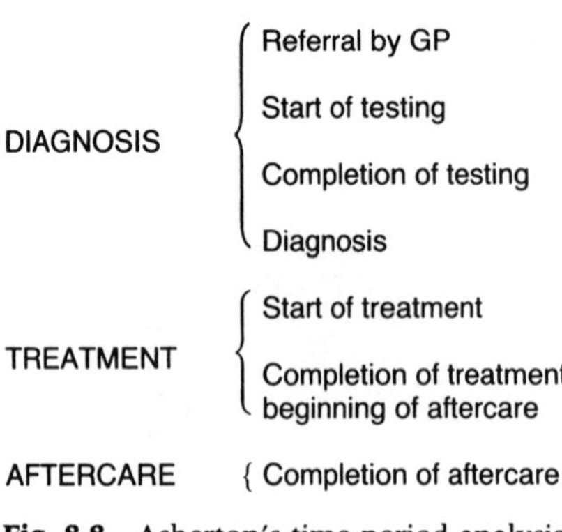


**Fig. 8.8** Asherton's time period analysis.

need recording for each case and each case type. Clearly, a hernia will have a very rapid treatment stage compared to a complex cancer, but the time between diagnosis and treatment may be substantial. Hernia cases, normally being non-urgent, may wait for months after diagnosis and before treatment.

At first Fred Asherton had been unsure how to obtain all the information he required concerning the timeliness of treatment. He had visions of endless piles of scruffy paperwork all written in blue ball-point. Then he thought of the computerized patient record system. One of the unit manager's sidekicks was always talking about getting more information off this system or an improved version of it. For the first time, Asherton began to see why. By slightly changing the way information was input the number of days between each stage of the treatment could be automatically recorded and the number of days calculated. After a chat with the computer department he was able to get some of the information he needed.

Table 8.6 is a copy of part of Fred Asherton's first time lapse summary sheet.

Many people looking at such a basic summary will feel that it is unrealistically simplistic. Appendicitis may be acute or rumbling and many ulcers will not need surgery now that anti-ulcer drugs are so affective. If there are useful subdivisions of diseases into different degrees of seriousness then the number of different outputs should reflect this. But there is another requirement of management information and that is that it should be simple and readily available. Too much detail is clearly incompatible with this need. Another possible way of categorizing hospital work is not by disease but 'class' of illness. General surgery work could be categorized into five classes, A to E, where A was minor illness and E was very serious. Asherton chose not to use this system for a number of reasons which are not discussed here.

From Table 8.6 Fred Asherton was able to see that gut cancer cases were taking 41 days before the commencement of treatment. What particularly worried and surprised him was that the period from the commencement of testing to start of treatment was 27 days or all but a month. Clearly this was a poor service. If he himself were treated like that he would have been livid with rage. He had always thought that the service for urgent cases was good. Now he could clearly see that it was not. He had learned something useful already. Only by recording the actual time

**Table 8.6** Average time intervals for treatments completed in period 13 199x–y in days

| | *Hernia days* | *Appendix days* | *Ulcer days* | *Cancer of gut days* |
|---|---|---|---|---|
| DIAGNOSIS | | | | |
| Referral by GP | 0 | 0 | 0 | 0 |
| Start of testing | 153 | 14 | 15 | 14 |
| Completion of testing | 154 | 15 | 27 | 26 |
| Diagnosis | 154 | 21 | 41 | 33 |
| TREATMENT | | | | |
| Start of treatment | 154 | 46 | 108 | 41 |
| AFTERCARE | | | | |
| Completion of treatment/ beginning of aftercare | 154 | 50 | 115 | 62 |
| Completion of aftercare | 194 | 75 | 175 | 529 |

lapse achieved is it possible to know clearly what is happening. And only once the truth is known can adjustments to practice be usefully made.

## Success rate

With these interesting discoveries about his own department Fred Asherton looked forward with some interest to measuring the success rate of the work they did. Again he decided to use the computerized patient records system.

For the less serious diseases success rates will be very high. But this is not a reason not to measure them. Perhaps there is a small failure on diagnosis, in which case, its true extent should be known. Or perhaps there are a significant percentage of complications in some of the more straightforward procedures.

At the other extreme the more serious diseases will have a significant mortality rate. Fred wanted to be able to compare his work with best practice achievements. He had recently come across some work comparing five-year survival rates in the USA and Britain. The results showed dramatic differences for some common cancers. The two survival rates are compared in Table 8.7.

Fred was surprised and a little annoyed that the rate achieved in the USA was about a third better than in the UK. He had always assumed that for urgent work the NHS and British doctors were second to none. Clearly, the health of different individual patients would vary before they develop the disease for which they are being treated. Nevertheless crude success figures such as those given above, were clearly a useful guide to achievement because they provided concrete information which could be considered and acted upon as necessary. Frederick Asherton was learning fast. Figures on achievement not only had the capacity to provide useful information but they were also rather interesting. Without figures one is forced to guess at success rates and guessing is likely to be considerably more inaccurate than calculated figures.

### *Success rates at Parkinson Hospital*

Using the patient records system, Fred Asherton calculated his first set of success rate figures. Table 8.8 shows how he recorded success rates of each output and each objective. More detail could usefully be given about these figures but as a first

**Table 8.7** Five-year survival rates in Britain and the USA

| | *UK* % | *USA* % | *Difference* % |
|---|---|---|---|
| Breast cancer | 58 | 72 | 24 |
| Melanoma | 71 | 82 | 15 |
| Cancer of the ovary | 26 | 36 | 38 |
| Cancer of the bladder | 54 | 72 | 33 |
| Cancer of the prostate | 36 | 65 | 81 |

**Table 8.8** Success rates of diagnosis, treatment and aftercare

| | *Hernia* % | *Appendix* % | *Ulcer* % | *Cancer of the gut, etc.* % |
|---|---|---|---|---|
| Diagnosis | 87 | 91 | 74 | 72 |
| Treatment | | | | |
| short-term success | 96 | 97 | 92 | 85 |
| Aftercare | | | | |
| long-term success | 75 | 96 | 94 | 32 |

attempt at measurement Fred was quite pleased. He was particularly satisfied with his ulcer results. The figures showed an aftercare success of 94% but a treatment success of 92%. This difference was because for one case the operation failed to cure the symptoms. Further treatment was, however, successful. He could have shown this as one protracted course of care but he chose to show it as two separate courses. Fred's figures could have shown more detail about the failed diagnoses. What were these patients actually suffering from? In Chapter 9 we discuss further how this more detailed information could be used to improve the functioning of the department.

## Patient satisfaction

In his late middle age Fred Asherton had the feeling that he was becoming quite a radical. He had just had an acrimonious argument with a colleague concerning the issue of patient satisfaction. The colleague was complaining that patients and relatives always wanted to know about everything and that they asked such stupid questions and wasted so much time. Fred had replied that he would not be complaining like that if patients had a choice of doctor because they would go to the doctor who gave them the best all-round service. People like him would be short of patients if there was real choice. Just to rub things in Fred had then said that under the new health reforms hospitals could not afford antagonism with patients because it would eventually result in fewer patients and hence less funding.

After the row Asherton wondered whether he was not beginning to display the attitudes of a shopkeeper. Perhaps he really considered that the only things that mattered were income and trade. But suddenly he realized that he had in fact been right. What made him so certain was the sight of a old couple staggering into the outpatients' department. Perhaps one of them was dying – he did not know, but it struck him very forcefully that if you were going to spend your last days in hospital then the quality of the whole service must be the best possible that can be obtained with the available resources. Patient satisfaction was of paramount importance. The success of the hospice movement demonstrated that, he thought. With his new flair for numbers and measuring achievement he now realized that the only way of maximizing patient care was to measure it and improve where the figures showed it was weak.

Patient satisfaction is perhaps the most difficult quality to measure accurately. This is because people expect their doctor to lay down the law about what is best for them; only in extreme circumstances will they voice concern although they may well feel that the service has not been to the highest standards.

Naturally timeliness of treatment and its success will affect patient satisfaction, but other more intangible qualities are involved such as politeness of staff, the interior design of the hospital and the general atmosphere. Attempts must be made to measure these things because they actually do matter. And in a time when people are getting more opportunity to choose from whom they obtain services the hospital or department with a bad reputation with the public will inevitably suffer.

Stimulated to further action Fred Asherton listed the measurements of patient satisfaction that he wanted to monitor. These are listed below.

### *Methods of measuring patient satisfaction*

1. Number of complaints received from:
   (a) patients;
   (b) relatives.
2. Market research questionnaires:
   (a) patients;
   (b) local population;
   (c) local GPs.
3. Rates of staff turnover.
4. Numbers of patients treated.

At various times all these methods need to be used. Trends and changes need to be monitored and studied for improvements and deteriotions in patient satisfaction. Staff turnover may surprise some readers as a measure of patient satisfaction. But it is highly unlikely that your patients feel they are getting a first-rate service if your own staff are deserting in droves. Staff turnover is a good measure of the general health of any organization.

The next evening Fred Asherton sketched out the following patient questionnaire. When it was typed it looked like this:

## Patient satisfaction survey

We are continually striving to improve the care we give you the patient. It would be a help to us if you could answer the questions below:

### *Medical and nursing care*

1. Were you given all the information you needed about the treatment you were having? Yes/No
2. Are you happy about the time you had to wait for treatment? Yes/No

3. Did you feel that your case was of importance to the doctors and nurses or did you feel you Yes/No [and so on . . .]

Fred was able to get some other useful quality data from nursing quality checking work done for the purchasers of health care, in this case the district health authority.

## Measurement of clinical output or productivity

Frederick Asherton commenced his departmental reforms with the issue of quality. This was because he felt more at home with this aspect of measurement than with unit costs for clinical outputs. The measurement of the quantity of work done for a given level of funding was an issue he still found rather perplexing.

The measurement of quality was relatively straightforward because much of the information required could be obtained off computerized patient record systems. In contrast, the measurement of clinical output required slightly more complex systems to measure the costs associated with individual cases. Fred Asherton needed the help of an accountant.

He was able to discuss his problems with Alice. She and John were coming to dinner. They were arriving separately and John had been held up. Fred was quite enjoying himself chatting to Alice.

'Of course the first thing you need to do is divide your costs between those that are fixed and those that vary with the amount of patients you have.' said Alice.

'Oh!' said Fred.

'Variable costs are expenditure which is specific to the work being carried out. For you they would be things like the costs of operating on individual patients, I suppose.'

'You mean that I have got to find out the cost associated with an anaesthetist, three theatre nurses, a houseman and me while we spend 45 minutes adjusting someones innards?'

'I don't really know what doctors do.' said Alice 'but that is the type of thing required. The point is that those types of expenditure are very different from costs that are fixed. I recently heard on the news that most of a hospitals costs are incurred whether or not there are any patients. You need to maintain and heat buildings, pay most of the nurses and ancillary staff regardless of patient load.'

'So what do I do with all the fixed costs then.'

'Well, since you cannot really control them – is that right? – you can ignore them.'

'Actually I can control some of them. For instance, I control use of beds and bed costs are in fact already calculated by the accounts department,' said Fred. 'In fact most of them I can indirectly control, for instance the cost of pathology work is very high and the more work I give them the higher it will be but I cannot control their actual costs.'

'From what you say I think you ought to use a standard cost for overheads based on the number of days each patient stays in bed. Say Joe Bloggs is in for a week then you should charge seven days at the average cost of a bed per day for the whole hospital.' said Alice.

'So all I would need to know was the number of days each patient was in hospital, right?' He thought he was getting somewhere. 'But what about the variable costs.'

'Presumably your variable costs would be mostly doctors' time and bandages or whatever hospitals use in the way of materials.'

'Yes, that's right, staff time, sterile supplies, drugs and things. And of course there are the costs from other departments which have an input into patients' treatment. I mean pathology, radiography, a consultant anaesthetist or any other people who become involved in a particular case.'

'Let's consider the staff under your own control first. The only way they can charge their time accurately is by using timesheets, I would have thought,' said Alice.

'But that sounds so terribly cumbersome,' interjected Asherton. 'More paper to process. Do you know that the health authority spends £900 000 or 2% of its budget on forms?'

'Well I doubt your timesheets will add appreciatively to that!' laughed Alice and then suddenly wondered whether she wasn't being rude. She continued hurriedly, 'All professional people have to record their time somehow because they are such an expensive resource. Lawyers, accountants, architects all use timesheets. Once you get a system for recording time and processing timesheets it is not difficult. I had one client with about twelve staff and a secretary spent about a morning a month processing timesheets.'

'Most of the nursing time could be included in the standard cost of keeping a patient in hospital for one night so I would only need timesheets for staff directly under my control,' mused Fred.

'What about the costs of other departments?' asked Alice. 'Are they charged directly to you or do you not know their costs at all?'

'They have just introduced an internal recharging system for some departments. We are charged £10 for simple blood tests for instance. But an anaesthetist's time is not charged. He looks after his own budget and I don't know anything about it'.

'Well other people's costs can only be accounted for by you if you can find them out. Clearly, the anaesthetist's costs cannot be included in your figures but blood tests could be if you recorded the number of tests each patient has.'

'More paper work!'

'Yes, but it should produce useful results. It won't be needless admin. for other peoples' benefit. You will be doing it because it will be useful to you.'

At that moment there were footsteps in the hall and at the door appeared John followed by his mother. Frederick rose and started to pour his lucky son a whisky.

## Costs

The next day Fred started by reviewing his costs. The expenditure of his general surgery department is shown below.

## *Expenditure for the year to 31st March 199X*

| Figures for a Budget Holder – General Surgery | | |
|---|---|---|
| Direct treatment services | | |
| Consultants | 263 | |
| Other medical | 206 | |
| Theatre services | 547 | |
| Pharmacy and other | 227 | |
| | | 1243 |
| Indirect treatment services | | |
| Radiology | 154 | |
| Microbiology | 79 | |
| Histopathology | 87 | |
| Chemical pathology | 54 | |
| Other pathology | 37 | |
| Physiotherapy | 74 | |
| Other | 43 | |
| | | 528 |
| Overhead Costs – Hospitals | | |
| Nursing | 1277 | |
| Medical records | 169 | |
| Cleaning | 270 | |
| Portering | 104 | |
| Catering | 206 | |
| Heating | 154 | |
| Maintainance and other | 405 | |
| | | 2585 |
| Overhead Costs – Administration | | |
| Administration | 20 | |
| Personnel | 31 | |
| | | 51 |
| TOTAL COSTS | | 4407 |

Let us review Frederick Asherton's costs. We can see that costs for the work of the department fall into a number of different types. We will look at each type in turn.

## *Direct staff time*

Much of the work of doctors of all grades and other medical staff will be done specifically for one patient. Such work will involve diagnosis, consultations and treatment procedures. This is all work for an individual patient case; that is it relates to one individual unit of clinical output. If this time is recorded on a timesheet costs can then be allocated to specific treatments. Note although the costs were incurred for specific patients they need only be charged to treatment types. Thus all the staff costs associated with a hernia patient would be charged to hernia treatment – not the individual patient.

Any time that is spent for the benefit of all or many patients in contrast is best looked at as overhead. This means that the cost is spread evenly between all patients, a process which is discussed below.

The cost of nurses may be specific to individual patients or alternatively nurses may staff wards ministering to all patients. The majority of nurses' time, with the exception of theatre nurses, will be of the latter type. It is therefore best treated as an overhead along with hotel costs (see below). Theatre nurses will be accounted for in the hourly theatre rate with which the general surgery department is charged.

## *Direct use of assets*

Patients will be operated on in an operating theatre. This large piece of 'equipment' will be available for a large number of different budget holders. The costs of this facility are probably charged to different users on an hourly basis. All you as a budget holder need do is divide the total usage between your different treatments (not patients) on a time and hence a cost basis.

There may be other pieces of major equipment that you use from time to time which you will need to charge in a similar way.

## *Pharmacy and supplies*

When drugs, sterile supplies or other purchased items are required then you will need to charge them to specific treatment types. This will require a form to 'Issue Note' whether the supply is from your own stock, the hospital store system or is specially purchased directly from the supplier.

Many small items such as syringes and small dressings may be used so often that it would be impossible to manage the paperwork if they were all charged to individual patients. Items worth less than say £5 are probably best considered as a departmental overhead. These are discussed later.

Say a specific treatment type requires a stores item costing £250 or a £50 dose of a drug. Each time such an item was used in a treatment an issue note would have to be written out and passed to the bookkeeper. He or she would then ensure that the cost was accounted for. Another method of achieving the same result would be to analyse a stores usage listing. All major issues could then be ascribed to specific treatments.

## *Work done by other departments*

Every treatment will involve testing or other work by radiologists and other specialist staff. There will also be pathology laboratory costs. You may already receive charges for these services in which case you will have to divide these costs between your patients on the basis of actual usage. If you are not charged then until the accounting system becomes more sophisticated ignore these costs.

### *Hotel costs*

One of the biggest costs of hospital treatment is the expenditure on buildings, heating, lighting, laundry and catering. As we discussed above the majority of nursing costs are probably best included under this category as well. These costs together can be referred to as hotel costs. In general they do not vary with the disease from which a patient is suffering; instead they are affected by length of stay.

When trying to account for hotel costs little work is needed to ascribe actual costs to treatments. Most expenditure will not relate to individual treatments because the costs are in many cases shared by a whole hospital. All that is needed is to calculate an average cost per patient day per hospital. This will have been done by the accounts department so all you need to do is record the number of days each patient stays in the hospital.

### *Other overheads*

There will be other costs not described above that a department incurs. As long as the costs can be easily ascribed to individual treatment types or are small, then the expenditure should be divided between patients on the basis of days spent as inpatients. Any other reasonable basis could be used. Included in this category of costs would be time spent by medical staff for the benefit off all patients.

The administrative costs of the whole hospital or unit are another source of overhead. For the purposes of this exercise it is probably best to ignore these costs because they are only distantly affected by the actions of your department.

## Summary

By now you along with Fred Asherton are probably thinking that you have quite enough work already without becoming an amateur accountant as well. How then are you going to practically implement measurements of clinical outputs in your department?

The first requirement is to seek advice from the accounts department or possibly from your internal or external auditors. Not everyone will be blessed with a daughter-in-law who is also a chartered accountant. There are a number of accounting problems to overcome and the early involvement of professional help will pay off.

To get useful data you do not need to wait for hospital-wide modern costing and resource management systems. Much can be done with a small personal computer with a 'spreadsheet' program or a proprietory time recording system. Such programs will be useful for many of the procedures that you will need to do. For instance the time recording system could be used for the following:

1. Processing timesheets by converting hours worked to costs;
2. Setting up records of specific treatment costs;
3. Allocating hotel costs and overheads to patients.

Once you have set up a system to calculate costs for each clinical output you need to think how you are going to operate the system. You have a number of options.

### *Use of a secretary part time*

Many of the most important figures could be collated by a secretary working a day a week. He or she could process timesheets for 15 to 20 staff and analyse operating theatre costs, laboratory costs and hotel expenditure. All the figures could be collated on a small microcomputer.

This option has the benefits of simplicity and control. But it lacks in comprehensiveness and probably accuracy. It is also a relatively expensive way of providing information since you would have to spend quite a lot of time assisting in the production of monthly reports.

### *Teaming up with other departments*

Another way of getting the information would be to team up with other interested departments so that the costs of obtaining management data could be shared. A book-keeper or part qualified accountant could be employed full-time to analyse costs and to present monthly reports. This is a much better solution that (1) above but could still lead to imperfect information. The cost, however, would be attractive at perhaps £20–30 000 a year or 0.25% of a combined budget of £12 000 000 for say three budget holders.

### *Unit costing for the whole authority or trust*

The ideal solution is that the whole authority or trust should set up an accounting system to measure clinical outputs. At the moment many authorities are not ready for this move because their accounts departments are still implementing the changes caused by the first phase of the internal market system. However, it is necessary that unit costing is implemented as soon as possible. Pressure from budget holders can only hasten that implementation.

## The results of measurement

What will the figures look like once all the procedures described above have been implemented?

After some rather half-hearted attempts at accounting for clinical outputs Fred Asherton's final monthly output figures were quite comprehensive. On Alice's advice he had managed to persuade the health authority accounts department to provide assistance. They had started to use him as an experimental department in the introduction of output accounting throughout the authority.

Table 8.9 is an example of the figures that Fred Asherton is obtaining. It shows the

**Table 8.9** General Surgery Department – surgical treatment of cancer of the gut, period 8

| | *Average for previous 12 months* | | | | *Previous period* | | | | *Period 8* | | | *Actual usage* | *Standard production* | | | | | *Quantity variances* | | *Price variance* |
|---|---|---|---|---|---|---|---|---|---|---|---|---|---|---|---|---|---|---|---|---|
| | *Price* | *Quantity* | *£* | *Usage* | *Price* | *Quantity* | *£* | *Usage* | *Price* | *Quantity* | *£* | *Hours* | *Price* | *Quantity* | *£* | *Usage* | *Quantity* | *Yield 000* | *Production 000* | *000* |
| Clinical output | | 16 | | | | 19 | | | | 21 | | | | 15 treatments | | | | | | |
| Direct treatment costs | | | | | | | | | | | | | | | | | | | | |
| Consultants | 35 | 88 | 3 080 | 5.5 | 35 | 96.9 | 3 392 | 5.1 | 35 | 102.9 | 3 602 | 4.9 | 35 | 75 hours | 2 625 | 5 | 27.9 | 73.5 | −1 050 | 0 |
| Medical | 17 | 115.2 | 1 958 | 7.2 | 17 | 138.7 | 2 358 | 7.3 | 17 | 153.3 | 2 606 | 7.3 | 17 | 105 hours | 1 785 | 7 | 48.3 | −107.1 | −714 | 0 |
| Theatre | 213 | 52.8 | 11 246 | 3.3 | 213 | 58.9 | 12 546 | 3.1 | 198 | 60.9 | 12 058 | 2.9 | 200 | 45 hours | 9 000 | 3 | 15.9 | 420 | −3 600 | 121.8 |
| Pharmacy and supplies | 81 | 16 | 1 296 | 1 | 70 | 19 | 1 330 | 1 | 75 | 21 | 1 575 | 1 | 71 | 15 units | 1 065 | 1 | 6 | 0 | −426 | −84 |
| | | | 17 581 | | | | 19 625 | | | | 19 841 | | | | 14 475 | | | 386.4 | −5 790 | 37.8 |
| Radiology and pathology | 275 | 16 | 4 400 | 1 | 275 | 19 | 5 225 | 1 | 275 | 21 | 5 775 | 1 | 275 | 15 units | 4 125 | 1 | 6 | 0 | −1 650 | 0 |
| | | | 21 981 | | | | 24 850 | | | | 25 616 | | | | 18 600 | | | 386.4 | −7 440 | 37.8 |
| Direct overheads (including nursing and hotel costs) | 1892 | 16 | 33 792 | 1 | 1727 | 19 | 32 813 | 1 | 1793 | 21 | 37 653 | 1 | 1760 | 15 units | 26 400 | 1 | 6 | 0 | −10 560 | −693 |
| TOTAL COSTS | | | 55 773 | | | | 57 663 | | | | 63 269 | | | | 45 000 | | | 386.4 | −18 000 | −655.2 |
| Average inpatient days per patient charged at a standard cost of GBP110 | | 19.2 | | | | 15.7 | | | | 16.3 | | | | 16 | | | | | | |
| Average cost per patient | | | 3 486 | | | | 3 035 | | | | 3 013 | | | | 3 000 | | | | | |

unit costs for surgical treatment of cancer of the gut. The year has been split into 13 equal four-week periods and comparative figures are given for the year as a whole and the previous period. The original budget together with standard cost figures is also shown.

Frederick Asherton now has average unit cost figures for each type of treatment for a period together with breakdowns of the reasons for variations in costs.

He is pleased with these figures because he has been able to reduce his costs by over 10% since the beginning of the year. His original standard gave a cost of £3000. This was in fact quite achievable but the figures at the beginning of the year averaging about £3300. They had budgeted for 16 days stay for each patient but patients were on average staying 19.2 days. On enquiry from ward staff Fred found that there was a problem notifying relatives when patients were to be discharged. Under the system they used a day's notice was normally given. This period was often too short and patients were kept in another two or three days while preparations were made for their reception at home. Once this became clear Fred arranged for relatives to be given proper notice and the results were immediately seen.

Other costs have been fine-tuned. One area of improvement that bodes well for the future concerns anaesthetists and theatre usage. Fred has started to interest one of the consultant anaesthetists in his management improvements. A result of this is an improvement in the efficiency of use of operating theatres. This can be seen from the favourable yield variance figures in Table 8.9. What other conclusions can you draw from the figures?

## Summary

Fred Asherton is beginning to be as professional in his management of resources as he has been for years with his surgery. In eight four-week periods he has increased his efficiency for treatment of cancer of the gut by 16%. He has analysed the times between referral, diagnosis and treatment and some of the results of this work have shocked him deeply. He has begun to measure the outcomes of the treatment he gives. There is much still to do but he is pleased to see that with effort the service he gives is steadily improving.

## Reader questionnaire

ANSWERS

1. Is your department or organization as successful as you are?
2. What is your 'waiting list' time?
3. If you were a client of your own department how would you judge your quality of service?
4. Are you prepared to stand up to your colleagues and insist on measurement of quantity and quality of services?
5. Are you prepared to set up productivity and quality measurement systems making the best of available resources or will you sit and wait until everybody is forced to measure achievement?

# Case study III – education: a school budget – Templeman Primary School

This case study is about a primary school with 238 pupils and ten staff. The school is managed by the governors and the headteacher and her staff under the 'Local Management in Schools' scheme set out in the Education Reform Act 1988. The case study is designed to illustrate how outputs could be measured in a school. It is not meant convey a particular educational message. The measurement techniques described can be adapted to the specific needs and philosophies of different schools.

The school is well liked in its area and is considered to be relatively successful. The school is not generally oversubscribed but it is unusual if there are more than 30 spare places at the beginning of each school year.

The headteacher, Hilary Kent, is aware that a good education is increasingly important to children as more and more jobs require people with some form of tertiary education. Traditionally the majority of Templeman Primary School pupils have left the education system at 16. This is not a state of affairs that Ms Kent wishes to perpetuate.

Parents of the children at Templeman are keen that their children are successful at school but at times they do not seem to fully understand the importance of tangible educational success. Hilary Kent puts this down to what she calls the English respect for amateurism and muddling through. Whatever the causes the parents at the school are caring about their childrens' happiness but a little unclear about the real advantages available to the well-educated young person.

## Quality and productivity

Hilary Kent is looking for a way of improving the achievement of her pupils at primary school. The option of attempting to encourage brighter children to enter the school at five is not a solution for her; she wants to serve better her existing clientele. To do this she must work for the highest standards and obtain the best possible use of financial and educational resources by improving quality and productivity.

Unlike at a hospital or a housing benefit office the definitions of quality and productivity in education can be complex. But the pupils must get good assessment results; if they do not then the goal of tertiary education will be denied them. The children must also be reasonably well behaved and show an independence and confidence of mind. In this way they are more likely to be successful in whatever they do.

So the quality of education Hilary Kent is trying to provide will involve achieving good exam results, and encouraging self-confidence and self-control in her charges. The 'productivity' so to speak will be the quantity of these qualities she can squeeze from the budget she is given each year.

Just as for medicine the term 'productivity' is inappropriate for a profession such as teaching. We will substitute the phrase 'school achievement' for the concept of productivity.

# Legal objectives

The objectives of the primary school system are laid down in the Education Act 1944 and the Education Reform Act 1988. They can be summarized as follows:

1. To promote the education of the people (s1 EA 1944).
2. To secure . . . a broadly based curriculum which
   (a) Promotes the spiritual, moral, cultural, mental and physical development of pupils at the school and society.
   (b) Prepares such pupils for the opportunities, responsibilities and experiences of adult life (s1 ERA 1988).
3. To secure . . . curriculum 'attainment targets', 'programmes of study' and 'assessment arrangements' (s2 ERA 1988).

Compared to many public services education objectives are quite detailed. This is because the Education Reform Act sets down a national curriculum and assessment systems. The improvements that Hilary Kent wants to make to the school must complement the national curriculum and the assessment process. In fact her wants for the school are very similar to those laid down in statute and we do not need to list any additional objectives.

# Educational achievement

In the housing benefit and hospital case studies the timescale between action and achievement was often very small. An expensive operation may take just four hours. In a school the achievement from four hours work will be very much harder to measure! Instead measurement of output must be over a longer period than we have seen so far.

Another major difference between this case study and the two before is the nature of the costs involved. In a hospital expenditure is relatively flexible. If a complex heart pacemaker is required then costs will increase by £10 000 instantaneously. In a school most of the costs are fixed costs and as long as there are no major purchases of equipment or books, costs will clock up at a relatively constant daily rate. For both these reasons this case study will be quite different from the two previous ones.

## Definition

As we discussed in Chapter 6 educational outputs are represented by the achievement of turning young and uneducated children into older educated individuals. The concept of output is obvious; it is the stimulation and development of individual children so that they can develop to the best of their ability. Although output is not difficult to recognize it is difficult to measure. In addition it is difficult to match the achievement of the output to the use of teacher time and materials. In the next section we look at how we can start to overcome this problem.

## Measurement

If achievement is the increase in 'education' of a pupil over a set period of time then we need to measure this achievement. When we have done that we can then look at how we can best use resources to maximize the achievements we measure.

If, for instance, we test or assess in some objective way a child at the beginning of a term and again at the end then it is possible to measure an increase in achievement over that time period. Over that same time period costs will be incurred. If we divide the costs for the period by the increase in achievement, we will get a 'productivity' or 'educational achievement' figure. Let us illustrate this with a small example.

Thirty pupils are assessed at the beginning of term. The class is given the total score of 95. This is the total of each child's individual assessment. It represents an average of 3.17 per pupil. At the end of term they are tested again. They obtain a score of 137 – an average of 4.57 each.

Teaching and material costs for the term were £34 450.

The 'Educational Achievement' is therefore 1.4 points per pupil at £820 per point per pupil (£34 500/137–95). This figure may compare with 1.2 points per pupil for the same class last year with a cost of £695 per point.

Of course, this form of measurement is extremely crude. Children will vary significantly from year to year and the assessments themselves will probably not be very accurate. But as with all management information it is better to have some objectively measured data than none. Even the crudest measurements are infinitely superior to inspired guesswork alone.

## The national curriculum and standard assessment tasks

Any attempts at measurement of achievement should be compatible with the assessment requirements of the Education Reform Act. At Templeman Primary School, Hilary Kent is attempting to base her measurement system on the Standard Assessment Tasks which have been set down by central government under the act. These tasks take the form of 10 levels of attainment covering performance from the age of 5 to 16 when GCSE examinations are taken. Hilary Kent intends to use the first five levels for her school.

As we can see in Table 8.10 a number of other measurements will also be taken of pupil achievement. These will include weekly tests in the main subjects taught, and subjective teacher assessments of each pupil's well-being and development. There will also be monitoring of staff turnover, and parents' and neighbours' complements and complaints.

**Table 8.10** Primary education – objectives

| *Objectives* | *Definition* | *Measurement educational achievement* | *Quality* |
|---|---|---|---|
| 1. Promotion of education | (a) Teacher assessments of:<br>– general education<br>– self-confidence<br>– independence and maturity | Marks are awarded on a point system for all three outputs as one.<br>One point represents one unit of output. | Quality will be measured under the following headings:<br>Timeliness – N/A.<br>Parent and Pupil Satisfaction<br>– Number of compliments and complaints<br>– Numbers on school roll<br>– Staff Turnover<br>Success<br>Short Term<br>– % of children reaching satisfactory assessments.<br>Long term<br>– Review of the achievements of pupils after leaving the school. |
| 2. Secure a curriculum | (b) N/A | N/A | |
| 3. Set assessment targets | (c) Assessments by teachers of educational achievement in Curriculum subjects. | Marks awarded on a points system.<br>One point represents one unit of output. | Quality will be measured under the following headings:<br>Timeliness – N/A.<br>Parent and pupil satisfaction<br>– as for 1. above.<br>Success<br>– % of children attaining grades at the expected age. |

Hilary Kent has devised the measurement system illustrated in this case study herself in response to the National Curriculum and her own views on the importance of education. She feels that it is not possible to leave the success of a child's education to chance. By measuring Templeman Primary School's success she feels that she is doing all that is possible to respond to her pupils real needs.

# Hilary Kent's assessment system

Hilary Kent's system of measurement works on the basis of assigning costs to raising children from one Standard Assessment Task to the next.

For the purpose of this case study only the three core subjects of the National Curriculum will be dealt with. These subjects are English, mathematics and science. We assume for simplicity that no other subjects are taught.

For the five complete years after the age of six that children attend Templeman Primary School there are five Standard Assessment Tasks – one for each year. When tested at the end of 'Key Stage 1' ideally all pupils will be able to achieve Standard Assessment Task 1. After 'Key Stage 2' at the age of 11 again pupils should be able to achieve Standard Assessment Task 5.

## Detailed measurement

The Standard Assessment Tasks are spaced at roughly yearly intervals. Hilary Kent needs information on a much shorter timescale that this so that she can continually monitor progress, control events and take decisions. She achieves this by the use of graded three-weekly assessments.

## Three-weekly assessments

Class teachers set a major piece of work every week for each core subject. This work is used to motivate children and to allow class teachers to monitor each individual child. Hilary Kent, as headteacher, reviews the results of the weekly pieces of set work but her main interest is in the three-weekly assessments that she uses as part of her overall measurement system.

The three-weekly tests take the same form as the weekly work but are more carefully set. The aim is to divide the Assessment Task for a year into ten graduated stages. For instance, after Assessment Task 3 there will be ten three-weekly pieces of work for each core subject until Assessment Task 4 is reached.

If a child obtains a mark of 60% (12 out of 20) or above in a three-weekly test then the Assessment Task will have been achieved. For instance if 60% was achieved for the third test after Assessment Task 3 this would give a level of 3.3. If a lower mark is obtained then the level below will be scored. If a child repeatedly scores low marks or poor assessments, say below 40%, then a subjective decision is taken as to which level is achieved.

At least for the purposes of the weekly tests children are streamed on the basis of ability. This means that children need not take a full year to cover one Assessment Task. If a child is particularly able only six or seven three-weekly tests will be needed to cover an Assessment Task. This means that children in one year can cover a wide range of Assessment Tasks at any one time.

## Costs

In order to decide how to run the school best with the resources available. Hilary Kent needs to know where to target resources. Should she try to maximize staff numbers by using 'classroom assistants' as well as qualified staff? This might be an effective way of helping the children at the lower Assessment Tasks. Another strategy would be to attract a few staff of exceptional ability perhaps by paying above the scale rate for the grade. A third method would be to invest heavily in staff training. There are many possibilities but their relative success needs to be measured.

Hilary Kent has eight forms at Templeman Primary School. Classes contain children at two or exceptionally three different Assessment Tasks levels. The class structure is shown in Table 8.11.

Ideally, from a measurement viewpoint, classes would have only one age group and teach only at one Assessment Task level. In most primary schools this is not possible although in a large secondary school with streaming, it is. At Templeman Primary School, Hilary Kent is content to assign costs to classes. In this way she will be able to connect one teacher and his or her costs including non-salary costs, with the achievement recorded on the assessments. Below we see how this was achieved in practice.

## Cost of achievement

In Table 8.12 we show an extract from Hilary Kent's management data for period 6. From this, we can see that Ms Kent has assigned costs to classes. Where teachers put

**Table 8.11** Class structure at Templeman Primary School

| *Class* | *Age* | *Assessment task* | *No.* |
|---|---|---|---|
| 1 | 5 | N/A | 25 |
| 2 | 5–6 | 1–2 | 31 |
| 3 | 6–7 | 1–3 | 33 |
| 4 | 6–8 | 2–3 | 36 |
| 5 | 7–9 | 3–4 | 29 |
| 6 | 8–10 | 4–5 | 25 |
| 7 | 9–11 | 4–5 | 33 |
| 8 | 10–11 | 5 | 26 |
| | | | 238 |

**Table 8.12** Templeman Primary School – educational achievement statement, period 6

| | *Annual budget total costs* | *Period budget* | *Period actual* | £ *Class 1* | £ *Class 2* | £ *Class 3* | £ *Class 4* | £ *Class 5* | £ *Class 6* | £ *Class 7* | £ *Class 8* |
|---|---|---|---|---|---|---|---|---|---|---|---|
| Teachers | 156 350 | 15 635 | 15 804 | 1766 | 1877 | 1455 | 2188 | 1989 | 1641 | 2477 | 2411 |
| Classroom assistants | 17 600 | 1 760 | 2 194 | 722 | 750 | | 722 | | | | |
| Teacher training costs (inc. costs of supply staff) | 22 400 | 2 240 | 1 323 | | | 670 | | | 653 | | |
| Supplies | 1 500 | 150 | 227 | 9 | 7 | 23 | | 130 | 5 | | 53 |
| | 197 850 | 19 785 | 19 548 | 2497 | 2634 | 2148 | 2910 | 2119 | 2299 | 2477 | 2464 |
| Other employees | 18 150 | 1 815 | 1 815 | 191 | 236 | 252 | 275 | 221 | 191 | 252 | 198 |
| Premises costs | 22 450 | 2 245 | 2 245 | 236 | 292 | 311 | 340 | 274 | 236 | 311 | 245 |
| Other costs | 5 700 | 570 | 570 | 60 | 74 | 79 | 86 | 69 | 60 | 79 | 62 |
| (A) TOTAL COSTS | 244 150 | 24 415 | 24 178 | 2983 | 3237 | 2790 | 3610 | 2683 | 2785 | 3119 | 2970 |
| (B) Number of children in each class | | | | 25 | 31 | 33 | 36 | 29 | 25 | 33 | 26 |
| (C) Total assessment score for period 6 for each class | | | | N/A | 60.45 | 82.49 | 107.28 | 110.78 | 112.25 | 170.94 | 154.96 |
| (D) Assessment score for previous period | | | | N/A | 55.80 | 79.53 | 101.16 | 108.17 | 110.00 | 166.98 | 152.10 |
| (E) Increase in assessment score for period (C–D) | | | | N/A | 4.65 | 2.96 | 6.12 | 2.61 | 2.25 | 3.96 | 2.86 |
| (F) Increase per child (E/B) | | | | | 0.15 | 0.09 | 0.17 | 0.09 | 0.09 | 0.12 | 0.11 |
| Cost per point per child Total costs/increase in assessment score (A/E) | | | | | 696 | 943 | 590 | 1028 | 1238 | 788 | 1038 |
| Previous period | | | | N/A | 668 | 1102 | 701 | 1110 | 1205 | 890 | 1001 |
| Average cost in year | | | | N/A | 681 | 1067 | 615 | 1231 | 1213 | 806 | 1085 |

time to a specific class this is charged to a class using timesheets where this is necessary. Some teachers spend all their time with their form or preparing work for it. Others put time into a number of classes. When a teacher takes assembly or another task which affects the whole school the time is split on the timesheet between classes on a pro rata basis based on the number of pupils in each class. Other direct costs are charged to the class that benefits. These costs include classroom assistants' time training and supplies.

The methods used by Hilary Kent are reviewed later. At the moment let us look at the results shown by the data.

## Review of the period 6 results

The key figures on the spread sheet are the 'Cost per Point' figures at the bottom. These show the educational achievement gained from the financial resources used. Before you read on it would be useful to briefly review the results.

We can see that a wide range of costs per point were obtained. The lowest was £590 and the highest was £1238. Let us look at the figures in more detail.

One of the highest cost per point figures was obtained from the relatively small top class. The children on average performed well. But the cost was high. The much larger Class 7 produced similar average achievements from the children also with a teacher with substantial experience. The cost here was £787 or nearly 25% less. The lesson here appears to be that for Templeman School it is best to use large class sizes to obtain the maximum from experienced staff.

The lowest cost per point came from Class 4. This was also a large class; it contains 36 pupils. Hilary Kent's idea of using a classroom assistant has paid off and despite the extra cost, costs per point are excellent.

Both of the classes subject to measurement with unqualified classroom assistants have produced good educational results and good costs per point. Ms Kent is considering using more assistants further up the school. At present, however, she thinks that larger class sizes and highly experienced staff have not only the cost benefits shown by Class 7 but also balance the staffing structure of the school. The benefits of mature staff are seen in her analyses of pupil self-confidence and behaviour.

Classes 3 and 6 have young teachers who are undergoing considerable training which is resulting in fees and heavy supply teacher costs.

The teacher of Class 5 has recently been on a number of training courses after a suggestion by Hilary. The teacher, Mr Appleby always had difficulties keeping order and this was reflected in poor results from his pupils and terrible cost per point figures. Since his return from a two-week residential course substantial improvements appear to be on the way. His cost per point dropped from an average of £1200 to about £1000.

Within the figures there are some quirks which probably do not represent an underlying trend. The results of Class 3 this Period look suspiciously good. In contrast the period 5 figures for Class 4 appear to represent a 'blip'. The same applies to the same period for Class 7.

## Producing the figures

When Hilary Kent had the idea of measuring the 'educational achievement' of Templeman Primary School she was not quite certain how to obtain the figures she needed. After talking to one of the school governors who is an accountant she began to understand what was required. With a rough idea of her needs she approached the accounts department of the Local Education Authority and after a morning's work together they created a system for producing the figures needed.

## Equipment

Hilary needed a small personal computer which cost about £700 including a printer and 'spreadsheet' software. Because the school is quite small even the most basic machine was adequate. In addition it could be used for the school budgets and for word processing. All that was needed in addition was a stack of timesheets.

What Hilary needed to be able to do was to allocate costs to classes. Figure 8.9 shows a timesheet as used at Templeman Primary School.

Ms Kent had to calculate the hourly rate for each teacher. Teachers are paid monthly thoughout the year whether it be term time or holidays. Ms Kent wanted to charge the cost of teachers to the lessons they taught and on which assessments were made. Since the assessment periods cover 30 weeks a year (10 three-weekly assessments) pay costs for the measurement system were calculated as follows: for example

| Paul Appleby – Teacher of Class 5 | £ |
|---|---|
| Gross salary per annum | 13 990 |
| Employers' National Insurance and Superannuation | 1 460 |
| Total pay cost | 15 450 |
| Days teaching class (FTE) | 150 |
| Cost per teaching day | 103 |

Name: Paul Appleby　　Three Week Period No.: 6

| Class | Days 1 2 3 4 . . . 13 14 15 | Total | Narrative |
|---|---|---|---|
| 1 | | | |
| 2 | | | |
| 3 | .5 .5 | 3 | English 3 |
| 4 | | | |
| 5 | 1 .5 .1 . . . .5 1 .5 | 12 | English 6.5<br>Maths 5.5 |
| 6 | | | |
| 7 | | | |
| 8 | | | |
| All | 1 1 1 . . . 1 1 1 | 15 | |

**Fig. 8.9** Templeman Primary School – staff timesheet.

Using the times from the timesheets we can construct the total cost of Class 5 for period 6.

| *Staff time* | *Subject* | *Days* | *Cost per teaching day* | *Total* |
|---|---|---|---|---|
| Mr Appleby | English | 6.5 | 103.00 | 669.50 |
| | Mathematics | 5.5 | 103.00 | 566.50 |
| Mrs Casanove | Science | 3.0 | 169.11 | 507.34 |
| Ms Kent | Admin | 1.25 | 196.53 | 245.66 |
| | | 16.25 | | 1989.00 |
| Classroom assistants | | | | |
| | | N/A | | N/A |
| Teacher training | | | | |
| | | N/A | | N/A |
| Supplies | | | | |
| English books | | | | 105.00 |
| Wall posters | | | | 25.00 |
| | | | | 130.00 |
| TOTAL | | | | 2119.00 |

Class 5 had no classroom assistant costs or teacher training and supply teacher expenditure. All staff costs whether they are qualified people or not are charged on the basis of timesheets. The cost of teacher training courses and supplies are charged on the basis of the amount billed.

In period 6 Class 5 was charged for 16.25 days of teacher time although there were only 15 working days in the period. This may appear odd until it is realized that with ten full-time teachers to cover only eight classes more time is spent than there is lesson time because teachers have to carry out some preparation and administrative work. In addition Hilary Kent charges administration time through her time sheets to all classes although she does like to take each class for at least one lesson a week. So what has Hilary Kent learned from all this analysis?

She has being running the system for just over a year now and she has already benefited much from the system. Until she started to calculate the cost of small class sizes she had not realized how expensive they were. Very much better results are required if they are to be cost effective. It was because of this that she considered using classroom assistants for the junior classes. That strategy has clearly paid off.

One of the benefits she most likes is the facility to monitor the benefits of training. This has allowed her to be much more selective in the courses she sends her staff on. Not all training produces results and with such tight budgets ineffective training is too much of a luxury. In contrast Mr Appleby's training course appears to be producing results. She will monitor the figures with interest over the next few periods before she draws a firm conclusion.

Although the system measures the relative increase in performance in the children there is one drawback Hilary Kent is aware of. A bright child may be at Task 4 whereas another child of the same age may be at Task 3. It will be easier to raise the bright child by one point than the other. In this respect Ms Kent's system relies on an even mix of abilities in each class. The system is much better than looking at exam grades achieved but those teachers with a predominance of under average children will still find it more difficult to produce good results. She is aware of this and tries to take this into account in her decision making.

## The measurement of general educational and personal qualities

The Education Act 1944 requires that a child receives an education rather than just obtains good exam results. In Fig. 8.10 it can be seen that Hilary Kent is attempting to measure the achievement of this objective by the use of a point based assessment system in the same way as she attempts to measure attainments under the National Curriculum.

The system works as follows. Every term each child is assessed for his or her general educational level and development using a questionnaire with multiple choice boxes for each answer. Assessment sheets are filled in by class teachers and are reassessed and altered if necessary by other teachers who also teach the child. In this way a balanced assessment is provided. A Part of the questionnaire appears as Fig. 8.10.

Points given range from 0 to 15 mirroring the assessment system used for the National Curriculum which was shown above. Hilary Kent produces a termly Achievement Statement in exactly the same format as the one in Table 8.12. The cost per point figures are carefully reviewed.

**Name**: Sydney Smith **Class**: 4 **Age**: 7 1/2

Mark each pupil on a scale from 0 to 15 where, as an example, 4 equates to the behaviour expected of the average child on his or her 4th birthday and 11 to that of a child on his or her 11th birthday. A 6 1/2 year old of slightly above average achievement might receive the score of 6.8.

A score must be given for each question.

| | |
|---|---|
| *General behaviour* | |
| Maturity of general behaviour: | |
| 1. In class | 6.9 |
| 2. Playing organized games | 7.2 |
| 3. At play | 6.5 |
| *Self-expression* | |
| 4. Use of vocabulary | 8.5 |
| 5. Lucidity of speech | 8.5 |
| 6. Confidence to speak in front of others | 8.0 |
| 7. Strength of written expression | |
| *General knowledge* | |
| 20. Grasp of general knowledge | 8.8 |
| TOTAL SCORE | 158.0 |
| ASSESSMENT SCORE (total score/20) | 7.9 |

**Fig. 8.10** Pupil general educational assessment questionnaire.

The results of this assessment have to be taken into account when making decisions based on the National Curriculum assessment we have already looked at. There are sometimes conflicts. For instance smaller classes produce better results when considerations of character and general education are taken into account. Other issues have been noted by Ms Kent for instance experienced teachers appear to produce better general results than younger individuals. The assessment system also supported Hilary Kent's decision to use classroom assistants.

## Measurement of quality

Hilary Kent has also produced methods of measuring the quality of Templeman Primary School's work under the headings of 'parent and pupil satisfaction' and 'success'. Let us first look at 'success'.

Under the systems used to measure 'school achievement' the relative quantity of education imparted in a period of time was measured. If the increase per period is satisfactory then the absolute level of achievement should also be adequate. However it is clearly important to measure the absolute achievement as well.

This measurement involves ensuring that each child is at the level that would be expected at his or her age. The National Curriculum set attainment targets at Key

Class: 4 Date:

| Name | Academic | | | General | | |
|---|---|---|---|---|---|---|
| | Points A | Expected B | (%) C | Points D | Expected E | (%) F |
| 1. Jason O'Donnell | 2.85 | 2.9 | −1.7 | 6.9 | 6.5 | +6.2 |
| 2. Kathy Wright | 2.98 | 2.7 | +10.3 | 7.0 | 6.8 | +2.9 |
| 3. Sidney Smith | 3.50 | 2.9 | +20.7 | 7.9 | 7.5 | +5.3 |
| 4. Vera Short | 2.53 | 2.5 | +1.2 | 6.5 | 6.5 | – |
| 33. Kylie Spagg | 2.98 | 2.8 | +6.4 | 6.2 | 6.8 | −7.8 |
| 34. Rachel Watmough | 2.80 | 2.8 | – | 7.3 | 7.0 | +4.3 |
| 35. Bill Nutton | 3.23 | 3.5 | −7.7 | 7.9 | 8.2 | −3.7 |
| 36. Boris Pavlov | 2.98 | 3.0 | −0.7 | 6.9 | 7.0 | −1.4 |
| TOTAL SCORE | 107.28 | 100.8 | | 269.1 | 270.0 | |
| AVERAGE | 2.98 | 2.8 | | 7.48 | 7.5 | |
| Percentage difference | | | +6.4 | | | −6.7 |

A = Actual academic achievement measured using three-weekly assessment procedures.
B = Expected achievement based on Standard Assessment Tasks.
C = 1-A/B, the percentage difference between actual and expected achievement.
D = Actual general behaviour assessment measured using the termly assessment sheets (see Fig. 8.10).
E = Expected general behaviour for age at each Standard Assessment Task.
F = 1-D/E, the percentage difference between actual and expected achievement.

**Fig. 8.11** Pupil achievement record.

Stages 1 and 2. All that Hilary Kent needs to do is to review the achievement of each child in respect of its age and any other matters of importance. Having done the assessment she then matches the results to an 'expected achievement profile'. This is a target level that she sets each year.

Again by making these measurements she can control the achievement of the school better and can make decisions based on objective information. Figure 8.11 shows a summary of results for Class 4. Academic results were good whereas the quality of general education was below standard.

## Long-term monitoring

Hilary Kent takes care to check the educational achievements of all the children that pass through Templeman. She collates their GCSE results and 'A' Levels grades for those that stay on as they progress through the education system. She also tries to discover whether they go on to further education. The results achieved are plotted on a graph which is kept on the wall of her study. Hilary produces these figures for three reasons. First, she has a natural interest in all her pupils; second, it provides some indication of the longer term success of her work and last, it allows her to suggest good secondary schools to parents. On the basis of these figures Hilary likes to think that Templeman Primary School under her control really does provide a good start to life.

## Parent and pupil satisfaction

A number of methods are used to try to measure this rather intangible quality. Hilary Kent monitors and collates all compliments and complaints received from parents and from those that live near the school. She produces a parent and pupil questionnaire to obtain directly the opinions of her 'clients'. She also keeps firm control over staff turnover. Before any member of staff leaves she carries out a debriefing interview where she asks probing and sometimes embarrassingly direct questions to try to discover where improvements could be made in the school.

# Summary

By now it must be clear that Hilary Kent is a determined individual who is not satisfied with second best. Neither does she believe in inspired amateurism. She is a professional who likes to take decisions based on evidence and not surmise.

All the different measurement systems she uses are bound into a coherent whole. In this way all control and decision making is based on a complete set of information. When making a management decision she will consider the cost per point data for each class, evidence for parent satisfaction, and the absolute attainment level for her school.

Altogether this provides a potent mix on which to base professional judgements. And this is a fact about which Hilary is justly proud.

## Reader questionnaire

ANSWERS

1. If you strive for excellence are you prepared to measure your achievement like Hilary Kent was?
2. Are you afraid of linking costs to human achievements and aspirations?
3. In a world of scarce resources is it moral to manage using 'inspired guesswork'? If not, what objective assessment techniques do you use?
4. Staff training is an investment. Its prime purpose is to cut costs and increase quality. Do you agree?
5. The public services need the best staff for the job. This means that the best qualified or the most experienced may be a wasteful luxury for many basic tasks. Could you usefully employ the equivalent of 'classroom assistants'?
6. Do your management methods provide a 'potent mix on which to base professional judgements'?

# 9

# Managing for excellence

In Chapters 6, 7 and 8 we were concerned with the practical problem of measuring productivity and quality. In this chapter we look at how this information can be used to improve the achievement of the organization to which you belong. It is about managing for excellence. We can use an analogy to explain what this means.

Let us assume you are trying to learn to run faster – perhaps you have entered a race to be held at the end of next month. You have some running equipment – shorts, vest and shoes but you do not have two things, a measured track to practice on or a stopwatch. This means that for training you just run for as long as seems reasonable over a distance that also appears adequate. You do not have to be an Olympic athlete to know that this is not the way to train. Ten days before the race you are a little worried that your running is unfocused and that you do not know your real ability. Then out of the blue a friend gives you a surveyor's tape and a stop watch. Now at least you can measure your real achievement and begin to work on those areas of your running that are weakest.

But there is more to the training of athletes than the measurement of abilities. Runners continue to break world records because training and management techniques continue to improve. There are always newer and better ways of using measurements of achievement to improve performance. The introduction of measurement is a first-rate start, but there is more to management and achieving value for money. The way information is used is important.

## Management and the social sciences

Considering that so much management is practised every day throughout the world it is astonishing how little can be agreed as objective truth. Management theory shares common weaknesses with all the social sciences. After the Second World War many hoped that a rational organization of the world through the use of economics, sociology and even political science would bring quick and lasting benefits. In fact, many people have been disappointed and major readjustments in thought have been necessary. Keynesian economics is no longer considered a solution to economic problems. But the period over which its fallibility was questioned was long and, for many, painful. Socialism appears to have done little to prevent poverty and crime in the big cities of the world. Political science would appear to carry little sway with our politicians or the electorate.

Compared to the hopes of the 1950s and 1960s this is perhaps a dismal picture. The centrally ordered world envisaged has not appeared. We still live in a world of diversity and at times chaos. But in many areas some of the beneficial changes that social science seeks to promote have been accomplished. The 1987 stock market crash was remarkable for its inconsequence rather than the catastrophe predictable from its illustrious predecessor in 1929. The world economy is being managed in a much more coordinated way than in the pre-war period. GATT and Bretton Woods represent very significant achievements. And in politics the norm of representative democracy has been relatively successful in a wide range of situations even before the revolutions in Eastern Europe. Throughout the world there is a movement away from dictatorship towards more pluralistic systems.

There is one common link between these changes. They were not in the main directed from the top by political, academic or intellectual leaders. They were generated from the bottom by the demands of society as a whole. The intellectual dogma of Keynsian economics fell not because academics decided on different approaches but because politicians found they could not win elections using reflationary policies. The dictatorship of Eastern Europe did not fall because of social scientific learning but because people took power into their own hands.

But just because the social sciences have not led these changes does not mean that social science is unimportant. We despairingly need ideas on how societies can better organize their activities. But we cannot generally expect these new ideas to be imposed from the top. Human activities are too diverse for this approach to be successful. Beneficial change is pragmatic. Academic and intellectual ideas are needed to cast reality into a clearer light and to suggest possible solutions which can be used as appropriate. They will not lead change, but they will give it direction.

We can see this happening in the public services. Measurement of productivity and quality is not some theoretical idea being demanded by intellectual opinion. Rather there is an insatiable public demand for higher quality services together with big productivity improverments. Since this is the case we must use the best of the methods academics have dreamed up to solve these challenges. Electorates are demanding higher quality and higher productivity. These twin goals are quite possible. To paraphrase President Kennedy, 'it is possible because we are American' (for American read human), or the renaissance Italian universal man Leon Battista Alberti who held that 'a man can do anything if he will'. And this leads us back to the mass of individual humans that make up the world. There is no more common a proverb than 'if there is a will there is a way'. Higher quality, cheaper public services are possible if we really want them.

# Trends effecting management

If the twin demands for increased public sector productivity and quality are not arbitrary and party political but rather demands of society itself, what are their causes? In Chapter 2, we discussed the effect that major changes in the way we live are having on all economic enterprises. It is these changes that are forcing 'bottom-up' changes in public services. The 'productivity divide', the 'demographic time-bomb' and the 'brain lust' are all demanding a management response.

## Management techniques

Powerful forces are already shaping the public sector and the way it operates. Issues of productivity and quality have raised themselves again and again and throughout the book we have stressed the idea of measurement as a prerequisite to all management reforms. This is because a constant theme in domestic politics is the public demand from their elected representatives for better more responsive services.

As the world becomes more complex and effective staff demand higher and higher salaries, there is pressure to cut the number of people directly employed in return for much higher achievement levels from them. A corollary of this is that contract staff are used to cover fluctuations in demand (remember the problem with the meat inspectors in Chapter 7) and to provide specialist skills. The introduction of compulsory competitive tendering was in part designed to accelerate the process of reducing the numbers of directly employed public sector staff.

Staff rolls will reduce further as productivity increases. More contract staff will be employed in a wide variety of roles – from solicitors to road sweepers. In this new dynamic world where costs are measured and known, where fluctuations in demand are catered for without large numbers of full-time staff, two points come into sharp focus. First, the art of management will get much more difficult. There will be a lot more measuring to start with, but communication with permanent staff and contract staff will be less direct and more subtle. Second, people will need to be trusted to act by themselves. This will be necessary because supervision will cost too much and also because the jobs being done will be too complex for more senior managers to comprehend quickly.

Some of these changes are already with us. All public sector managers know that the demands on them are increasing. More statistics are needed, good staff become more difficult to recruit and pay and conditions become individually negotiable. The days of fixed union rates are fast disappearing. The second aspect – more 'trust' in staff – has long existed in many parts of the public sector. Often this trust was more in the nature of abandonment. People are left to get on with the job with the assumption that everything is under control unless a disaster happens. The chief executive of a local authority will normally take very little interest in an environmental health department unless there is fraud or major public complaint. This form of trust is not the type of trust required. Rather people need to be left to take their own decisions but with the results of their decisions being closely monitored. We have yet again returned to the necessity to measure.

This new form of management is much more flexible than most people are used to. If you employ 1000 manual workers to do simple repetitive tasks clear orders are needed by managers to direct them. Obedience is a necessity of that method of organization. If you employ five people, three of whom hold degrees to do 100 difficult administration jobs then the concept of orders from above becomes difficult to understand. Rather you must encourage enthusiasm for their work, pay them well, treat them as individuals and expect high productivity and a first-rate service. You measure this achievement in the ways discussed in Chapter 7 and 8.

## Management by objectives

In the late 1950s and thereafter 'management by objectives', or MBO, was developed and implemented. This view of management was a formalization of management techniques developed over a long period of time. The idea was that management effort was concentrated on the key objectives of an enterprise. Those objectives were driven home with the full vigour of corporate might behind them.

Within the public sector a watered-down version of management by objectives is effectively in force. In many cases objectives may be poorly defined, but the emphasis is on top-down management. Looking back in time it can be seen that MBO worked very well in the mass production industries of the post-war period. It was a period of unparalleled growth and success, but one has to remember that Western countries were actively importing cheap labour from their, or other peoples' colonies to staff expanding industries. An immigrant peasant is a very different employee to a motivated graduate. This is not because one could be considered intrinsically more valuable as an individual than the other – one hopes that few people now hold such views – but because the type of work done by each is very different. The Algerian in a French car factory in the 1960s may have had as his sole 'responsibility' the provision of hub caps to wheels. His daughter perhaps a young graduate could be organizing a small sales department in a biotechnology company. His son, less academically able, might be a contract plasterer with irregular but good wage levels. The old simple full-time jobs are being replaced by high calibre office or technical jobs and contract work.

This change in the way enterprises staff themselves is having effects on the way in which they are managed.

## Staffing changes in the public sector

Until recently the public sector had shown very little change in its staffing structure from that inherited from Victorian times. Many public services were and still are very labour intensive. If we review the public sector outputs described in Chapter 6 this can be easily confirmed. Health, education, social work – all these activities tend to resist automation.

But change is affecting even the most resistant, and public sector enterprises are beginning to adapt to the use of much more flexible work forces. Local authorities no-longer employ manual staff directly. Many in the south of England have a few tens of manual staff whereas in the early 1980s a district council might have employed 800. In hospitals the reduction is at present less marked although this is certain to change. In the armed services the numbers of staff have been cut by a quarter, but cost will only fall by 6% because people are being replaced with expensive machines. You could argue that the Gulf War was won by 2000 pilots. This was productivity on a grand scale.

But whereas manual staff levels in public bodies have fallen we have yet to see reductions in the clerical, technical and professional workforce. The people at these grades have very tenaciously held onto their traditional perks so that while the private sector has had a decade slimming down middle management – British Airways sacked 20 000 managers after privatization, staff establishments in the public sector have remained static while real wages rose steeply.

This steep rise in salary costs cannot continue. Much of it was financed from buoyant tax incomes, steep rises in rates and community charge and interest receivable at high rates on the massive reserves held by many local authorities. If the status quo cannot continue how then will public sector enterprises work, especially if the demands on them increase, as they are bound to do?

In Chapter 6 we contrast an efficient industrial concern with an imaginary housing benefit department. There was a quantum difference between the management systems in the two organizations. One measured, set standards and monitored achievement; the other muddled through. Public sector bodies will move from one method of management to the other. The change will take place over the next five to six years. It will be rapid but it will not be ruthless. Attitudes will change fast, those who are unhappy with the new arrangements will go voluntarily leaving a small efficient dedicated workforce.

For all this to happen management methods must change. Rigid top-down orders will not produce the high productivity high quality public sector we need. This can only be achieved using small teams of people organizing themselves but monitored closely in terms of quality and productivity by senior management. The team will be paid on the basis of results not time put in.

All this seems very different to the public sector we know. But change will happen. No Western country can continue modifying one half of its economy but not the other. A new management system is needed for the public sector. It will be some form of 'total quality management'.

## Total quality management

Think for a moment about errors. How much of your time is spent rectifying misunderstandings, wrongly processed paperwork, taking inquiries about when a service will be delivered. Now guess the cost of all this as a percentage of the total cost of your department.

If your answer is 5% you need to think again. If your answer is 20% you are being or attempting to be realistic. If you say 40% this will probably be correct for many organizations. Walk into nearly any administrative office and the staff will be solving problems, not creating output. Clerks are on the telephone answering queries about delays and misunderstandings. Others are hunting for files. The manager is discussing why the books do not balance. Very few people will be assessing and processing productive work. The 40% figure is quite realistic for many service industries.

The major productivity and quality gains needed in the public sector will be obtained by reducing the 20–40% of costs spent rectifying errors. In Chapter 3 we said that a 20% improvement in National Health Service productivity would pay for the entire cost of primary education in Britain. This is not only a statistic; it needs to be an NHS goal to be achieved in the next ten years. It is the aim of total quality management (or TQM) to make these productivity and quality achievements possible in both service and manufacturing enterprises.

## *The history of TQM*

In Britain TQM has been fashionable over the last three years, but its origins are much older. It is a story of missed opportunity and belated reform.

During the 1950s and 1960s in the United States it was begun to be realized that after a certain point it was difficult to improve quality in manufacturing. By looking at the psychology of working in an organization some Americans realized that people felt that if say a 5% error rate was acceptable then it was clear that errors generally were acceptable to management. In addition waged employees quite rightly considered quality a management issue; it was not a personal responsibility. Management, not surprisingly took the opposite view.

W. E. Deming was one of the first to formalize these ideas and produce a solution. Philip Crosby was another who had similar thoughts while working with ITT. These and others realized two things:

1. Employees need to be given responsibility for their work. In this way quality becomes their responsibility too.
2. Increased quality saves the very substantial costs associated with the rectification of errors.

This, one would have thought, was a heaven sent gift to management, a 'win-win' situation. Costs would go down, sales up and profits would spiral. But things did not work out like that. In both the USA and Europe few took any notice of these ideas. But it would be quite wrong to think that Deming *et al.* were ignored; they were not.

In Japan post-war industry was notorious for its shoddy goods. I remember as a child considering the label 'Made in Japan' as an equivalent to 'Made in Hong Kong'. It was all cheap, cheerful, nasty and probably came from a corner shop. Much more than in the West the Japanese needed to make major management changes to improve the quality of their output. Once they heard about the benefit of managing for high quality they began to implement TQM ideas as a matter of urgency. In the 15 years from the middle 1960s to the beginning of the 1980s Japanese industry was transformed.

By the early 1980s the US was ready to reimport its own ideas. The success of Japanese industry was so prodigious that America badly needed to understand the management techniques that made it possible. American ideas such as 'quality circles', 'zero defects' and TQM began to be relearned from the Japanese. If these ideas had been British the whole saga would have made a very good sob story to be told to demonstrate British genius along with hovercraft, Concorde, television and transistors. But in Britain, few had heard of TQM even five years ago.

## *TQM management structures*

There is a saying in the army that 'there are no bad men, just bad officers'. When I was in the cadet force at school I remember being told this simple truth after a practice attack I was leading failed dismally. I had overrun the enemy position single-handed, but the rest of my attacking force were in disarray. In that situation the truth of the remark was all too clear.

TQM works on the basis that managers take this army proverb to heart. All too often it is the junior staff who are considered to manage time poorly, who are blamed for poor quality output or who are seen as impossible to motivate. As we learnt in Chapter 3 these are all management failings not staff failings. Nor is it difficult to see why it occurs. Philip Crosby in his book *Quality Without Tears* observes that when employees enter a company they are highly motivated. This enthusiasm for the job wears off with time as the imperfections of life in an enterprise take their toll. He likens this situation to a school playground full of pleasant children and also one or two bullies. But when the *joie de vivre* of the children falls away it is not the bullies who are blamed but the bullied. Returning to the business world, it is the junior staff who are often blamed for low motivation not the senior managers. Again and again those in a position of authority forget that people are rational. Everyone serves their own interest first; they will only be motivated if it benefits them to be motivated. Unless work is recognized as valuable there is often little point in being motivated. Managers the world over constantly fail to recognize this simple truth.

## *Change starts at the top*

If there are 'only bad officers' change must start at the top with the most senior management. But it is useful to remember that in many public sector situations departments are small and relatively autonomous. A meat inspecting department of perhaps seven people would be a viable TQM unit. A social security office in a small town is relatively independent, as is a Family Health Authority responsible for paying pharmacists, dentists and GPs. So although TQM starts with senior management this could well be a third or even fourth tier officer, not just a chief executive, general manager or permanent undersecretary.

## *Implementing TQM*

If change must start with managers what must you do? The weakness in many organizations is with the leadership. Although large numbers of people are joined in common cause there is often no real sense of teamwork. Each level of staffing in an organization can easily work at odds with each other rather than together. In these situations TQM will never take hold; it will remain a meaningless cliché used by the trendy to alienate further the majority.

## *Leadership*

Leadership in modern enterprises needs to be democratic if it is to succeed. This is a heartening development because for much of this century we have had democracy in private life but often quite autocratic dictatorships at work – the place where so much of our life is lived. As we have already said democratic leadership is required because the work we do is too complex for our 'superiors' to properly understand. We can illustrate this type of leadership diagrammatically.

But what is involved in leadership? What is it composed of? After the egalitarian 1960s leadership has become something to be embarrassed about. This may help to account for the weak leadership seen in much of the private and public sectors. But the old autocratic class-dominated view of leadership which this phobia feeds on is now irrelevant. That type of leadership belongs to the left end of the diagram in Fig. 9.1. We need to concern ourselves with the right end, with democratic leadership. Leadership is a management function. In fact it is a number of functions as shown in Fig. 9.2.

The modern leader holds the team together by organizing its activities so that it can attain its goals with as much certainty as possible. To use a phrase from John Adair, a key figure in recent work on leadership in management, the manager must look after the 'group needs' of the team. He illustrates this concept using three circles (see Fig. 9.3).

Whenever a group of people assemble to achieve an objective they will balance the objective, the 'task', with their individual needs and the maintenance of the group. We discussed this in detail in Chapter 4. The leader's role is to personify these needs for the benefit of the group as a whole.

Consider an administrative office in a public organization. As in any office there is the continual stream of minor problems. Perhaps there is too little room for filing, regulations keep changing and the computer does not work very well. If there is to be an improvement in the situation leadership will be required because the whole team will have to pull together. Those that lose faith or never had it in the first place must be persuaded to support the group. Perceived external difficulties, such as perhaps the computer, must be faced with a united front. Teams can only act in this way if they have effective leadership.

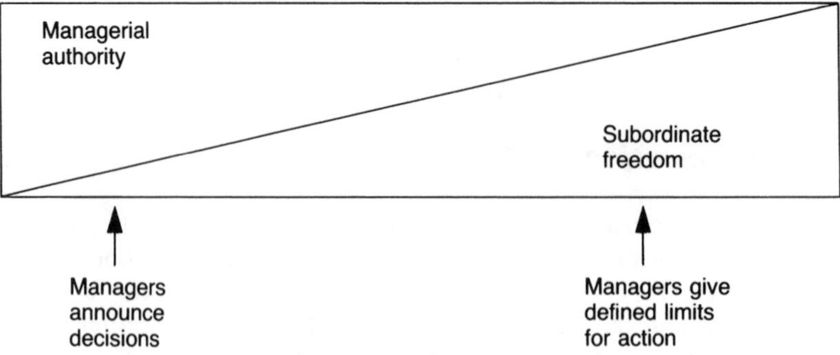


**Fig. 9.1** The leadership spectrum.

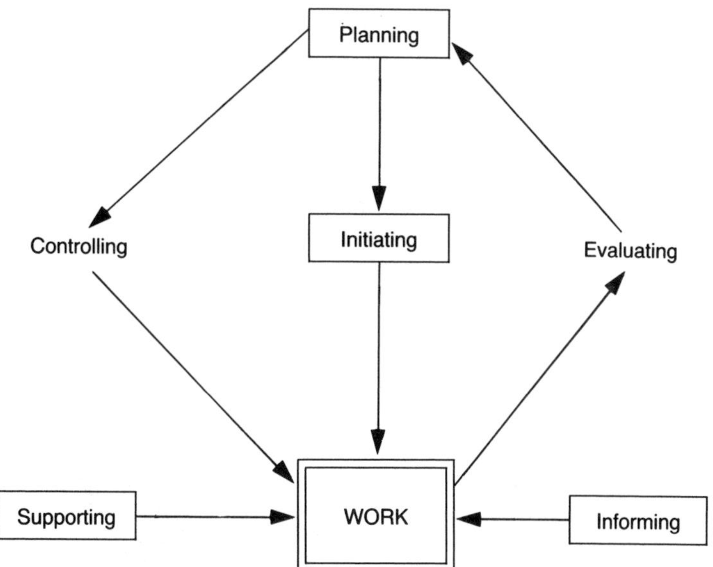


**Fig. 9.2** Leadership functions.

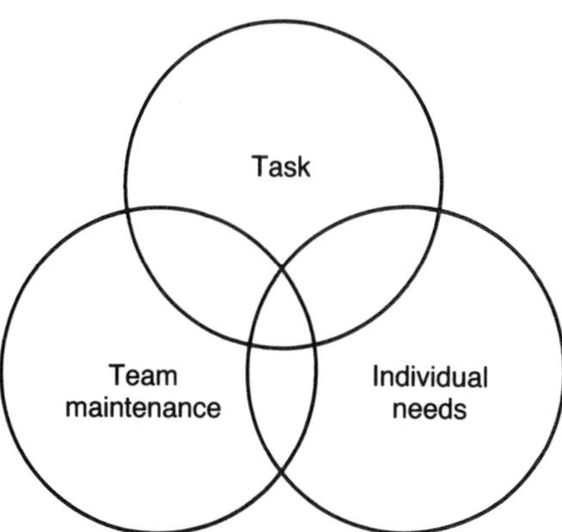


**Fig. 9.3** The interaction of group needs.

We have used the word team to describe the people in an organization. This is because in modern organizations teamwork is the only viable method of working effectively. So many modern 'managers' either ignore their team or abuse it. Managers or leaders must work with the team. It would be extraordinary if the captain of Liverpool Football Club ignored his players in the middle of a match. It would be just as ridiculous if in the middle of a game he were to punish players he felt were performing badly by making life more difficult for them with poor passes or failure to support their attacking play. And yet these are the methods used in many attempts to 'manage'. Ideas from junior staff are spurned. The personal needs of staff are ignored. Promotion of staff is determined on the most tenuous of evidence for fitness for the job. Nearly everyone has worked in an organization where these and other management failings are an everyday occurrence. In these circumstances a radical overhall of the senior management is a precondition for total quality management or any other attempt at reform. Change must start at the top; to use an old saying, 'Physician, heal thyself!'

## *The '14 steps' to total quality management*

It is widely considered that there are 14 stages in the development of a management system that will reduce errors and costs and will increase quality. These steps are highly practical. Quite realistically the first step is 'management commitment'. This means commitment to team work and the concept of 'zero defects'. The 14 steps are listed below

1. Management dedication.
2. The TQM improvement team.
3. Quality measurement.
4. Cost of errors.
5. The quality message.
6. The quality feedback system.
7. Zero errors committee.
8. Training.
9. Zero errors introduction day.
10. Short-term targets.
11. Error elimination.
12. Recognition
13. Quality circles.
14. Don't stop.

Full explanations of what the 14 steps entail is given in the first case study at the end of the chapter.

This programme of management reform is worth analysing more concisely. In essence three management functions are being perfected: measurement, communication, and recognition of achievement. This process of perfection is being carried out with one objective uppermost – the elimination of errors, or 'zero defects'.

Something needs to said about the idea of zero defects. It does not mean perfection; it does mean 100% compliance with a specification. Thus a housing benefit claim need not be assessed immediately on receipt, i.e. perfection. It can be assessed within ten working days. As long as no assessments exceed this period there will be zero defects.

But the following is not acceptable. It would be possible to have a policy of requiring a minimum of 90% of claims to be assessed in ten working days. This would mean that a 10% error rate would be considered acceptable. TQM works on the basis that no errors are acceptable either by management or workforce. Only by a total ban on 'defects' can the message that quality is important be understood by the team. Subjectivity is eliminated. Everyone understands that they must strive to work within the specification.

Of course errors will not disappear overnight. Quality demands constant work. Progress is measured by accounting for the cost of errors. Slowly a figure representing perhaps 35% of total costs is whittled down to a more acceptable 5–7%.

The management structure required for TQM is illustrated diagrammatically in Fig. 9.4.

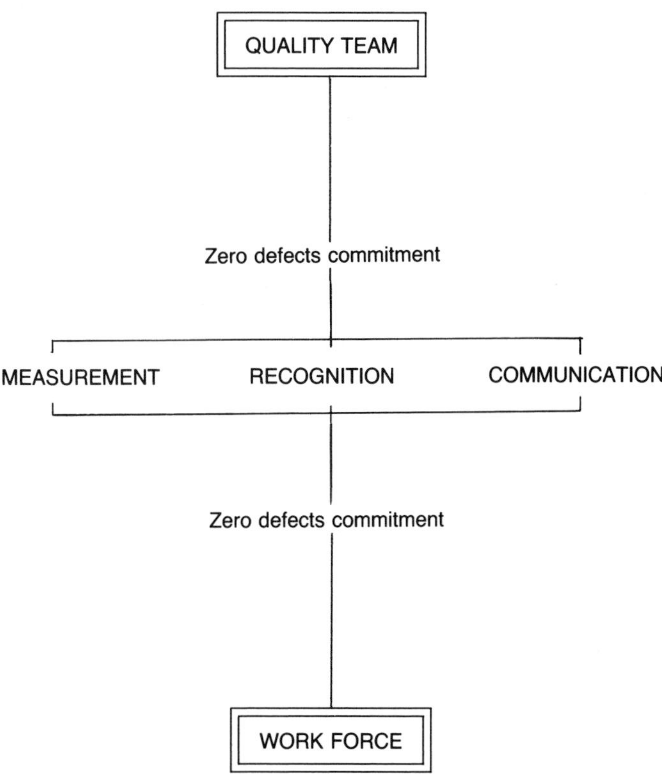


**Fig. 9.4** The total quality management: (TQM) management structure.

## Proof that total quality management works

It is one thing to say that organizations should reduce the number of errors they make and thus save money. It is quite another matter to actually save up to 40% of total costs. What proof therefore is there that TQM is effective?

Proof is normally very close at hand. Most wages and salaries departments have long operated under a policy of zero defects. The importance of properly and accurately paid salaries is understood by both management and staff. Neither are tolerant of errors. Using conventional wisdom we would expect to find that a large army of clerks would be needed to check individually each payment made. In fact, even for quite large organizations two or three people are normally all that are required to carry out all the staff payment functions. The amount of checking is minimal because only by getting the pay right first time can it be guaranteed correct.

As an auditor, I have reviewed the workings of many payroll departments in both the public and private sectors. I can remember no occasion where there was not a strong feeling of team spirit and calm professionalism amongst all grades of staff. The payroll department in your own organization almost certainly shows similar traits.

If you are the manager of a relatively autonomous department or section within an organization then you too can learn the virtues that your colleagues in the payroll section of the accounts department mastered long ago. You cannot use the excuse that your superiors prevent action being taken. The wages and salaries people are at everyone's beck and call. Things become more difficult if you are perhaps the second in command of a larger department with a wide range of duties. Examples would include being a deputy planning officer in a local authority or a deputy treasurer in any organization. In these situations you will have to win over your superiors as a prerequisite to departmental change.

### *Large organizations*

If there is ample proof that total quality management is effective in small organizations what evidence is there that it can be effective in major enterprises? If the public sector as a whole is to provide the major quality and productivity gains that the public are demanding TQM must work in major hospitals, in the police and fire brigade, in the prison service, in education and in the armed services. What evidence is there that this is possible?

At present there are few examples of TQM in the public services. In the USA the Federal Reserve Board is implementing TQM as is the Department of Agriculture and the Department of Energy. It is too early to see the results in these American central government departments. However, in the US a small number of private hospitals have introduced TQM with excellent results. Medicine is an area where a commitment to excellence is particularly effective.

Excuses will have to be very persuasive if any area of the public sector is to validly exclude itself from a commitment to zero defects, improved quality and higher productivity.

# Summary

Immutable economic and social changes are placing the public sector under great pressure. In this context the concept of zero errors within a programme of 'total quality management' is a useful tool. Total quality management is a way of solving the 'impossible' demand for more public services, of much higher quality, for less money.

Traditional views within the public sector assume that additional funding is the prerequisite of improved quality of service. In many cases where an effective service is more or less absent, this view is correct. But in many other cases additional funding is not the solution to low productivity and quality of service. Additional public spending is a matter of priorities. In this situation a commitment to zero defects is a much more attractive method of reviving a service than addition allocations of cash. As a voter and taxpayer it is difficult to disagree!

# Case studies

In Chapter 8 we saw how a number of typical public sector activities were able to measure their productivity and quality of output in simple but effective ways. In this chapter we continue the same case studies and see how they introduce management improvements to make the best use of the new information they have at their disposal. In all the case studies the management improvements are based on a commitment to zero defects and a policy designed to reduce the cost of errors.

The first case study continues the housing benefit example. The full 14-step implementation process for total quality management is illustrated. This case study is designed to provide a practical grounding in TQM implementation. The other case studies assume that the processes illustrated in this first example have been understood. The second case study continues the illustration of the management of the general surgery budget in the health service. This study focuses on the process of measuring the cost of errors. The primary school case study in Chapter 8 forms the third example.

In all three case studies figures have been given for the cost of errors in the different departments and professions discussed. These figures are estimates of the cost of errors likely in average departments. They are designed to illustrate the process of implementing total quality management in a realistic way. They are *not* designed to be reference points with which to compare your own achievements.

# Reader questionnaire

This questionnaire looks at your views on the cost of errors, leadership and finally, quality management.

1. Errors if quantified would be found to cost the British public sector about £70 000 million. This is approximately the gross domestic product of what was East Germany.

ANSWERS

(a) How much of your work is concerned with solving routine problems as opposed to productive work or policy formulation?
(b) Do your staff have long periods of uninterrupted time when they can get on with the job in hand or do they constantly have to stop work to answer other peoples' problems?
(c) 'For want of a nail the shoe was lost, for want of a shoe the horse was lost . . . for want of a rider the battle was lost.' In your work how costly are errors?
(d) If the payroll department in most organizations can be almost error free why can't your department be the same?
(e) What could you spend the money on that would be saved by reducing errors – new, badly needed services to the public, a new computer system, reduced waiting times for customers?

2. As a public sector manager you are responsible for leading your organization or department. A good leader will be able to control his or her staff so that excellence is achieved. To what extent can you get the results you want from your people?

ANSWERS

(a) Do you see yourself as a technocrat or a leader? Are your staff your responsibility or just a paid workforce?
(b) Is your management style autocratic, democratic or just weak?
(c) As a leader your job is to plan, initiate, control, evaluate, support and inform. Do you carry out these functions passively or do you actively manage the people in your department to get the best out of them?
(d) To want extent do you consider you work as the leader of a team?
(e) As a team leader how do you make sure that the members of the team are bound into an effective whole and how do you ensure that the needs of individual members are looked after? Does the team have a clearly understood goal?

3. The public sector traditionally works at its best when it is pursuing goals that society as a whole strongly supports. The ideal of cheaper, higher quality public services is becoming just such a public objective. How are you responding to this?

ANSWERS

(a) Quality management starts with management dedication. Is this likely in your organization?
(b) In a public sector that is subject to competition how long will it be before quality management becomes the only way to keep your department or organization in business?
(c) Holding British Standard 5750 could be the only way that your department could win at competitive tender in future. Do you agree?
(d) An enabling public sector should make it a condition in all its contracts that those tendering hold BS5750 and have implemented a quality management system. As a taxpayer and user of public services surely you would agree?
(e) When are you going to start implementing quality management within your department and organization?

# Case study I – housing benefit administration

Abigail MacGovern was quick to introduce TQM into her new department. She wanted to control the achievement of her people so she needed good communication and pertinent recognition of success (see again Fig. 9.4). She also was determined to produce first-rate results. Having given so much abuse to her superiors in the past she was not going to produce second-rate results herself.

After a considerable amount of research in her spare time Abigail decided that TQM and the concept of zero errors were just what she was looking for. Her boyfriend, if that is the right description of a 48 year-old Marxist out-of-work docker, was horrified. There before his eyes was Abigail joining the ranks of the exploiters of the working class, or so it seemed to him. At least with old-fashioned management systems all the workers knew that management were half-boiled. The evidence of their inefficiency was forever before ones' eyes. Job demarcations for instance gave a man a sense of his own worth because it allowed him to demonstrate to management his power and their foolishness. With the type of thing that Abigail was suggesting the workers were all about to be brainwashed into holding management's view. What would happen to working-class solidarity then? He knew the answer only too well.

Abigail and Sid had lived together for nine years. Both had had little formal education but both had read voraciously once they were adults. Sid had a superb library of socialist and communist literature and could even read Russian slowly. Abigail was more eclectic. And whereas he had become more and more fanatical, she had become relatively tolerant with success.

Abigail MacGovern's achievements at Senforth District Council had become known throughout the region. At one of the regular meetings held by the region's housing benefit managers she had been asked to give a talk on introducing TQM into housing benefit departments.

She started her talk stressing the importance of measuring outputs and having available an effective management information system. She then went on to talk about the introduction of a 14-point action plan.

Below are the notes she handed out at the meeting.

## 1. Management dedication

TQM starts at the top with the absolute commitment of senior managers. In the case of a housing benefit department the commitment must be from the housing benefit manager and his or her deputy. The support of the treasurer or deputy treasurer is not necessary unless the whole of the finance department is involved in the TQM programme.

Once the housing benefit manager is committed to the introduction of TQM and is prepared to act, it is possible to move on to the next stage.

## 2. The TQM improvement team

The manager cannot implement TQM on his or her own. A coordinating and monitoring team is needed to push the message through and control the TQM process. The message will be that errors are not acceptable in the housing benefit department and that everyone in the team is working to that end. It is useful to have an easily remembered slogan to represent this idea. Such phrases as 'Right every time' or 'Once satisfies if it's right' can be helpful to reinforce the message in everybody's thoughts. The role of the team is the implementation of total quality management affecting every aspect of the department's work.

## 3. Quality measurement

Much of the quality measurement needed for TQM has already been talked about (see Chapter 8). No addition analysis of the quantity and quality of outputs is needed. The results of output measurement need careful analysis. In particular the analysis of the quality of outputs will need to be carefully reviewed.

## 4. Cost of errors

A new financial measurement is needed and that is the 'cost of errors'. This is the expense the department incurs as a result of doing things incorrectly. This figure is a key indicator in monitoring the effectiveness of the management process.

## Calculation of the 'cost of errors'

When measuring the quantity and quality of outputs it was relatively simple to record achievement because the computerization of the department was already geared to outputs. But if we are interested in errors the computer is likely to be less helpful.

In a housing benefit department errors will result in time spent reworking assessments, answering unnecessary queries from clients, searching for files in a defective filing system and all the other duties that result from a failure to provide an error free service. The cost of these errors will be seen in the main as wasted staff time. There with be other costs such as additional use of the computer, the telephone and stationery. Also because of the extra staff needed to rectify errors, premises costs will be effected since an error free department might need 30% less staff.

When we measured outputs all the cost of errors was incorporated in the cost of producing one unit of output. In this second measuring exercise we need to analyse the proportion of output unit costs between doing the job for the first time and the subsequent cost of improving or redoing the job if it is not up to standard. Thus for assessments of claims we need to divide our costs as follows:

| | £ | £ | £ |
|---|---|---|---|
| *Cost of getting job done once* | | | |
| Cost of first assessment | | | XX |
| | | | XX |
| *Cost of putting right subsequent problems* | | | |
| Salary cost of: | | | |
| 1. Answering queries associated with | | | |
| (a) Mis-assessment | XX | | |
| (b) Slowness | XX | | |
| (c) Poor communication | XX | | |
| (d) Poor customer care | XX | | |
| | | XX | |
| 2. Reassessments after queries by claimant | | XX | |
| 3. Substandard office organization, | XX | | |
| namely | XX | | |
| (a) Poor computer software | XX | | |
| (b) Insufficient terminals | | | |
| (c) Poor filing systems | | XX | |
| Computer, supplies and premises | | | |
| costs resulting from the above | | XX | |
| Total cost of errors | | | XX |
| TOTAL UNIT COST OF OUTPUT | | | XX |

How do we make this analysis of costs? The first thing to make clear is that unlike output measurement the cost of errors need not be computed all the time for all transactions; it can be measured on a test basis. But how do we get the information at all? The answer is time sheets.

## Data collection

In the department there are 25 staff. As well as their normal time sheet staff fill in an 'Error Timesheet' on two days every month. Not all staff fill in their error timesheets on the same day. Rather a spread of days is used every month. An example of an Error Time Sheet for the housing benefit department is shown below.

### *Timesheet – cost of errors*

Name: Date:

*Assessments*

1. (a) Pre-assessment work
   (b) First time assessments
2. Queries – mis-assessment
   (a) slowness
   (b) poor communication
   (c) poor customer care
3. Reassessments after claimant query
4. Time wasted from:
   (a) computer software
   (b) insufficient terminals
   (c) poor filing systems
5. Other – please specify

ERROR TIME

TOTAL ASSESSMENT TIME

*Payments*

6. (a) Preparation of payment runs
   (b) Checking runs
   (c) Deletion of incorrect payment from runs
   (d) Reconciliation of payment runs to accounts

TIME SPENT ON ERRORS

TOTAL PAYMENTS TIME

*Overpayments*

7. (a) Overpayments caused by claimant
   (b) Overpayments for other reasons (ERRORS)

TOTAL TIME

TOTAL TIME SPENT ON ERRORS

GRAND TOTAL

At the end of each month the error timesheets are summarized to give the total amount of time spent on error work. Extrapolations to provide estimates of the total time worked in a month can also be made. Below are the total extrapolated hours for the department for the month of March.

## *Timesheet – cost of errors*

Name: Extrapolated totals Date: March 199X

| | |
|---|---|
| *Assessments* | |
| 1. (a) Pre-assessment work | 573 |
| (b) First time assessments | 1673 |
| 2. Queries – mis-assessment | 58 |
| (a) slowness | 152 |
| (b) poor communication | 151 |
| (c) poor customer care | 76 |
| 3. Reassessments after claimant query | 217 |
| 4. Time wasted from: | |
| (a) computer software | 92 |
| (b) insufficient terminals | 62 |
| (c) poor filing systems | 272 |
| 5. Other – please specify | 14 |
| ERROR TIME | 1094 |
| TOTAL ASSESSMENT TIME | 3340 |
| *Payments* | |
| 6. (a) Preparation of payment runs | 47 |
| (b) Checking runs | 57 |
| (c) Deletion of incorrect payment from runs | 15 |
| (d) Reconciliation of payment runs to accounts | 23 |
| TIME SPENT ON ERRORS | 95 |
| TOTAL PAYMENTS TIME | 142 |
| *Overpayments* | |
| 7. (a) Overpayments caused by claimant | 115 |
| (b) Overpayments for other reasons (ERRORS) | 51 |

| | |
|---|---|
| TOTAL TIME | 166 |
| TOTAL TIME SPENT ON ERRORS (34% of total) (1094 + 95 + 51) | 1240 |
| GRAND TOTAL | 3648 |

We can see that out of the 3648 hours worked 34% were concerned tasks associated with errors. The next job is to calculate the cost of this error-associated work.

Costs will include supplies, premises costs and computer time as well as salary costs. Figures will be calculated in the same way that they were in Chapter 8. For the housing benefit department the following figures were produced extrapolated over a whole year:

| | *Productive* £'000 | *Errors* £'000 | *Total* £'000 |
|---|---|---|---|
| Salaries | 160.8 | 90.5 | 251.3 |
| Computer costs | 33.9 | 11.3 | 45.2 |
| Supplies and services | 20.4 | 10.2 | 30.6 |
| Establishment expenses | 16.5 | 8.5 | 25.0 |
| | 231.6 | 120.5 | 352.1 |
| | 65.8% | 34.2% | 100% |

It may well be that the figures produced are not completely accurate. Judgements will have to made in deciding whether time spent was due to misunderstandings on the part of claimants that could not be prevented or due to poor communication and mistakes on the part of the department. Nevertheless the figured produced will do two things:

1. The major causes of wasteful expenditure will be indentified.
2. Staff will understand very quickly the message of zero errors.

# 5. The quality message

Point 5 is the stage where the commitment of management is communicated to the rest of the staff. It is done now because only at this stage is all the information available to convince the staff of the seriousness of managements intentions.

Remember, we now have a substantial amount of evidence about the performance of the department. It is worth listing the achievement.

1. Monthly management accounts showing details of productivity;
2. Monthly analyses of quality achievements;
3. Monthly approximations of the cost of errors.

Grassroots staff may well be less surprised by the findings from the three measurement systems that have been set up, than management. After all managers are usually desperately 'fire fighting' if productivity and quality are low and errors high. Productive staff on the other hand are often only too aware of the waste in the department due to say, poor application forms or defective software. Their interest will not be in putting these problems right; but they will want to know if management are. Quality awareness is a matter of communicating intentions through staff meetings, through written notices and memos and by managers being seen to care.

# 6. Quality feedback system

After the awareness stage there needs to be action. The three management functions – measurement, communication and recognition all need to be implemented. Measurement is now firmly in place. Recognition will be addressed later. Now is the turn of communication.

A point so often missed by managers is that if a policy requires implementation it will be implemented by grassroots staff. Managers can only organize; they cannot do. So if having measured performance we wish to improve specific areas of activity this can only be done if the staff become involved, understand management's intentions and communicate to management the problems involved in achieving. For instance errors may arise because claims are wrongly input into the computer. The error timesheets highlight this difficulty and management decide to tackle the problem. It is no good saying to staff 'do it better' because nothing will happen. Rather you must ask them why it is difficult to get it right.

Thus, the second key management tool, communication, must be developed. This can only be done by having mechanisms to locate and transmit concerns and ideas. Weekly staff meetings with brief written minutes is one method. Direct access of staff to managers at least at pre-set times is another. Managers should have a short meeting every Monday morning with supervisors to set targets and to solve problems. The most important point is that a habit is formed of isolating problems and then putting them right.

# 7. Zero errors committee

In larger organizations a subcommittee of the quality improvement team may be needed to analyse more completely the consequences of zero errors. In a housing benefit department there is probably no need for a separate committee although it might be useful if detailed analysis of the problem of errors was left to the deputy manager.

# 8. Training

Supervisors need to fully understand the idea of zero errors. And they need to be able to fully explain the idea to the rest of the staff. In particular they must be able to explain that by reducing errors there will be more time and money available to improve the service further. The benefits of this will be amongst other things a lot less rude telephone calls from disgruntled claimants! These are a source of unpleasantness that all benefits staff dislike.

## 9. Zero errors introduction day

Once the measurement and communication systems have been set up it is possible to start the zero errors programme. You can never introduce a TQM system in stages or piecemeal. Errors are either acceptable or they are not – there is no middle way. This means that the change from the old regime to the new must take place suddenly and publicly. This is done by assigning a day as zero errors day. On that day everyone knows that errors are unacceptable in the organization.

Of course there will still be errors. Clearly they cannot be removed instantly. But whereas before zero errors day a certain probably undefined level of errors was probably considered acceptable, afterwards none are. Remember the salaries and wages department. They do not consider a 5% error rate acceptable, but when very occasionally mistakes are made with pay an attempt is made to learn from the error so that it is not repeated.

## 10. Short-term targets

Once the zero errors regime is in place there need to be realistic objectives for staff to meet over the short to medium term. Suitable targets could involve reductions in the costs of errors. Perhaps the time losses as a result of the poor filing system are targeted to fall by 50% in the next month. Another target could be to cut input inaccuracies and thus start to cut the cost of mis-assessments and reassessments. A 25% cut in error costs in three months could be realistic if the precise causes of inaccuracy could be found and corrected.

## 11. Error elimination

Alongside the system of targets and the new communication system there is a need for a formal attempt to remove the cause of errors. All staff need to list on a standard form the matters that are causing them the most problems in avoiding errors.

Causes of errors might be as follows:

I don't fully understand the computer system and this means that I am slow and make mistakes.

Claimants always misunderstand question 5 on the form so I am always chasing them for more information.

> When claimants ring in with a query it takes me 5 minutes to find their file. By that time they have become unsympathetic to our needs and more time and effort is wasted.

Unless management have this type of information the problems cannot be solved.

## 12. Recognition

Recognition is the third main management function which was shown in Fig. 9.4. Once people are starting to analyse problems, chart achievement, and set themselves goals it important that success is rewarded. There is nothing more dispiriting than meeting a goal through conscientious hard work and then being ignored. Unless an employee is hoping for promotion, which most junior staff are not, there is only one reaction to unrecognized success. It is typically expressed as follows: 'Sod the b. . . . s! That is the last time I bother for them.' Management excuses for not recognizing good work are based on the idea that staff are paid to do a good job and that it is all in the line of duty. *You* may think that, but your junior staff will not. What is more they will prove you wrong.

Many commentators feel that recognition should be financial in the form of performance related pay. Others feel strongly that money should not be involved. What is clear is that money by itself is not an adequate form of recognition. There needs to be a clear human input; people need to feel that they are worthwhile individuals who add to the team. Financial reward may damage the sense of team effort, but substantial financial savings from the success of TQM must in some way be shared with the people responsible for them.

## 13. Quality circles

Since elimination of errors has become a key element within the housing benefit department there needs to be a structure to channel issues of error reduction up and down from management to workforce. The vehicles for this are the famous Japanese quality circles. These are small groups of people from all levels within the department who discuss problems and results and who agree future courses of action.

## 14. Don't stop

These first 13 points are needed to set up the TQM system in the housing benefit department. But they are also needed to maintain TQM in the department. Once the quality circles have set up it will be necessary to go back to point 1, reinvest in management commitment, appraise the quality improvement team and review the measurement systems in force. The quest for zero errors is continuous. It is also important to remember that it all takes time.

## Reader questionnaire

ANSWERS

1. Is your department or organization struggling to meet targets and to provide an adequate service?
2. What sort of solutions to this problem were you considering before you read about Abigail MacGovern's successes? Do you still think they are a good idea?
3. If you can think of four or five areas of work where errors may cost a few per cent of total costs you are half way to a quality management approach. Can you list these areas now?
4. What is your likely cost of errors? Guess!
5. Are you worried that your staff will think you hair-brained if you take on a quality management approach? Remember the majority of staff will welcome the communication and recognition that a successful change must bring.

# Case study II – a health service budget: general surgery department

In the previous chapter, Frederick Asherton the consultant surgeon in charge of the general surgery department at Parkinson Hospital discovered how well suited medicine is to measurement of 'clinical output' and quality. In the Case Study in this chapter we learn how Mr Asherton further developed his management skills when he discovered the concept of zero errors and total quality management.

If it is not surprising that an administrative function can make substantial improvements through the determined elimination of errors then many in the medical profession would express doubt that the hard pressed National Health Service could save a large percentage of its costs through the elimination of errors both in medical practice and in administration of that practice.

Clearly, the types of errors to be eliminated will vary from specialty to specialty. Most will not be examples of medical negligence; they will mainly be trivial malpractices that lower the quality of service and waste money. But it is worth considering how such errors add up to become a significant proportion of the total. Five different causes of errors each of which has only a small effect by itself could easily total a fifth of potential achievement or a quarter of that actually achieved. In a service as big as the NHS this amounts to billions of pounds wasted.

## Better management at Parkinson Hospital

Frederick Asherton had pioneered the use of management information at Parkinson Hospital. For the first time in his medical career he could monitor his achievements.

He knew his success rates for different diseases. He was beginning to reduce waiting lists and impressively he was within his budget. Even late in his career he was finding that the practice of medicine could throw up considerable challenges and surprises.

A subject he found particularly interesting and perplexing was communication and control within his department. On the one hand, he had his management information and on the other, there were the consultants, junior doctors and nurses who did most of the work. Even when the causes of inefficiencies were highlighted in the figures it was always very difficult in communicate and implement improvements. It was as if he were trying to fly an aeroplane with elastic between the controls and the wing flaps. You made an adjustment and then gritted your teeth while you waited to see if anything happened. As often as not nothing did or there was an undesirable knock-on affect. He found this aspect of managing rather annoying and at times he was beginning to look foward to retirement again.

One Saturday afternoon at home he was flicking through an old copy of *The Times*. It had been left by one of the armchairs and was the previous Wednesday's edition. There was a brief article on changes in management practice. Like all such journalism the article assumed you already knew most of what the article was about. Fred always wondered whether this was because everybody actually did know or whether the journalists used false confidence as a cover for their onw incertitude. The gist of its contents was that total quality management was the salvation of all businesses and that anyone in a management role should be introducing it now just a decade after the Japanese. Perhaps this TQM was the answer to his management problems?

Parkinson Hospital is not far from a university library. On the off-chance Fred decided to call in on his way home one evening. With the help of a librarian he located a number of modern management journals and a couple of trendy volumes on management practice. He spent an hour and a half dredging this material for TQM and better communication methods.

## The importance of the team

From this reading Fred obtained his first formal management training. It was quite a revelation. People always said that management was just common sense. Now having read a little on the subject he could understand why people who held this view always seemed to have such miserable departments. They were not the sort who believed that management was about sharing achievement within a team. It was about instilling a sense of mission and corporate responsibility. Management was definitely nothing to do with pecking orders and medical hierarchies. On the subject of TQM he discovered it was about eliminating costly errors through the use of teamwork and clear-cut objectives.

A day or so later Fred wrote off for two books on introducing TQM and from this point began the management revolution that transformed his department.

## Zero errors

Fred had always assumed that in medicine an error was amputating a foot instead of doing a thyroid operation. It had never occurred to him that minor imperfections were effectively management errors.

Inefficient bed allocations were costly errors. Infections after surgery represented errors. Striving overzealously to cure the dying was often expensive and unkind waste. More serious errors resulted, he found, from performing operations on patients with rare diseases. In these situations he sometimes found he was lacking in experience. He was also seeing from his quality statistics that success rates were lower than those reported in the medical press.

There were a whole range of areas where imperfections were resulting in needless waste. The problem was how to improve these areas. What he required was a dedicated team striving towards perfection. Once areas of weakness had been identified they could all work to avoid mistakes in future.

## The 14-point plan

Because of his inexperience as a manager Fred Asherton was keen to implement TQM methodically as suggested in his newly arrived books. This involved a 14-point plan.

### *1. Management dedication*

Fred Asherton was fully committed to excellence. Since his conversation with the unit manager which had sparked his enthusiasm for management and since Alice had become his management accountant daughter in law, he had become fascinated by management in the NHS. Total quality management now formed his major interest and concern.

### *2. The TQM team*

Somehow his fellow consultants, the senior nurse and the other senior staff in his department would have to be converted to the concept of TQM. This was not going to be easy.

Fred took his chance just before the Easter holiday. Non-emergency work had ceased and the majority of the department were together. He explained the idea of zero errors, the savings to be made, the higher quality of treatment that would result and the need for a team approach based on communication, measurement and recognition of achievement. To put it in perspective he showed how by reducing errors by 10%, the non-essential surgery waiting list could probably be eliminated.

The following is Fred Asherton's example to demonstrate benefits of TQM:

| | Existing workload % | 10% Savings workload % |
|---|---|---|
| Urgent work | 66 | 60 |
| Non-urgent work | 34 | 30 |
| | 100 | 90 |

| | New workload % |
|---|---|
| Urgent work | 60 |
| Non-urgent work (old case load) | 30 |
| Additional people from waiting lists | 10 |
| | 100 |

If the average waiting list period is one year then the department could expect to provide immediate access to all treatment in three years time. (30% non-urgent work/10% additional capacity = three years.)

Of course, this was rather simplistic if only because if all work was done without delay more people would probably opt for NHS treatment. But the principle was the thing that mattered. If errors could be eliminated much more medical care could be given.

Parkinson Hospital's general surgery department went into the Easter holiday that year with the message that team work and zero errors were the way they would manage in the new financial year.

## 3. *Quality measurement*

Fred Asherton has already implemented most of the quality measurement systems he will need for TQM (see Chapter 8).

## 4. *Cost of errors*

The TQM programme would need information on the cost of errors. This type of information is not available from the systems Fred Asherton had already set up.

Asherton decided that he would collect information on five different sources of errors. These were as follows:

1. Infection rates after surgery;
2. Wastage of bed space;
3. Patients missing appointments;
4. Unnecessary medical procedures;
5. Resources wasted due to slow diagnosis.

A sixth source of errors, the treatment of rare diseases that might be better handled by a hospital specializing in such work he left for a second TQM review. This was because the quantification of the waste would be difficult to achieve. It would involve quantification of the cost of lower success rates and measurement of excess times spent on the work.

Fred's methods of measuring the cost of errors were as follows:

### Infection rates

Infection rates will be measured by ward sisters. Every day they will record the number, if any, of beds occupied by patients suffering from infection. This will be used to calculate a % figure which will be applied to all budget costs. This system will have the benefit of simplicity, although as Fred Asherton realizes it was unlikely to be completely accurate.

### Wasted of bed space

When each patient is discharged the ward sister and a houseman will assess the case to discover whether bed space has been wasted. Fred has devised a small questionnaire for the purpose. At the end of the month all wasted bed space will be aggregated to give a percentage of all occupied bed space. This figure will be applied to total hotel costs at the end of each month.

### Patients missing appointments

The percentage of patients missing appointments will be recorded every day by the ward staff. The lost capacity resulting from this will be expressed as a percentage and applied to all departmental costs at the end of each month.

### Unnecessary medical procedures

Whenever a patient dies in hospital Fred Asherton assesses the case to ensure that the hospital took all proper actions. After the introduction of his TQM initiative he will also record an assessment of whether unnecessary treatment had been carried out.

The type of thing that he will look for are resuscitation of very old and infirm heart patients and costly operations on those with terminal cancers. He will also keep an eye open for indications of surgery on relatively healthy patients which is unlikely to produce useful results or where drug treatment is preferable such as for many stomach ulcers. Fred Asherton's view is that excessive use of life-support machines and the unending care of the dying can be degrading to the human spirit. It is also terribly wearing for relatives as they endure protracted waits for the final liberation of death. If he can reduce waiting lists by preventing the misery associated with unnecessary medical work this seems to him to be a worthy goal. That said Fred is no supporter of euthanasia.

At the end of his assessment Fred Asherton will be able to produce an estimated figure for the cost of unnecessary work done in each period. He will then express this as a percentage of a normal month's total costs.

### Resources wasted due to slow diagnosis

Every month a houseman will review the cases where the length of time taken for diagnosis and treatment are in the highest quartile. He or she will obtain these figures from the timeliness monitoring schedules that were described in Chapter 8.

Where a patient is in this category and his stay in hospital is above the average for that case type the additional days over the average will be recorded. This will then be expressed as a percentage of the total occupied bed days. Fred hopes to computerize this procedure in the near future since no medical judgement is needed.

Fred Asherton hopes that these five areas of monitoring, together with the quality data he produces already, will provide the basis of the measurement processes required for his zero defects programme. If he can cut errors and improve the timeliness and success of the treatment provided, then he will be well pleased. If patient satisfaction also improves he will be happier still.

## 5. *The quality message*

Fred was adamant that all the staff should be aware of TQM. To achieve this he and the senior nurse arranged three meetings so that his full-time staff and his more regular contract or temporary staff whether they were doctors, nurses or ancillaries could all understand that there were going to be changes. Asherton had mentioned his management plans to a friend. The rather crusty retort had been that he would never get it past the unions. In fact Asherton was only asking for a recognition that quality matters in all aspects of the medical service from serving of meals to complex surgical procedures. Much to his surprise it was the lowest grade staff that received his message best. He was quite gratified.

## 6. *Quality feedback system*

At the three staff meetings Fred outlined his ideas for a method of exchanging ideas between all grades of staff on a regular basis. He was trying to implement an effective communication system within the department.

It was important that his ideas on where improvements were necessary should be understood and acted upon. But it was also equally important that where implementation was difficult or where there were other problems he should be aware of this. Regular staff meetings lasting only ten to 15 minutes were needed. In terms of his aeronautical analogy he was introducing this system as an attempt to stiffen up the elastic that connected the pilot with the wing flaps. If he, Frederick Asherton, wanted change then he could only achieve it if the staff implemented it.

The type of meetings Frederick envisaged were to be held once a week either by him or a senior doctor or nurse at the beginning of shifts. To keep the duration of these meetings to a minimum speakers would be asked to notify informally their intentions before the meeting. Discussion would be limited and to the point. Major issues could be discussed at subsequent meetings and between staff on an individual basis between meetings.

In this way Fred hoped that a real feeling of professional teamwork would be developed. Moaning and negative dissatisfaction were to be replaced by positive involvement in a team initiative were everyone had their own part.

## 7. *Zero errors committee*

Fred wanted to reduce the bureaucracy of TQM to a minimum. The TQM team would act as a zero errors committee. Individuals from the team could use their specialist knowledge as required to investigate areas of concern.

## *8. Training*

The major areas where TQM was likely to give a benefit were:

1. More responsive and hence better care of both urgent and non-urgent patients (e.g. reduction in waiting times).
2. Reduction in hospital infections.
3. Better use of hospital resources (poor and unnecessary treatment).

These areas affected all grades of staff. It was the responsibility of doctors to ensure testing, diagnosis and treatment all took place in the minimum possible time. It was nurses and administrative staff who had to ensure effective and rapid processing and delivery of information to those that needed it. And infections were a problem for nurses as well as doctors and surgeons.

Fred Asherton was in two minds concerning how to provide the necessary training to make the TQM programme successful. Some errors resulted from carelessness but others were due to ignorance and lack of knowledge. In the end he thought that the major problem lay not in formal training – programmes of training could be provided as specific needs were identified, but with the concept of 'zero errors'.

In a service such as health care where there are endless unmet needs, the practice of compromise is common to everyone. It is deemed quite acceptable to leave patients with uncomfortable non-urgent conditions to suffer for months or years. If first-rate drugs are too expensive then cheaper ones are used instead. If a bed is needed urgently then the fittest patient is discharged early. These are all everyday compromises that the NHS, and in fact most health services, are forced to practise every day. How is this attitude and practice compatible with zero errors?

The main point that all staff had to fully comprehend was that an 'error' was not a deviation from perfection but a lapse from a stated and probably imperfect practice standard. The waste of a bed day might actually benefit one patient, probably at the expense of another, but if the requirement was to maximize bed usage within a regime of good medical practice then one patient staying an extra day perhaps because test results were not ready would count as an error. Unnecessary treatment was an error as more obviously was a patient acquiring an infection after surgery.

The concept that Fred had to communicate was that each patient had to be considered both individually and in the context of the total pool of patients waiting to use the hospital service. He wanted to produce a catch phrase that could be used to imprint the idea of zero errors onto everyone's mind. 'Controlled compromise means better health care' seemed to say everything but it was not the type of message that the public would appreciate. In fact any form of slogan was unlikely to be acceptable. In the end he asked senior nurses to spread the message that 'A better service provides more for less'. This combined the idea of better patient care with the requirement for efficiency.

After all this Mr Asherton was ready for the formal implementation of TQM in his department.

## *9. Zero errors introduction day*

Fred Asherton was very conscious that his TQM initiative should be introduced with a bang and not a whimper. This was not to be just another nice idea that would fade away when the going got tough. This was for real.

Fred Asherton set Midsummer's Day as the first day of TQM at Parkinson Hospital. The night before, Midsummer's Eve, the whole department had had a barbeque. Fred had provided a disco from money held in a small staff welfare trust fund topped up by him personally. And just so that everyone would remember what the jamboree was in aid of, Fred had got some balloons printed with the following: 'ZE = More for Less'. People were invited to buy a balloon and label. At midnight they were all released into the beam of a small searchlight that pierced the night sky. Fred wondered what the public would think of the somewhat cryptic message they would find on the balloons when they eventually landed.

## *10. Short-term targets*

The next day back in the hospital TQM started in earnest with the setting of short-term targets. In the period between Easter and Zero Errors Introduction Day, Fred Asherton had been pulling together data on the cost of errors. He had found the summarized results quite startling. Table 9.1 shows Fred's first ever cost of error figures.

Fred's rather conservative calculations of error costs showed that 25% of his budget was being wasted. There was no one cause of waste. All five sources of errors isolated in point 4 were contributing.

Fred isolated the people who could help prevent each type of error. At the first quality feedback meetings held after ZE Day the different groups of staff were shown Table 9.1 and then a breakdown of the figures for which their section was responsible. Each section set itself, some with more than a little encouragement, modest targets to improve procedures. Improvements were to be measured over the next four-week period.

## *11. Error elimination*

During that first four-week period, Fred Asherton produced yet another questionnaire. The idea was to encourage staff to highlight particular problems they faced in eliminating errors. He was not looking for highly structured answers, just indications of the causes of problems. Why did patients miss appointments? Was it because they had moved house or was it that they were frightened of treatment or perhaps they were even in prison. His staff needed to find out and tailor the appointments system to tackle these problems. The same applied to unnecessary treatment, slow diagnosis and all the other problems. The questionnaires aimed to make people think about these problems so that solutions could be found.

## *12. Recognition*

Mr Asherton was very aware that staff usually got very little recognition from their seniors for the hard work they put in. He had spoken about the best ways of

**Table 9.1** Effect of errors on medical costs

| | *Total costs* | *Types of error* | | | | | *Cost of errors* | *Cost of useful work* |
|---|---|---|---|---|---|---|---|---|
| | | *Infection* | *Wasted bed space* | *Appointment missed* | *Slow diagnosis* | *Unnecessary work* | | |
| % total costs resulting from each error type | | 0.06 | 0.06 | 0.05 | 0.04 | 0.07 | 0.25 | |
| Direct treatment services | 1243.00 | 74.58 | | 62.15 | 49.72 | 87.01 | 273.46 | 969.54 |
| Indirect treatment services | 528.00 | 31.68 | | 26.40 | 21.12 | 36.96 | 116.16 | 411.84 |
| Hotel costs | 2385.00 | 143.10 | 143.10 | 119.25 | 95.40 | 166.95 | 667.80 | 1717.20 |
| Total costs | 4156.00 | 249.36 | 143.10 | 207.80 | 166.24 | 290.92 | 1057.42 | 3098.58 |

Total percentage errors 25%

providing recognition for nursing and junior medical staff with Alice. The problem was that the NHS was not set up to give rewards to its best employees.

'Alice, what do I do about rewarding staff achievement.'

'I would say thank you if I were you', replied Alice half joking. It was the middle of August and John and Alice had been married for three months. Fred had invited them both to Sunday lunch because they had not seen them since they had got back from their honeymoon. John and his mother were in the kitchen and Fred and Alice were drinking gin and tonic in the garden.

Fred continued, 'What just say, "Thanks I'm off home now".'

'I think you would have to say a little more than that. What about "Thank you for cutting error rates by 0.67% last month and saving £10 000".' Alice could not be very serious. She found it amusing that her father-in-law kept asking her all these questions when they met.

'Hmm' mused Fred.

'Well I bet you don't even say that now. Most nurses and junior doctors I have met say they get no thanks from anyone except the patients.' Alice had suddenly become serious.

'No, you are right Alice I don't think we say thank you enough. One always thinks it will sound rather false but I know that when people do thank you it always makes one feel better.'

'The other thing people want is a fair system of promotion so that success brings a tangible result in the longer run', said Alice.

'Yes, you are quite right there. That is something the NHS has been struggling with for years.'

'Can't you provide a reward system based on access to interesting and challenging work? You could arrange secondments to other departments, promote training in specialist skills and generally encourage employee development. Regular staff assessments are a useful method of solving problems and encouraging performance. I think that would help people to think that their efforts were noticed.'

'I dare say I will try that, Alice', said Fred. 'That is what I will do'.

## *13. Quality circles*

The final items Fred needed to slot into the TQM jigsaw were quality circles. He had been a little worried about adding yet more meetings into already crowded routines. Then he remembered the communication problems that the department had been plagued with. Staff meetings, staff assessments, staff error questionnaires and finally quality circles were all essential aspects of the drive to introduce confidence and reassurance into the ways staff all worked together.

One quality circle was set up using staff from all grades and professions. It met in the evenings once a week for an hour. It formed yet another useful way of spreading information around the department and for providing recognition for achievements.

## *14. Don't stop*

By Christmas, Fred Asherton and his department had learned a lot. The days when they had measured nothing and had no management development programme seemed to be years ago. In fact it has been just 18 months.

The thing that struck everyone most strongly was that it had all been so enjoyable. To start with people had been frightened by the thought of what the management information system might turn up. If the figures were bad they thought they were in for a telling off. Of course in fact it was not like that. When figures were poor it required a team effort to improve them. Those that were not game for this type of management system tended to leave the department. Those that were, found that work became a source of interest and challenge – not all the time but significantly often to be satisfying.

On Boxing Day Fred and Patsy, his wife, went to John and Alice's for the day. Fred did not mention work to Alice. No one wanted them to start talking shop again when it was Christmas. But it came up just once. They were playing scrabble in the evening by the fire. John had just won and they were clearing the board away.

'What letters did you end up with?' Alice had asked Fred.

Fred showed her his final hand. 'I can't believe it', she exclaimed, 'Look what the captain of industry's got!'

Fred pushed his counters forward for everyone to see. They stood out clearly. The letters, TQM.

'I've planned the programme for next year', he quietly told Alice, 'I going to repeat the whole exercise and treat 7% more patients.'

## Reader questionnaire

ANSWERS

1. Are you successful at influencing how your staff work? Do you invariably get what you want from them?
2. Do you consider that you work in a team?
3. Is the total quality approach too rigorous for you?
4. If you had to go into hospital would you rather you were cared for by a highly motivated medical team or by the minions of an authoritarian senior consultant?
5. Do you fully comprehend the cost of staff time and hence the cost of errors? Do you realize that if you left your pocket calculator in another part of the building you work in it would theoretically cost more for you to collect it than it would to buy a new one? Namely:
   £40 per hour × 10 minutes = £6.66. My calculator cost £2.80!

# Case study III – introducing total quality management – Templeman Primary School

In Chapter 8 the education case study looked at the effectiveness of a measurement system. In this case study we recount how Hilary Kent learnt about total quality management and how she introduced it into Templeman Primary School.

As a headteacher much of Hilary Kent's time was spent sorting out problems brought to her by staff. One day she was complaining to a friend that her teachers never seemed to solve problems themselves. They always seemed to bring their queries to her. The friend said that it was unlikely that she solved all the problems in the school because if this were the case her staff would be sitting around doing nothing. After a slight deflation of ego this idea came to facinate her.

Perhaps it was true that there were problems that her staff were solving all the time. And if this were the case an eradication of these problems would give them all a lot more time and energy for the job. After this she asked some of the staff at Templeman Primary School if they spent much of their time on solving one-off difficulties. The answer was that the whole day seemed to be spent solving problems. A common answer was that a difficulty, perhaps with discipline, caused two problems. First, time was wasted; but second the wasted time made things more difficult with the rest of the children. This in turn could lead to greater problems in future.

The question Hilary Kent then wanted the answer to was, how much time was wasted? And how much was it all costing? She mentioned her concerns and interest in this problem to some colleagues at the next area heads meeting. The general view appeared to be that they considered problems and time wasting a natural part of school life. What could you expect with children drawn from so many backgrounds?

After this piece of very obvious observation Ms Kent started to forget about the cost of errors. But at a very boring dinner party given by a work colleague of her husband's she heard two of the guests talking shop. The conversation was based on the fact that a competitor company was very vociferously selling a commitment to defect free engineering goods. What was worrying was that all the clichés about 'total quality' that this firm were using did in fact seem to be having an effect. Forced by necessity one of the two men talking had been sent on a total quality management course and had just returned. When Hilary Kent heard the words 'cost of errors' without hestitation she forced herself into the conversation.

In fact the individual who had been on the course was soon quite happy to explain TQM to Hilary because the other chap was not terribly interested in modern management jargon; he prided himself on being a doer not a talker. In contrast Hilary Kent was both and it was not long after that office dinner that she began her first attempts at measuring the cost of 'errors' at Templeman Primary School.

## Measuring the cost of errors

Before she introduced TQM at the school Hilary Kent wanted some evidence about the cost of errors actually suffered. To find out something about the real cost she arranged for some data to be obtained on a sample basis.

She devised a timesheet (see Fig. 9.5) and gave copies to two of her staff to fill in for two separate days one week. She filled two in for her own time on the same basis. At the weekend she summarized the results for the two classroom teachers. These are given in the last column of Fig. 9.5.

The results from these time sheets were simply staggering. Over 50% of all teaching time was being wasted, 30% of administration time and 30% of other time including planning time. What made all this so extraordinary was the fact that Hilary

Name: Summarized results | | | | | | | | | Date:
|---|---|---|---|---|---|---|---|---|---|
| Hours | 1 | 2 | 3 | 4 | 5 | 6 | 7 | 8 | Total |
| *Error time* | | | | | | | | | |
| – Illdiscipline in class | | | | | | | | | 1.2 |
| – Illdiscipline out of class | | | | | | | | | 0.3 |
| – Time loss to class due to individual tuition | | | | | | | | | 1.5 |
| – Time loss due to poor timetabling of lessons | | | | | | | | | 0.2 |
| – Poor timekeeping by pupils | | | | | | | | | 0.1 |
| – Wasted administration | | | | | | | | | 0.2 |
| Total | | | | | | | | | 3.5 |
| *Effective time* | | | | | | | | | |
| – Teaching | | | | | | | | | 2.9 |
| – Preparation | | | | | | | | | 1.1 |
| – Administration | | | | | | | | | 0.5 |
| Total | | | | | | | | | 4.5 |
| GRAND TOTAL | | | | | | | | | 8.0 |

**Fig. 9.5** Timesheet to measure the cost of errors.

Kent prided herself on having a well-run school. If she was getting figures like this what were less successful schools doing?

Of course what she was recording was everyones' school experience. At school we all remember timewasting in class. Sid Wheel used to try to bate Mr Smith the science teacher who could not stand him. Felicity was always moaning because she said the boys were nasty to her. And everyone knew that Belinda was thick and the teacher had to go through everything with her about three times.

But it was a very costly school experience as we can see now in retrospect. And a lot of it was damaging particularly to the weaker pupils who could not catch up after the time was lost.

It was the realization that it would be the weak to average pupils that were suffering from the problems illustrated that drove Ms Kent to introduce TQM in a formal manner. The majority of pupils at Templeman Primary School were probably in this category because the school did not tend to attract the most able who normally seemed to be attracted to a school in a neighbouring area.

# The 14-point plan at Templeman Primary School

After due planning Hilary launched her 14-point plan to achieve zero errors. In such a small organization as Templeman Primary School with its team of able and fairly willing staff it was relatively easy to obtain the committment so necessary for total quality.

Nevertheless, the concept of zero errors in an organization so 'error' prone as a school was initially difficult to communicate to the staff. The ideal of 100% good behaviour amongst pupils in all classes all the time seemed so unattainable by some teachers that Hilary Kent foresaw problems. Her concern was that if there was a committment to anything less than perfection then the whole idea would fail. In this concern she was quite correct.

Success was achieved in the end when she told the story of a small and in many ways rather insignificant physics mistress at her old grammar school who could achieve instant quiet and attention with one word. Even if her physics was pretty unsophisticated her ability to obtain control was shattering. After this reminiscense the concept of zero errors in a school suddenly appeared much more realistic and the staff began to realize that they were in fact familiar with quite a number of teachers who probably quite subconsciously used the maxim of zero errors every day to influence various aspects of their work.

# Implementation

The actual mechanics of implementation were very similar to that in the housing benefit case study. These stages are not repeated here. What is of particular interest are the cost of error figures achieved over the first year of TQM. Just as the housing benefit department measured cost of errors on a sample basis so did Hilary Kent. At three-weekly staff meetings where the cost per point data was considered (see Case Study III in Chapter 8) Hilary Kent also produced a brief report on cost of errors (see Fig. 9.8).

The level of errors recorded broadly followed the results found in the measurement of educational output. There were differences because some teachers can teach a lot in a short time and hence can suffer a high error rate; others impart information more slowly. Not surprisingly, Paul Appleby with Class 5 recorded a high error rate although it was dropping substantially after his recent course. Class 4 had very low error rates with the combination of a good teacher and a classroom assistant paying off again. Class 8 had the next best score. The small class size and a mature teacher gave the good results expected even if cost per point figures and value for money (see Chapter 8) suffered. The arrangement in Class 4 on balance gives the best results.

Once the school started to produce these cost of error reports staff took a strong interest in trying to reduce costs in specific areas. At each three weekly management meeting they set themselves targets and discuss their successes and failures.

# Summary

Using a form of TQM Hilary Kent was able to build up a sense of trust at Templeman Primary School. Together the staff look at their achievements and plan how to

**Table 9.2** Templman Primary School – Cost of errors report, period 6

| | Annual budget total costs | Period budget | Period actual | *Cost of errors taken from specially designed timesheet* Illdisc. in class | Illdisc. outside | Individ. tuition | Time table | Time keeping | Wasted admin. | Total cost of errors | Effective time cost | Error % | Taarget % |
|---|---|---|---|---|---|---|---|---|---|---|---|---|---|
| | *A* | *B* | *C* | *D* | *E* | *F* | *G* | *H* | *I* | *J* Sum (D:I) | *K* C–J | *L* J/C | *M* |
| Class 1 | 29 200 | 2 920 | 2 983 | 567 | 119 | 358 | 89 | 113 | 119 | 1 366 | 1 617 | 0.46 | 0.45 |
| Class 2 | 31 400 | 3 140 | 3 237 | 514 | 101 | 348 | 97 | 103 | 129 | 1 292 | 1 945 | 0.40 | 0.45 |
| Class 3 | 29 500 | 2 950 | 2 790 | 528 | 112 | 430 | 84 | 114 | 100 | 1 367 | 1 423 | 0.49 | 0.55 |
| Class 4 | 36 900 | 3 690 | 3 610 | 403 | 144 | 433 | 108 | 81 | 144 | 1 314 | 2 296 | 0.36 | 0.45 |
| Class 5 | 24 700 | 2 470 | 2 683 | 670 | 107 | 510 | 80 | 134 | 107 | 1 609 | 1 074 | 0.60 | 0.65 |
| Class 6 | 23 900 | 2 390 | 2 785 | 722 | 111 | 529 | 84 | 144 | 111 | 1 702 | 1 083 | 0.61 | 0.65 |
| Class 7 | 34 250 | 3 425 | 3 119 | 467 | 125 | 468 | 187 | 93 | 125 | 1 465 | 1 654 | 0.47 | 0.50 |
| Class 8 | 34 300 | 3 430 | 2 970 | 374 | 119 | 356 | 94 | 75 | 119 | 1 136 | 1 834 | 0.38 | 0.40 |
| Total | 244 150 | 24 415 | 24 177 | 4 245 | 939 | 3 432 | 823 | 857 | 955 | 11 251 | 12 926 | 0.47 | 0.51 |

overcome their problems. The regular cost of error reports focus attention very strongly on eliminating waste. And if a teacher has a less than ideal cost per point then the error reports are of real assistance in helping to put the problem right.

Hilary Kent was worried initially because the cost of errors report was put together on the basis of each teacher assessing him or herself. She expected that there would be accuracy problems. In fact teachers know that Hilary has a pretty shrewd idea about what goes on in a class and little difficulty has been found with self-assessment.

Hilary Kent has a lot of work ahead of her. It will be difficult to achieve her goal of tertiary education for all her pupils. But without the three components of TQM, that is *measurement, communication* and *recognition* she knows she hasn't a chance. She thinks that she will succeed. We can only hope she will.

## Reader questionnaire

ANSWERS

1. To achieve high quality performance effort is always needed from those involved. What is the best way of getting people to give fully of the skills and abilities they possess?
2. There is never an easy way to obtain excellence. A formal structure is needed into which people can channel their best efforts. If not TQM what other methods do you think would work?
3. In the public sector the cost of errors is often suffered by society at large as well as in the body responsible. How does this truth effect the way you work?
4. Professional people need to exhibit the same professionalism in management as in the skills for which they were specifically trained. Do you?

# 10

# A new public sector environment

## Introduction

In the last two chapters we have seen how any organization can achieve high levels of efficiency. We have also seen that modern management methods tend to give the individual employee a sense of purpose and a large say in the running of his or her work routine. All this is highly encouraging.

But we would be naive to think that once the public sector finds out about quality management techniques all the inefficiency problems discussed in Chapter 3 will naturally disappear. When individual managers implement the changes we have discussed they will benefit personally. But other managers may well find other ways of promoting their careers. The self-seeking characters we discussed in Chapter 3 are not going to be stamped out by management reform alone. Reform of the environment in which the public sector operates is also needed.

### An environment for measurement and quality management

All public organizations need motivating to work for public goals. We need an environment in which to place 'measurement' and quality management so that:

1. Their use is promoted;
2. They are used to the public benefit.

Traditionally there are two methods of ensuring management efficiency and the achievement of common goals. The first is adequate accountability and the second is competition or a market. Until recently many hoped there was a third way of obtaining efficiency and goal congruence. The idea was to use central planning.

Central planning is still very much in use in the British public services and in most other countries including the USA. But you can only plan when you have a high degree of control over peoples' actions. But by the nature of things governments have very little control over the hearts and minds of public service managers. After all the doctrine of neutral competence was devised to ensure that politicians did not influence public servants.

The relationships between management achievement inside a public body and the accountability and competition environment in which that body operates can be show diagrammatically (see Fig. 10.1).

## Accountability

All public sector bodies need to be accountable. In a democracy most should be accountable directly to the public in a meaningful way; all should be accountable to elected politicians.

At present accountability is generally weak both to politicians and public. The example from the diaries of Richard Crossman quoted in Chapter 3 makes this quite clear and in our own everyday lives we know this to be the case. In addition the lack of management information available means that even if they wanted to, most public sector managers would be unable to properly inform the public and politicians on their actions. These issues were discussed in Chapters 4 and 5.

The management systems already discussed in this book would help provide for the deficiency of information. But the political will must be there to demand it. Later in this chapter we suggest a possible structure for reporting to the electorate.

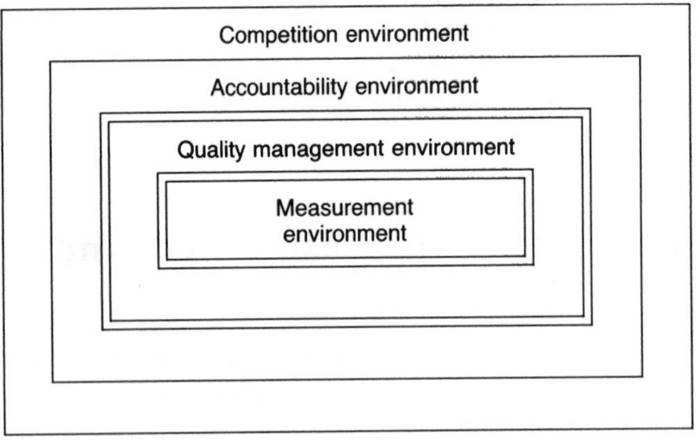


**Fig. 10.1** Layers of 'environmental control' over public services.

## Competition

Accountability is the first and important rquirement for monitoring management achievement. In a sense it is an extension of the techniques described in Chapters 8 and 9 to include a non-executive management made up of politicians and public. But for much of the public sector and for most human activities, more than accountability is needed. We also need something that the traditional public sector has come to dread – competition and the market.

Markets are disliked by producers and welcomed by consumers. Businesses continually attempt to remove competition by increasing market share. In contrast consumers welcome the responsiveness, choice and low price that the market gives. But an unregulated market often fails to provide these benefits to consumers for long. In the civilized world more and more regulation is needed if a market is to provide the things we want from it. It is important to remember that there is nothing sacred about the concept of competition; it is the benefits that matter.

The public sector has now come to the stage when it is ready to work under a series of highly regulated markets designed to provide specific benefits. The success of these markets will depend on the clearsightedness and subtety of the regulations draw up. Later in this chapter we look at some of the options available, but first we consider accountability and reporting in more detail.

## Accountability and reporting systems

The Citizens' Charter requires public bodies to develop reporting systems so that they can be compared with each other. Unfortunately this is easier said than done. We have already mentioned the reasons for this difficulty but they are worth restating.

First, output is difficult to measure when there are no trading profits. Profits are a very efficient way of measuring achievement when there are near perfect markets. Second, within public bodies there is a scarcity of management information available. Lastly, there are no standard accepted ways of presenting data on public sector achievement.

The problem of a lack of 'profit figure' will always be with us. Even where large parts of the public sector have been privatized the newly calculated profit has often been of little use because many of the privatized companies do not operate in a perfect market. The profit generated may not be a measure of achievement but of monopoly. Many consider British Telecom a good example of this phenomenon. Even when regulated markets are introduced profit is still unlikely to be a useful measure unless the market is open to all. There may be scope for more compulsory competitive tendering throughout the public services. But it is the author' view, having reviewed the performance of a number of local authority inhouse 'direct service organisations', that in a genuinely free market many inhouse teams have little to offer. Unfortunately for a range of reasons many will go out of business. This means that only a minority, although probably a substantial minority, of public sector bodies will participate in this type of open market public sector. Profit then, is unlikely ever to be a useful measure of achievement for the public sector.

The other two problems affecting accountability are a lack of management information and a lack of standardization where there is information available. Clearly these are areas were much work is still required.

## Government action

Public services are only accountable if accountability is a statutory requirement. The situation is similar to asking people to disclose their income to the tax authorities; it is only done if it is mandatory. Luckily it looks as if public bodies will soon have to disclose more of their achievements. It is likely that any government regardless of political complexion would legislate in this area in the near future.

## Freedom of information act

At this point it may be useful to mention a topical issue, a freedom of information act. Much is made of the secrecy of central government in the United Kingdom. One particular area of concern was s2 Official Secrets Act 1911 which made it an offence to disclose any information from a central government source. In 1989 s2 of the old Official Secrets Act was repealed and replaced by the Official Secrets Act 1989. The sole effect of this piece of legislation appears to have been to change half a page of script into 17. As a result those in favour of a changed approach are little further forward. But it is useful to consider some of the issues.

A freedom of information act would clearly be an important step forward in improving public access to information. As an example, for the first time it would be possible to assess the information used by officials to make decisions. But there is another issue which is just as important. We need audited accounts from public bodies that show the real achievement of the organization over a period. This is not what people usually consider when they demand freedom of information. Much information needs processing before it is in a form usable by the public. A programme of freedom of information legislation needs to contain a set account and audit regulations setting out in broad terms a proper level of disclosure for outputs and achievements for all public bodies.

In contrast to central government, local government in Britain is already reasonably open. This openness has in practice resulted in few benefits because the public and journalists make no good use of the right. Doubtless in central government there would be greater public and newspaper interest. And conversely if the local government rights were to be threatened with withdrawal, quite rightly, there would be an outcry. The point is that the quality of reporting by local government is little better than that from central government. It is important that people demand access to processed information from public bodies. Access to unprocessed data, although useful to journalists on specific occasions, will do little to make government more accountable.

# Possible new reporting structures

In February 1991 central government departments started to produce separate departmental annual reports. Previously reporting has been limited to audited accounts which gave no narrative and summarized expenditure into enormous totals. The new unaudited reports have started to give some detail on outputs but in no context. The first Department of Transport report stated that 79 'equivalent route miles' of motorway had been renewed in 1989/90. This is an interesting 'Trivial Pursuits' type statistic but is of little use in judging the efficiency of the Department of Transport or of deciding who to vote for in an election. For information on outputs to be of any use it must be in a context that gives the figures meaning.

As a further example of the problems associated with reporting, the annual report of the Crown Prosecution Service is instructive. The 1991 report provides good entertainment but little useful information. Under s9 Prosecution of Offences Act 1985 the Director of Public Prosecutions 'shall make a report to the Attorney General on the discharge of his functions'. Obviously, the Attorney General is assumed to like light reading with strictly nothing numerical. The report costs £12.50 and for that you get among a few other things a charming description in the 1991 issue, of a murder case that took place in 1980. The BBC television programme 'Crimewatch' became involved and we are given a moody photograph in full colour of a grey haired boffin in half glasses eyeing up the skull of the victim. It is all fascinating stuff for only 40 times the price of a popular newspaper.

What we ought to be finding out is whether the prosecution service compares well with the major firms of solicitors who are its opponents. We need to know how for instance the cost per case for the prosecution compares to the cost of legal aid used for the defendant. This information could then be divided between cases lost and cases where conviction is achieved. As useful would be information on the cost of different case types in different regions of the service. Perhaps the cost of the average actual bodily harm case in Manchester is double that in Newcastle. Disclosure of this type of data together with explanations would be instructive. Manchester may in fact be unreasonably wasteful but at present we are unlikely to find out.

We can say that the essence of accountable reporting is as follows. There must be:

1. Simple concise disclosure of information;
2. Disclosure of output unit costs (or profit if this is meaningful);
3. A meaningful context in which to view the information, i.e. comparative data.

## Reporting

Any reporting structure that is intended to promote accountability must deliver a simple message. The reader needs to be able to see at a glance whether the reporting organization is performing acceptably.

In a set of company accounts the net profit figure, the so-called bottom line, performs this function. Other key pieces of information are the earnings per share figure and the level of turnover. Any public sector reporting structure needs an equivalent level of summary though clearly the important figures will not be profit or turnover but some figure representing value achieved.

Behind the summary there then needs to be detailed breakdowns of figures that can be referred to to provide back-up information and provide answers to particular queries.

Next, in a non-market situation the reporting structure must give unit costs of output achieved in the period. The report must be factual and objective. Subjective reviews of performance, such as a chief executive's report, can only be subsidiary to the factual information provided.

Last, the figures reported must be placed in a meaningful context. This means that there must be,

1. Comparative figures from previous years;
2. Comparisons to objective standards set by auditors or other objective bodies;
3. Comparisons to the results of other organizations carrying out the same work.

In not all cases will all three sources of comparison be necessary. Commercial accounts only give comparative figures from previous years. In the public sector one would expect previous years figures and at least comparisons with objective standards, or comparisons with other organizations.

## Example of effective public sector reporting

What then will an effective public sector report look like? Below we give the summary sheet from the accounts of the housing benefit department used in the case studies in Chapters 8 and 9. The figures are for Abigail MacGovern's department at Senforth District Council. She would be pleased to know that she is well within the top quartile of authorities.

### *Summary sheet from housing benefit annual report*

| | *£'000* 199Y | *£'000* 199X |
|---|---|---|
| A. Total cost per year of department | 352.1 | 360.9 |
| B. Cost of best practice standard (achievement exceded by top quartile of authorities) | 381.2 | 370.7 |
| C. Money 'saved' in Year (B–A) | 29.1 | 9.8 |
| D. Efficiency percentage (C/B) | 7.6 | 2.6 |
| E. Quality rating | 9.5 | 9.1 |
| F. Top quartile of authorities | 8.7 | 8.4 |

This summary gives us very clear evidence about the performance of the housing benefit department over the year 199Y. We can immediately see that the department is achieving significantly above best practice both as regards productivity and quality of service. Senforth District Council is 7.6% more efficient than the best practice standard. Best practice is represented by that level of achievement exceeded by the top quartile of all authorities. Comparison has been made in comparative terms by use of figures from the best practice authorities and in absolute terms by giving a figure representing money saved.

The comparitive figures from the previous year show that the productivity performance of the authority is continuing to improve for both productivity and quality of performance. As a summary these figures give all the information we need for effective reporting. The detail supporting the summary would give further breakdowns of the figures.

## *Derivation of the figures*

Anyone who has worked in a housing benefit department will be wondering how it is possible to produce cost figures for different departments that could be described as comparable. Some authorities will handle many more cases than others. Another source of problems would be differences in case mix. One department may deal with many relatively simple applications from council house tenants. Another may have a predominence of more complex cases from private tenants. At first sight the two departments are not comparable.

It is one of the roles of accountancy to make sense of raw data from different sources. Departments that handle different quantities of a given output can be compared by the calculation of a quantity variance. This allows comparison on the assumption that both process the same number of claims and payments. Because quite often comparisons are required between two sets of figures that are made up of a varying mix of different outputs accountants calculate mix variances. Again the object is comparability and analysis of achievement.

## *Calculation of the figures*

This book is for public sector managers. It is therefore unlikely that many readers will want to construct their own reporting documentation if only because there will be a lack of data from other organizations available for comparison. Clearly, it is up to central government to lay down guidelines for reporting and subsequent audit. That said it is important to explain how figures could be produced for a straightforward example.

In Table 8.2 the different outputs from a housing benefit department were listed against the objectives of the department. The chapter then went on to describe how to calculate unit costs for each output and to measure output quantities.

The department had the following unit cost figures as shown below. These are similar to the unit costs shown in Table 8.3 but vary slightly because they are for the full year rather than for just one month.

**Cost breakdown for housing benefit department**

| | Outputs as shown in Fig. 8.5 £ | No. | Total cost |
|---|---|---|---|
| 1 | 24.87 | 1 514 | 37 653 |
| 2 | 32.16 | 802 | 25 792 |
| 3 | 54.99 | 492 | 27 055 |
| 4 | 55.50 | 884 | 49 062 |
| 5 | 42.22 | 1 416 | 59 784 |
| 6 | 66.03 | 754 | 49 787 |
| 7 | 0.49 | 28 262 | 13 848 |
| 8 | 0.11 | 84 102 | 9 251 |
| 9 | 1.09 | 20 287 | 22 113 |
| 10 | 1.14 | 26 987 | 30 765 |
| 11 | 50.44 | 364 | 18 360 |
| 12 | 1.07 | 8 065 | 8 630 |
| TOTAL | | | 352 100 |

By multiplying the number cases of each type by their unit costs the total cost of the department is given.

Now if a comparison is required to a performance level given by another authority with different costs and caseloads this is easily done by substituting the other authority's unit costs but retaining the first authority's case load (see below).

**Cost breakdown for housing benefit department using unit cost data from a comparative authority**

| | £ | No. | Total cost |
|---|---|---|---|
| 1 | 28.71 | 1 514 | 43 466 |
| 2 | 29.17 | 802 | 25 394 |
| 3 | 55.10 | 492 | 27 109 |
| 4 | 63.17 | 884 | 55 842 |
| 5 | 48.17 | 1 416 | 68 208 |
| 6 | 73.10 | 754 | 55 117 |
| 7 | 0.35 | 28 262 | 9 892 |
| 8 | 0.09 | 84 102 | 7 569 |
| 9 | 1.22 | 20 287 | 24 750 |
| 10 | 1.35 | 26 987 | 36 432 |
| 11 | 51.11 | 364 | 18 604 |
| 12 | 1.09 | 8 065 | 8 791 |
| TOTAL | | | 381 174 |

What we have done is to say that the authority with the unit costs we have substituted, if it had the same case load and mix as the authority used in our case study, would have costs totalling £381 174.

The beauty of this method of comparison is that differences between organizations which are doing the same work can be eliminated so that valid comparison can be made. Whereas in the past when crude parallels were made it was always possible to believe that there were mitigating factors that had not been taken into account, with the method described above few such complaints would be valid.

### *Obtaining comparative data*

In the summary on page 230 we show comparative data entitled 'Achievement exceeded by top quartile of authorities'. How could this data be obtained and calculated?

To be able to report using data derived from other authorities clearly everyone would have to communicate their year's results to a central office so that the achievement of the best quartile of authorities could be calculated. This process would require significant organization but conceptually would provide little problem. An alternative would be to use data from the previous year by way of comparison.

A more interesting problem would be how to calculate achievement from the data provided by each authority. The difficulty is this. If one authority has a unit cost for one output that is very cheap but for another output its unit cost is expensive how do you compare this to an authority with two moderate unit costs? There is in fact no correct or definitive solution to this problem.

A reasonable solution would be to compare all authorities using a standard caseload and mix which was perhaps the average for the country. In this way best practice unit costs for the top quartile of authorities could be calculated and used as the basis for local reporting in the way shown in the summary.

### *Quality ratings*

In our example we show a 'quality rating' figure as a method of comparing the quality of service of an authority against a best practice figure. The figure has been calculated using an assessment system whereby different aspects of quality of service are given a score according to a set of rules.

Quality could be assessed using a number of different means. Departments could be required by regulation to measure their quality in some of the ways shown on Table 8.2. The results of these measurements would then be fed into a formula to give an overall score. The whole assessment calculation would then be subject to audit to ensure figures were properly and fairly produced.

A less complete quality assessment could be obtained by auditors completing an assessment questionnaire. This system would have the benefit of relative simplicity, but it would have a number of drawbacks. First, it would be based on less objective data than an assessment system based on mandatory test checking of quality of service. Second, it would do little to encourage departments to monitor their own service quality.

## Competition

The concept of competition flows very naturally from the achievement of accountability. By comparing data on outputs the environment necessary for effective competition is being created. If one organization is seen to compare badly with another then this is only a thinly veiled challenge to compete.

Traditionally we think of competition involving profits and probably profiteering. We forget that we competed in races at school and competed in exams throughout our early life without money being mentioned. Competition in the public services will be much more like competition at school than the Victorian marketplace one tends to envisage.

## Compulsory competitive tendering

Where jobs that a public body needs doing are simple and self-contained then the possibility for public tender exists. Public bodies have always used this method obtaining value for money. Early examples include defence contracting with military uniforms being a good case in point.

More recently the majority of jobs requiring manual labour have become subject to mandatory tender in the British public services. Normally this type of work can be tendered for successfully and although certain interested parties may object to the introduction of the chill wind of competition few can rationally object in principle. In the author's experience many of those involved in the old local authority manual labour workforces will openly admit that work practices were long overdue for change.

But how far can competitive tendering be taken to provide competition in the public services? The Citizen's Charter makes clear that Conservative politicians envisage tendering for 'lawyers, accountants, architects and surveyors'. Experiments in these fields are already underway. Some professional work can clearly be tendered for because it is by nature fitted to the tendering process. Examples would include architects' departments, internal audit departments and surveyors. But other work is difficult to tender for. The central accounts department of a public body would be difficult to 'privatise' because its work is complex, although often mundane, and because it depends on a large range of personal relationships with user departments at all grades. Labour hired on the basis of a tender is unlikely to be able to quickly take up where a previous tenderer left off. In addition because of the complexity of the job tender prices would be set high to absorb uncertainties.

## Contract staff

There are clear boundaries beyond which tendering is unlikely to provide value for money. Not even the most rabid right winger would consider putting the work of the Chancellor of the Exchequer out to tender. But there is a middle way between the use of permanent staff and tendering. This is the use of individual contract staff to provide specific services when required at a market price. In Chapter 2 and 9 we discuss how workforces are changing due to the pressures in society to achieve increased efficiency. Clearly the use of contract staff helps to even out changes in workload. Specific skilled jobs requiring an expert can also be efficiently carried out using a contractor.

Contract staff fulfil a need and allow the payment of a market rate for a job as long as the employer negotiates realistically. The use of contract staff will increase bringing with it its own relatively benevolent form of competition.

## Employed staff

The issues of tendering and contract staff are likely in the long run to resolve themselves and a natural level of usage will result. Where tendering is likely to bring benefits it will be used and where contract staff are advantageous they will be sought. Conversely, if tendering and contract staff do not bring benefits they will not be used as a method of introducing competition.

But what other competitive methods are there? At the beginning of this section on competition we said that competition followed naturally from accountability because accountability involved comparison.

## The status quo

At present there is significant competition in the permanent workforces that operate the major public services. This competition involves working for promotion and recognition in the workplace. These form influences on personal behaviour as staff compete with one another for favourable outcomes. The problem with this form of competition is not that it is weak but that it encourages suboptimal results. As we explained in Chapter 3 under the traditional competitive public sector system the result was achievement of personal goals at the expense of public goals. There was little goal congruence.

As we have said, in this respect it is not difficult to see that the status quo is unacceptable.

## The branch system

Many organizations operate through a series of branches. Examples are shoe shops, supermarkets, insurance companies and social security offices.

In commercial branch structures it has long been recognized that there is considerable scope for competition between branches even though the environments the branches operate in may differ considerably. By completing branch returns on a regular basis branches are compared and targets set. In a shoe retailing company with which the author was involved the management found that a change of branch manager could regularly lead to a doubling of sales if the right candidate was chosen. As a young auditor I remember being staggered that this was possible with a conservative product such as footware.

Clearly the competitive capacity of a branch structure has considerable scope in central government. The main requirement is that branches are compared over a number of criteria that promote the public interest. Managers and staff should be compared on the basis of productivity and quality of service. The ambition and personal qualities of the staff are of little interest to the public. They just want good services.

In Chapters 2 and 9 we discussed some of the current influences affecting all organizations. We saw how staff hierarchies were being removed and how the need was for small teams of staff that could be trusted to achieve goals without supervision. The concept of total quality management was then found to fit well with this type of highly professional organization which controlled itself through a combination of trust and measurement.

The idea of splitting up parts of large organizations into small competing branches is thus attractive from more than one viewpoint. But how would it work in practice?

## Splitting up major organizations

There have always been decentralized public bodies. The local authorities and health authorities are the most obvious examples. The problem with these organizations is that they have used their geographical locations as a method of preventing competition between themselves. Even in the major cities where it would be relatively easy to make valid comparisons there has been almost no competitive pressure between authorities this century.

The first attempts to make existing branch structures compete in the public sector came with the Education Reform Act 1988 which introduced 'Local Management in Schools', and the National Health Service and Community Care Act 1990 which set up an internal market in the health service. The basis of both these reforms was that suppliers of public services would compete with each other at a branch level for children and patients respectively and that the funding for the service would depend on the success in attracting clients. It is worth looking at the similarities and differences between the two schemes.

### *Local management in schools*

The Local Management in Schools (LMS) system had already been used in the education system within the universities, in a simplified form, and within the polytechnics. The essence of the system is that educational establishments are free to attract pupils by advertising their qualities. The incentive for the universities was a chance to benefit from the cream of the nation's up and coming intellectual generation. For the polytechnics and schools the incentive was more mundane – money. The pupil or parent or both chose a polytechnic or school on the basis of its advertised qualities; the educational establishment gets paid on the basis of the number of pupils it bags. Theoretically, the system works for the public good. And the indications from the polytechnics are that the scheme is successful since the number of students has doubled for little increase in real costs and no noticeable reduction in standards. As yet it is too early to discover whether the same can be said of the school system. However, after the many complaints that greeted the scheme when it was proposed it is probably fair to say that in practice it appears to work better than many expected.

## *The national health service reforms*

The health service reforms took the education reforms one step further. Whereas a school could only attract 'clients' and therefore funding on the basis of the perceived quality of the school, the hospital could attract on the basis of quality and price. The NHS reforms were thus considerably more sophisticated than their education counterparts. This has also made them more difficult to introduce.

The NHS reforms needed to involve a control over price because one of the main concerns was that governments were unable to control NHS spending. In education by contrast, spending has been better controlled. The issue was that schools were seen as failing to provide the type of education that electors wanted. For the NHS the service generally pleased the electors but the waiting lists and cost of the service were considered unacceptable. The whole issue of reform of the health service is made more complex because there is probably not a country in the world that runs its state, voluntary or private health care services on an efficient patient orientated basis. The hospital, doctors or charity, depending on the circumstances, always seem to take the first priority. There is thus an unusual shortage of models of effective provision to follow.

In the long term it is probable that the internal market system will be successful. This is because most of the disciplines of the market structure favour improved patient care and improved administration while retaining substantial government control over total spending. In the short term there will be controversial difficulties as inconsistences in the market structure are revealed and as those with fixed interests in the old system voice their concerns over the changes. This phase may last three or four years as difficulties are slowly ironed out.

## *Market systems for the other major services*

How will these experiments in internal or social markets affect the other as yet unreformed services? What lessons can be learned and what changes are desirable?

We can divide the remaining public service into a number of categories. These categories will cover a wide range of organizations but will share a common task. The following have been identified:

1. Armed services;
2. Police and firebrigade;
3. Regulators (e.g. planners and inspectors);
4. Social security administrators;
5. General administrators in different areas.

The armed services, police and fire brigade are relatively specialized services. For simplicity we consider only the last three categories here.

## *Regulation, social security and general administration*

These categories all have one aspect in common. They all involve an interpretation and clerical implementation of government regulations. A building inspector assesses a new drainage system to check that the building regulations have been complied with. A passport office clerk checks that an application for a passport is in compliance with statute and regulation before issuing a new one. There are a vast variety of jobs like this and it matters little whether they involve slaughter houses or labelling of children's toys.

To understand how we can improve these services it is useful to look at their evolution and history. Traditionally societies have assumed that the law will be upheld; only when it is broken is official action taken. With the major changes in life which resulted from the industrial revolution this *laissez-faire* system broke down and governments began to take direct and precipitate action to prevent the law being broken. This was an important change. As we mentioned in Chapter 1 the Child Labour Act 1833 established inspectors to ensure that factories obeyed the new law. The traditional method would have been to let aggrieved parties take court action if the law was broken. When poor parents sent their children to work in a market desperate for cheap labour the old system was clearly inapplicable. This was because the problem was widespread and because the parties directly involved had no interest in complying with the law. But what can we learn from this which is relevant to our present circumstances?

First, we must still rely on inspectorates; they are still an efficient method of upholding the standards the law requires. But second, the traditional system of both defendants and claimants hiring specialist legal advice has much to offer. If you do not like your solicitor you can sack him just by picking up the telephone. This option is not open to those using government inspectorates or clerical offices. The inspector or administrator in theory stands halfway between the 'inspected' or 'administered' and the law; he or she is both councel for the prosecution and the defence and is expected to be fair and efficient. The problem is that very often this paragon of virtue falls down and injustice and waste of public resources results.

If as a society we want efficient public administration then a middle way is required whereby it is possible to inject some competition into the service. It may also be desirable to have a choice over which inspectorate the client uses. Imagine the following conversation:

Denis Smith has just be made unemployed after a long period of sickness. He is rather disillusioned with the world and to make things worse he is rather worried about claiming all the benefits he thinks he is due. They are vitally important to him because they are all he will have to live on. He goes to see an old friend of his, Reg Greenstreet, who was unemployed recently and knows most of the problems of being on benefits.

> Hello Reg. Well they sacked me at long last. 'S'pose I shouldn't complain but there you are.
>
> 'Well, how are you bearing up then, old chum?
>
> Fair to middlin' I suppose. What worries me is those sods in the benefits. Not so bad when I get my pension but 'till then . . . But I came for some advice about what to do.

Under the present system Denis will have to use his local office whether he likes it or not and Reg's advice will be rather limited. But the conversation could continue as follows:

> Well, Denis, I tell you straight don't go near the ones they call Department B. They'll call you in every couple of days and keep you waiting for hours and hours. I used Department A. They were alright.
>
> So I have a choice of benefit offices do I? And if I don't like one I can change to another. Treat you like a king, they do, once you're on the scrapheap
>
> Come on Denis, you knew they would not keep you on forever. You'll get some part-time work. A few fivers in the back pocket. You'll be alright. I was talking to Sid's wife Margie the other night up at the *Alma*. She said her boy's between jobs and is claiming benefit from a private agency. I don't know if they are any good but you could give them a try, Den.

There are a number of options available if we want to introduce an element of competition into these types of services. Privatization, the most radical option, may be possible in some situations but might not be the most cost effective method. We will consider the possibilities in turn.

We have said that all public organizations must be properly accountable. Accountability involves comparison. Competition could be injected into administrative bodies by targeting branch managers to achieve improved results. Clearly there would have to be rewards and recognition of success for those that improved the productivity and quality of the service that their branch offered. Just as the successful manager of the branch of a shoe retailing chain is rewarded with performance related pay and ultimately promotion, so must the benefits or inspectorate manager be recognized.

This system may seem little different to that already employed to motivate and promote staff. But the key point is that the promotion and increased pay are not judged on a subjective assessment of worth as they tend to be at present but on an objective and published achievement clearly compared to best practice. A well-planned scheme of this type that is clearly explained to staff before introduction will in some cases produce dramatic improvements in achievement.

This limited form of competition will enhance the services it is applied to at least in total. But it will not help those individual clients who are forced to use the least efficient offices because there is no choice. A stronger competitive influence could be injected in public service provision by giving clients a choice of branches. This is the situation described in the middle of the narrative when Reg warns Denis not to use Department B. For some services the idea of customer choice will seem ridiculous but it is worth bearing in mind that in some areas there is already competition between local authorities for the provision of services some of it of dubious legality. I recently needed an old cesspool emptied before a new septic tank was fitted. I rang my local council and was told that they would have to send me a form before anything could be done. I rang a neighbouring authority and immediately arranged to have the service the next morning. As a consumer of a public service I benefited greatly from having a choice. Choice is a right it is difficult to deny to any user of a public service because it tends to enhance the efficiency of the producer and the quality of life of the consumer.

A problem arises when there is a choice between a number of public services. What happens to the inefficient ones that would naturally 'go out of business'? If they do close due to lack of custom then the choice is reduced. Since the service is not in an open market new service providers cannot set up in business to replace them.

An answer to this problem would be a 'market' in branch managers. If managers of branches were on fairly steep scales of performance related pay then an unsuccessful branch manager would be paid at an unattractive rate and would consider leaving the job. A new manager would start at this low level. Ambitious individuals would be attracted to these branches because of the scope for increasing their income and saleability in the job market should they be successful in turning the branch round. There is little new in this idea; it is the method whereby the high-street banks keep a branch in every town. They do not close unsuccessful branches; they change the managers.

For many public services this would be the most competition that could be reasonably introduced because the risks of security leaks, fraud or political embarrassment would outweigh the benefits of allowing a genuinely open although regulated market.

## Open markets

An open market in the provision of public services would require the registration of private operators followed by their regular audit. This is marginally different from a tendering situation because with an open market service the public deal with the operator whereas with a tendered service they deal predominantly with the public sector client. As an example if a road is flooding the public inform the highways authority. They then ask the winner of the gulley-emptying tender to clear the drain. In contrast the tenant of a council house now run by a housing association will deal with the new landlords.

Open market provision of public services may in many cases provide a cheap and high quality service. Examples that have been relatively successful for many years include doctors, dentists and pharmacists in general practice and lawyers providing legal aid. There are few conceptual reasons why schemes such as these could not be expanded to cover benefit administration and much other government administration. In the dialogue above, Reg suggests to Denis that he uses a private administrator of social security benefits. At present none exist and the evidence is that the private sector is little interested in entering this field.

An area where there are more conceptual difficulties is the area of government regulation. How feasible would it be to have private sector planning departments to replace those at present run by local authorities? Could they be trusted to be unbiased? It probably is possible to set up regulatory regimes to provide free market control of planning, building, food premises, and so on. Companies have used private auditors in a similar way for a century and a half. However, the system is not perfect as many commentators have noted after recent spectacular collapse of a number of high profile companies which had all received clean audit reports in the recent past.

Each case would have to be looked at on its merits. The benefits of choice and competition would have to set against the likely costs of effective regulation and the expected level of tenders.

# Summary

This final chapter has attempted to suggest solutions to the problems of effective public sector provision raised at the beginning of the book. It has also tried to place the management techniques illustrated in the rest of the book in a context. The public sector will never be able to maximize its achievements by management reform alone. Reform of the environment in which the public sector operates is vital if public servants are to work reliably for the public interest.

There is not one single method of reform; each public sector activity needs to be individually considered to find the best method of enhancing the quality of service it provides and obtaining the best value for money. Some services are very effective at present. Others are obvious candidates for improvement. However there are a number of general rules that every organization should comply with. Every public body must:

1. Be 'goal congruent' with the public interest;
2. Have comprehensive management information for both *inputs* and *outputs*;
3. Promote initiative and flair in its staff.

The book has attempted to show how these characteristics can be encouraged. It has attempted to dispel some of the myths about how the public sector works so that it is possible to concentrate on better public services for everybody at a price that is reasonable and affordable.

We are living in a time of flux. The 'Triple Squeeze' on resources described in Chapter 2 has already started to make reform of the public services inevitable. Our job is to manage that reform so change is rational and well organized, so that the best is built upon and the worst is quickly discarded.

If you are a public sector manager who cares for the service you provide do not wait for reform to happen. Others less informed than yourself may unwittingly damage the best of the service you provide. Agitate for effective change; persuade your staff, your superiors and politicians to take a rational course that clearly benefits the majority of the public, that makes full use of management information and that encourages individualism and flair.

Engineer reform. Don't be the victim of inevitable change. *Make sure you can manage.*

## Reader questionnaire

This questionnaire reviews the key messages the book seeks to impart. It is brief because at this stage you should be starting to implement change in your own organization.

ANSWERS

(a) Do you and your staff have a clear set of objectives?
  (i) do these comply with statute?
  (ii) have you categorized them into priorities?
(b) Have you and your staff defined your departmental/organizational outputs?
(c) Have you started to design and implement a management accounting and information system to measure
  (i) outputs, as well as
  (ii) inputs.
(d) Have you produced a statement of quality standards for your department/organization?
(e) Have you considered compliance with British Standard 5750? Have you looked for and found organizations similar to yours which use the standard? How have they benefited?
(f) What steps have you taken to introduce a total quality management system? Have you begun to estimate the cost of errors in your department/organization. Which are the types of error most easily eliminated? Have you discussed the subject with your senior staff?
(g) Do you know how the achievement of your department/organization compares with other similar organizations? What steps have you taken to obtain information on best practice output costs?
(h) Have you taken steps to introduce an element of competition between different sections of your department or organization?
(i) Are you confident that your department or organization can meet the challenges that it will face it in the medium term? Will it be setting standards of excellence that others will envy?

# Bibliography

## 1. The rise of the public sector

Jenkins, K., Caines, K. and Jackson, A. *Improving Management in Government: the Next Steps*, HMSO, 1987.
This is the important and interesting report prepared for Margaret Thatcher which clearly analysed the problems in public sector management. Well worth reading.

Peacock, A. T. and Wiseman, J. *The Growth of Public Expenditure in the UK*, Unwin, 1967.
This provides an good introduction to public spending policy.

Public Expenditure White Papers. HMSO. Yearly.
This publication gives government spending figures and comparisons for the UK.

## 2. Why value for money is important

*Citizens' Charter*, HMSO, 1991.
This is the document which has been responsible for the latest emphasis on management reform in the UK.

*Competing for Quality*, HMSO, 1991.
This is the White Paper that discusses the introduction of compulsory competitive tendering (CCT) into management of local authorities.

Handy, C. *The Age of Unreason*, Business Books, 1991.
A provocative and popular book that considers management (and living) in the near future.

Jones, P.C. and Bates, J. G. *Public Sector Auditing: Practical Techniques for an Integrated Approach*, Chapman & Hall, 1990.

Designed for audit professionals, Chapter 10 provides a succinct introduction to VFM useful to all managers.

*Social Expenditure*, OECD, Paris, 1985.
A clear analysis of the dangers of increasing public expenditure.

# 3. Self-interest and shared opportunities

Butler-Sloss, Lord Justice. *Report on the Inquiry into Child Abuse in Cleveland*, HMSO, 1987.
The much quoted but little read report that analyses many of the defects of bureaucracy, as well as discussing child abuse.

Chapman, L. *Your Disobedient Servant*, Chatto & Windus, 1978.
A key work in initiating the reform of bureaucracies in the UK. Good reading.

Crossman, R. H. S. *The Diaries of a Cabinet Minister*, Hamish Hamilton & Jonathan Cape, 1975.
A detailed but amusing day-by-day description of the work of the UK government in the 1960s.

Knott, J. H. and Miller, G. J. *Reforming Bureaucracy*, Prentice-Hall, 1987.
This book discusses motivation in public bodies controlled by democratic governments. Provocative reading.

# 4. What makes an organization function?

Clegg, W., Kemp, N. J. and Legge, K. *Case Studies in Organisational Behaviour*, Harper & Row, 1985.
Useful for managers who wish to appreciate how organizations function practically.

# 5. Accounting

Henley, D., Holtham, C., Likierman, A. and Perrin, J. *Public Sector Accounting and Financial Control*, Van Nostrand Reinhold, 1986.
This is a straightforward introduction into the technicalities of present day public sector accounting.

# 6. The structure of output-based management

There are a large number of books designed to help non-financial students and managers understand the basics of accountancy. There are also some good training videotapes. Perhaps the best are from Video Arts whose material stars John Cleese. Some books are:

Dyson, J. R. *Accounting for Non-Accounting Students*. Pitman, 1991.

Kellock, J., Harrison, J., Horrocks, J. and Newman, R. L. *Accounting: a Direct Approach*. Pitman, 1987.

Langley, F. P. and Herdern, G. S. *Introduction to Accounting for Business Studies*. Butterworth, 1990.

# 7. What do *you* get from output-based management?

Audit Commission. *Performance Review in Local Government*, HMSO, 1986–89.
This is a useful introduction to measurement in local government.

Audit Commission. Management Papers. HMSO 1988–to date.
The Audit Commission produce a continuing series of papers looking at various aspects of management in the public sector.

Audit Commission. Occasional Papers and Reports. HMSO, 1984–to date.
These papers and reports discuss current and best practice in specific public sector services. They are required reading for all public sector managers.

National Audit Office. Various Reports. HMSO 1984–to date.
More specific than Audit Commission reports, NAO material is a valuable source of data on central government management.

# 8. High quality public services

British Standard 5750 Parts 0–4 Quality Systems. British Standards Institution 1987–1990.
The British version of the international standard ISO 9001–9004 which allows organizations to advertise independently checked standards of quality.

For those who need quality control procedures two texts are given below:

Grant, E. L. and Leavenworth, R. S. *Statistical Quality Control*, McGraw-Hill Kogakuska, 1980.
A straightforward text text aimed principally at manufacturing industry.

Banks, J. *Principles of Quality Control*. John Wiley & Sons, 1989.
This is a comprehesive book that considers service industries as well as manufacturing.

# 9. Managing for excellence

Crosby, P. B. *Quality is Free: the Art of Making Quality Certain*, McGraw-Hill, 1979.
This book is one of a series of easily read and successful books on total quality management.

Deming, W. E. *Out of Crisis*, Cambridge University Press, 1986.
This book is a quality management text from one of its inventors.

*Management Decision*. MBC University Press.
This is an easily read monthly journal of management. Although you may not agree with many of the articles in an issue it is a valuable source of ideas for all managers.

# 10. A new public sector environment

There are few books on the most recent changes that are occurring in the UK public sector. However, there are articles constantly in the serious newspapers and the public sector professional journals. Reading these is the best way of keeping up to date.

# Index